Straight Sense
Volume 2

Robert F. Simms

ISBN 978-0-9858233-8-2
Published in the United States

Subjects

INTRODUCTION

Why I Criticize

My father used to sit in his easy chair on Sunday nights after everyone had gotten home from church, eat hamburgers with the rest of us, and as Pa Cartwright, Hoss, Little Joe and Adam (or probably the anonymous crowd in the saloon instead) occasionally would pour a stiff one, Daddy would mutter, "Drink, drink, drink!" Daddy was down on drinking. It didn't keep him from watching Bonanza, but he wished television wouldn't promote alcohol consumption. Daddy was a teetotaler, as I am, and for a long time he wouldn't eat in restaurants that served beer or any other kind of alcohol. That changed over the years as eventually there almost weren't any restaurants that didn't serve alcohol. In his last years his favorite restaurants were Applebee's and Fatz, both literally built around bars. Culture didn't go his way, or mine for that matter, but the way of "the opposition" instead.

I still prefer not to eat in bars, but I would be limited to about two places in my hometown if I ate only where no alcohol was served, and all Mexican restaurants would be eliminated—and that just wouldn't do.

If I were discouraged by the fact that few things I complain about ever change to suit me, I would be continually in the dumps. However, I don't critique culture only because I expect it to go my way in response. I critique it because it needs critiquing. I live in a world where the various cultural cancers that have been eating away at refinement, morality, and good sense are destroying and disfiguring the nation and Western civilization itself. As they do, the Nixonian silent majority shrinks and feigns indifference or even tacit approval, afraid to disagree much less to oppose actively , lest they be marginalized or persecuted.

In such an atmosphere, I have to critique, criticize, preach and prophesy. If I don't, I might be assumed not to care.

An old story told of a prophet who spent every day in ancient Sodom walking through the city streets preaching loudly. After many years someone from another city asked him why he did it. He said, "At first, I preached to change them. Eventually, I preached so they wouldn't change me."

I'm somewhere in the middle at this point in my life. I'm realistic enough to know that I won't change the world around me much even if I am very vocal and very active, either in a negative or positive way. However, I can see that if I stopped caring enough to complain about the direction of our culture, I would eventually conform to it, even if only by default.

For that reason, I continue to speak up and invite ridicule and condemnation as I see the forces of the homosexual revolution overrunning the ramparts of morality.

For the same reason, I continue to say that I believe alcohol is a major part of the ruination of the country.

And for the same reason, I express my opposition to a variety of other things that contribute to the coarsening of our culture, the loss of our liberties, and the promotion of libertine living.

So, I write this in praise of criticism. As self-contradictory as that might seem on first glance, it makes serious sense when you think about it ever so briefly.

Unlike my first volume of *Straight Sense,* the chapters ahead of you are organized into topics. They were written between February, 2013, and April, 2016, and they were driven most of the time by then-current events. I realized when I pulled together all the little essays I wanted to publish in this volume that a great many of them had to do with a handful of subjects that weighed on my mind continually, and still do. I don't apologize for this, though I do promise to widen my field of insensitivity and intolerance for the next volume, if there is one.

For instance, President Obama merited his own subsection, because of the violence he has done through the "dreams of his father" to the lofty dreams of our forefathers for this great land. Also, homosexuals and their near cousins the transgendered folks got their own subsection, simply because they have made themselves the topic of debate of the last quarter century or more. And Islam and terrorism, while mentioned in some other contexts, merit their own grouping of brief essays because they are only slightly more dangerous phenomena to the world than the homosexual agenda.

As I write this, the 2016 elections have not yet taken place, although the final candidates *seem* to be certain. I suspect that one of two things will happen to my writing once a new president takes office: either I will write more about politics, or I'll write much less. I'm toying with the idea of declaring another moratorium on news as I did when Obama was first elected. I had had it with the news, with the idiocy of an electorate that seemed giddily determined to opt for "hope and change" irrespective of what that change was going to be, and with the utter folly of sociological and political liberals who were bound and determined to trash the shining city on a hill in their march to embrace the causes that destroy the American Dream. The day after the 2008 elections, I didn't watch TV news, listen to radio news, didn't even listen to talk shows that contain news, didn't read a newspaper, and would not allow discussions of news in my household. I didn't want to know anything going on in the world outside my immediate surroundings. It was an experiment to see if I felt happier not knowing. It was a retreat from the world that had beat like an ocean storm against my emotions, my thinking, my very spirit, to the point that I was becoming comprehensively pessimistic.

The moratorium lasted a year. When I came out of my self imposed cocoon, I found that nothing had needed my attention during that year that didn't get it, that no one suffered for my having been out of pocket, and that I felt refreshed, as if I could re-engage with the world without quickly becoming burned out. I was able to return to my subsidiary mission in life, to cry out like Lot in Sodom, to the sinful city that is the world, about its myriad iniquities and inequities, about its stupidity and pride, about its villains and its devils, and about the self-absorbed fools who imagine that their irrational tolerance is equivalent to love and peace.

And along the way, I'll throw in some superficial pet peeves that pale in comparison to what's really ruining the world.

Barack Hussein Obama

How Bad Obama Is — or Was

It's always nice to share core values with your co-workers; it usually makes for nicer conversation at work, and it makes expressing your gripes easier—you don't have to stifle yourself to avoid starting an argument.

Unfortunately I have a co-worker with whom I share next to no political values: we are at opposite ends of the political spectrum. However, we have learned to avoid getting into political spats, mostly because we otherwise like each other a lot. But if we ever get into it over some lightning rod figure like Barack Obama, I'm sure I would find it frustrating not to be able to get through to him about how wrong this man has been for America. (By the time this goes to print, Obama will be out of office, praise the Lord, and I sincerely hope his party will be as well.) Part of the reason I would have difficulty convincing my friend of the folly of his being a fan of Obama is that he has a different idea of what the country should be. When your philosophical destinations are vastly different, your routes and road maps simply can't coincide.

But opening people's eyes to how bad Obama has been for this nation is difficult if they have been emotionally committed to him. In the case of my co-worker, he is emotionally attached. Not only is my friend a dyed-in-the-wool Democrat (which is usually also true for emotional rather than rational reasons), he is also Black, which increases the likelihood of his being a fan of Obama, who is, well, not White. Blacks who haven't done their own thinking typically root for Obama mostly because he's Black, not because he has done anything that they really agree with or like. (Ask ten Black persons what accomplishment of Obama's they like most; I predict that besides Obamacare they won't be able to really settle on anything else, unless it's because he's given them Obamaphones and other free stuff.)

Emotional attachment is nearly impossible to break, apart from an Newtonian event—an equal and opposite emotional experience that confronts the irrational affection. It's something like the old saying that a liberal is a conservative who hasn't been mugged yet. Converting a liberal Democrat who supports Obama (or Hillary, or any other liberal Democrat politico) requires being mugged by that same liberal Democrat, in an economic sense or any other way that will invoke repugnance or a feeling of fear.

Nevertheless, I'd like to be ready to unleash a flurry of actual reasons that Democrats should be kicked out of the White House as soon as possible. Should Hillary succeed Obama, she would be an extension of his destructive policies, so the reasons Obama should never have been president would be the same reasons no Democrat should be elected to replace him.

I would have preferred not ever to have let Obama in the White House, but that would require time travel and interference with historical events (which is one good reason I hope our physicists will discover how to go Back to the Future, and vice versa). I would have liked to have seen Obama impeached once he got there and started misbehaving, but Republicans, though they have had plenty of cause, have been weenies on that matter. I'm left with a list of reasons to urge upon my readers.

My nature is not to keep active records of offenses on my brain; they cause headaches. But after a while it becomes necessary. Still, I'm not in practice at it because I don't engage much in debate, day to day. I shall endeavor to make a short list, however, of the reasons that Democrats should be defeated in the fall and that Obama should go down as one of the worst and most dangerous presidents ever to hold the office.

First, there's the fact that, whether through deliberate strategy or incompetence, Obama's policies have resulted in phenomenally worse statistics with respect to the economy and government assistance than any president in my lifetime. More than eleven million Americans have left the work force since Obama became president, and fewer are working today than the year before the World Trade Center buildings came down. At the same time, food stamp recipients have grown to comprise twenty percent of the American population. Part of the reason for the unemployment figures is the imposition of new regulations on business that have dramatically increased their costs by nearly fifty billion dollars per year. Paired with this has been the Obama Administration's continued blocking of the Keystone Pipeline, which would reduce oil prices in this country. Higher oil prices trickle down into higher costs for everything that moves by truck, train or airplane—which is mostly everything.

Second, Obama promised, when running for president, that he would nix tax increases on the middle class. He hasn't. Have your taxes stayed the same? Mine haven't, and I'm in the middle class. Instead, my taxes went up to pay for bailouts and to send more and more money overseas to other countries, some of which—admitted Secretary of State John Kerry—is being used to fund terrorism.

Third, when he ran for president Mr. Obama said he would cut the deficit by half during his first term. Instead, the deficit is twice what it was when he was elected (maybe more by the time you read this). Perhaps Obama just confused his division with multiplication. The administration simply proposes and orders spending that far outstrips revenue. Do that in your own family and see what happens. Obama is enslaving my children and grandchildren and probably endangering the very future of the country by putting us in that kind of debt.

Fourth, under Obama the IRS has targeted Christian groups and others perceived to be political adversaries of Democrats and the President. The director of the IRS was unapologetic about any of it. The IRS disobeyed subpoenas to produce documents and emails about this illegal activity of theirs, and the Obama Justice Department has done nothing about it. Surprise, surprise.

Fifth, need I say Obamacare? Obama lied to get it passed, saying "you can keep your doctor," when he knew that the effect of his plan would be to cause a mass exodus of doctors from participating in the program, making it significantly unlikely that you could keep your doctor and still be covered. Obama promised also that the Affordable Care Act would be just that, affordable, when what has happened is that the program costs the average American much more than his previous private insurance. And after the bill passed, Obama made two dozen changes to it by himself, without going through Congress, which is patently unconstitutional.

Sixth, Obama reversed himself on his campaign claim to be against homosexual marriage. Like Hillary Clinton, who said the same thing to voters she thought it would help her with, and then did an about face when the tide in the country turned, Obama discovered that the gay lobby was more powerful than he thought. He saw the gay light, so to speak, and now supports homosexual marriage, as well as championing every major tenet of the LGBTQ "community."

Seventh, Obama vilified George W. Bush for military involvement in the Middle East, got us out of Iraq, and then we watched Iraq be taken over again, this time by ISIS, which wants it as the core territory of a new Caliphate, with the intention of precipitating the Last Days, Islamic style. As of six months before his presidency is over, Obama hasn't made good on his promise to utterly defeat ISIS, and there's no prospect that he will. It will take someone more dedicated to the security of the U.S. and our allies to do that.

All over the Middle East the pattern is the same. Obama's timidity in international affairs has resulted in the strengthening of ISIS and other terrorist groups, and the situation is heating up in Europe as well. To the south in Africa, terrorists burned the U.S. Embassy in Lybia and killed our Ambassador and others. Obama echoed the now infamous and completely debunked notion that it was a spontaneous demonstration set off by an Internet video critical of "the Prophet." Obama, his Secretary of State at the time, Hillary Clinton, and his Ambassador to the U.N., Susan Rice, all parroted this explanation to the media, and Obama and all the rest of them knew it was a lie. His own administration had sent out emails urgently telling their people to draw attention away from the administration's policies and to blame an Internet video instead.

Eighth, Obama champions any and every method of allowing wholesale illegal immigration from Mexico and other points south. He has directed his own Justice Department not to deport illegal immigrants, and he has filed suit against states that are upholding their own laws with respect to illegal aliens. It is difficult to argue persuasively against the proposition that Obama's main reason for these actions is to win for Democrats the votes of Hispanics in general and illegal immigrants in particular once he manages to give them the vote, unconstitutionally. They already get government benefits that I pay for, even though they're breaking our laws just by being here.

Ninth, Obama champions the diminution of Second Amendment rights. He used to say otherwise, but he's dropped any pretense these days. Any time some criminal shoots someone and it makes the news, Obama goes out and self-righteously lobbies for gun control. Never do we hear him acknowledge the fact that thousands of times per year lawful gun owners and concealed weapons permit holders use their guns to prevent or foil crimes against themselves, their loved ones and their property. We only hear about the occasional nut case, and although some people think those cases are on the rise, statistics do not agree. There are fewer "mass shootings" now than in decades past. We *hear* about mass shootings now because of 24-hour news stations and the Internet, where before, the news of shootings out in the hinterlands often didn't make it through the local news filters and capture the interest of the broader public. In any event, the instance of a mass shooting now and then by a criminal does not in any way militate for a government grab of guns belonging to law abiding citizens who, after all, are the people threatened by those maniacs. Neither does a crime using a gun in any way justify the government's making it harder for people who obey the law to own or carry a weapon. We're the good guys.

Operation Fast and Furious was the Obama Justice Department's scheme to get American semi-automatic weapons into Mexico with the hope they would wind up in the hands of the drug cartels. It sounds insane, but the idea was that when the bad guys were caught with the weapons and the weapons were identified, average Americans would be up in arms, so to speak, against the terrible proliferation of guns. Only thing is, U.S. Border Patrol Agent Brian Terry was killed with one of those weapons, exposing the scheme. On the stand about the sneaky plan, Attorney General Eric Holder claimed he didn't know about the operation. He also wouldn't turn over the many documents that related to the operation, thus defying a court order, for which he was placed in contempt of court. Guess what happened because of that? Nothing.

By the way, this maddening, repeating event of Obama's doing something, a court ruling it unlawful, and nothing happening in consequence, makes me think of baseball. Under the new video review provisions, a team can challenge a ruling, the umpires gather on the third baseline to listen to a team of impartial umps in New York as they review the play, and then the spokes-ump takes off his headphones and either calls the runner out or signals that he stays on base (the typical situation). What if, when the ump makes a fist and calls the runner out, the player were to remain on the base anyway? It wouldn't happen, because *somebody* would go out and haul him off forcibly, if necessary. But that's what's going on in America with Obama. Courts say, 'That's wrong; you can't do that,' but nobody interrupts the process he has set in motion or undoes an order he has issued. What's going on, here?! And even if the process is stopped, the one who set it in motion goes on, planning his next violation of the Constitution. Why hasn't he been impeached?

Tenth, Obama's concept of America in the world is rotten to the core, and it has strengthened the hand of those who wish to destroy us. Obama thinks America is part of the problem, not part of the solution, that America is to blame for some people's hatred of us, and that America should apologize around the world for what we've done to them. He doesn't believe in American exceptionalism and he wants us to blend into the world community, not lead the world in illuminating the path to prosperity and freedom. What his philosophy does out there in the world is cancerous.

For one thing, it increases terrorism. Because of his philosophy, Obama will not call Islamic terrorists what they are, which affects the way the administration is behaving toward Islamic extremists, which has been timid, apologetic, and ineffective. In one example among many,

Nidal Hasan's attack on fellow soldiers at Fort Hood was labeled workplace violence, not terrorism, although it was manifestly the latter. This is not a matter of mere semantics: evasive and timid characterization of terrorism as something less than that creates an international impression that the United States is afraid to confront Islamic extremism for what it is. It's not just an impression: it is, in fact, the case. The result, if we don't act to reverse U.S. policy and activity on the international front quickly, may well be our national demise.

I tire of this list, and you tire of reading it. (It's okay, I understand.) But the list, you should understand, goes on. And on, and on, and on.

The bottom line is that when Obama leaves office, his work must be largely undone by someone who will work doubly hard to reverse course and fix what Obama has wrecked. That means the citizens of the U.S. simply *must not* elect a Democrat, in the first place, but it also means we need desperately to elect someone who will cancel nearly every executive order signed by Obama and steer us out of the terrible storm that lies in our path if we continue on the course that Obama set. If we do not succeed in doing this in November, then in the next four or eight years we may, in fact, have that Newtonian event that shocks the nation and convinces us our wagon has been emotionally hitched to the wrong political star. But even if that happens, it might be too late for the United States of America. God help us.

Just Say No to Obama and Garland

After the untimely death of Justice Antonin Scalia, political figures and pundits argued about what could happen, should happen, ought to happen, ought not to happen, with President Obama's fairly rapid nomination of Merrick Garland, a Federal Appeals Court judge, to replace the eminent deceased justice.

"I simply ask Republicans in the Senate to give him a fair hearing, and then an up-or-down vote," Mr. Obama said. "If you don't, then it will not only be an abdication of the Senate's constitutional duty, it will indicate a process for nominating and confirming judges that is beyond repair."

The Senate positioned itself on the opposite side: "Whether it's before the election or after the election, the principle is the American people are choosing their next president and their next president should pick this Supreme Court nominee."

McConnell even invoked what he calls the "Biden Rule," which is not a rule but a statement by Biden when he was a senator in 1992 that expressed the Democrats' position that in an election year a Republican president should not even nominate a Supreme Court replacement. McConnell's strategy illustrated that the Senate's delay in considering a nominee for the High Court—or any court—was a tactic employed by both parties under the same or similar circumstances. It's simply hypocrisy for anyone, Democrat or Republican, to condemn the other party for denying confirmation to the adverse party's presidential nominee to the Supreme Court.

Nothing could be clearer to the objective—or even the partisan but *reasoning* mind—than that the Senate's opting to refuse to hold confirmation hearings when a president is a lame duck and there's a vacancy on the Court is a valid way for the majority party to conduct business. The Constitution does not demand that the Senate fast-track a nomination or even that it hold hearings. It's one of the ways that this federal government, set up by some mighty smart people, exercises its system of checks and balances.

The refusal of the Republican majority in the Senate to hold hearings on Garland has actually resulted in SCOTUS decisions not generally liked by Republicans. A deadlock on the Supreme Court gave organized labor a victory by allowing a lower court decision to stand that public sector unions could collect dues from non-members to pay for collective bargaining activities. But another case under consideration may yield other results conservatives will not rue at all. A 2013 Texas law required abortion clinics to meet medical standards that outpatient surgical centers work under, and mandated that abortion-performing physicians have admitting privileges at a hospital within thirty miles. If the appeal to the Supreme Court results in a tie vote, the Texas law would stand.

So, having only eight justices on the high court is a mixed bag for Republicans and conservatives. But the Senate's strategy is not aimed at particular cases. It's a principled stance with the most obvious of justified motivations: to keep Obama from placing on the Court a jurist who will shift the highly predictable political philosophy of the Court to a leftist view. As McConnell put it, "I can't imagine that a Republican majority Senate, even if it were soon to be a minority, would want to confirm a judge that would move the court dramatically to the left."

Denials of Democrats that they have done the same thing in the past, implying they would never do such a thing as the evil Republicans are doing, are simply disingenuous.

Harry Reid said recently that Democrats "have never held up a Supreme Court nomination." I'm not going to use pretty circumlocutions to label this statement. It's simply a bald faced lie. Robert Bork, President Reagan's nominee to the High Court in 1987, was the subject of an absolutely unprecedented resistance movement by Democrats, who conducted a grilling that turned the confirmation hearings into what both parties say the process should not be—political—and then smiled as they consented to a vote, in which Bork lost. The man whom Reagan then nominated and who eventually got the seat Bork would have filled was Anthony M. Kennedy, who cast the deciding vote in one case that benefitted the pro-abortion movement and who since then has cast three deciding votes that advanced the homosexual agenda. Reagan has probably turned over in his grave.

The circumstances of this particular vacancy/nomination in 2016 are not unique. If the Senate doesn't hold hearings at all, that particular part of the process may be technically unprecedented, but the strategy is just the logical extension of the principled resistance of the Republican Party to cooperate with the leftist commitment of the current president. Rather than hold hearings and subject Obama's nominee to the kind of examination that might well ruin his career the same way that Democrats ruined the advancement of Robert Bork's, Republicans might even be doing Judge Garland a favor.

Not only so, but Obama knew that Garland was not going to be the next Justice. He knew it from the start. No doubt Garland knew it, too, and he agreed to be nominated as a sacrificial lamb anyway. I'm not sure why, except to hope, on a wing and a prayer, that the serious split in the Republican Party might result in a Democrat victory in the fall, and that perhaps, just perhaps, Garland might be re-nominated and confirmed by the next president, whether a him or her. (God help us.)

As I wrote in an earlier chapter, I have a friend in my profession who is on the diametrically opposite side of all things political from me. He rues the current division in the country and condemns conservatives for their having caused it. He's wrong about the cause and he's wrong to rue the division. From his perspective, I understand that he wishes we would all get along, and that as a result we would all vote Democrat, love Obama, and move farther to the left. I regret the division only because I regret the inability of conservatives to convince liberals that they, liberals and Democrats, are destroying the country. The division is necessary, because it is essential that conservatives stand fast against every leftist cause and maneuver. That includes the nomination of a liberal jurist to the Supreme Court.

He Had Help Crying

I do not for one moment believe that President Obama cried genuine tears of emotion in his speech January 6, 2016, announcing new executive orders regulating gun sales. He had help crying.

In the first episode of TV's NCIS, Agent Gibbs pulled Secret Service Agent Kate Todd aside and very bluntly broke the news of her boyfriend's sudden death by poisoning. Todd, clearly shocked, broke into tears and cursed Gibbs for his heartless attitude, but Gibbs didn't really know Todd yet, and she was already a possible suspect. So, Gibbs explained himself immediately: "I gave it to you cold. Wanted to see your reaction. "Liars can't pale on cue," he said. That's the truth. A good actor can act shocked, but going pale is an autonomic reaction, not something people can fake suddenly.

Neither can most people cry on cue. No one I know can, though some actors are reputed to be able to work themselves up to it. As a community theater actor with a college degree in theater, I've been fairly convincing myself on occasion, but shedding tears on cue is a rare talent. That's why movie actors have help. The standard aid used to be glycerine, though I don't know what it is now. But I'd lay odds that President Barrack Hussein Obama didn't cry spontaneously from emotion. If I were a betting man—and I'm not; I've never even bought a lottery ticket—I would lay good money on a wager that Obama had medical help in producing tears when he began to try to wring the same thing out of Americans when attempting to justify more restrictions on gun sales.

His show of what he wanted us to think were genuine emotions was like so much of the other fakery of his presidency: the public pretense of concern, concealing the actual purpose.

My suspicions are borne out of my certainty that Obama is not committed to reducing gun violence, only to reducing gun ownership. Like any big government Democrat, Obama is afraid of rank and file Americans who, in his words, cling to guns and religion. Liberals and Democrats (often the same thing) fear the theoretical revolt of independence-minded Americans who will at some point reach the limit of their tolerance for the Constitution-eroding, rights-grabbing, power hungry Federal Government (and some state governments as well). It has been pointed out often that one of the first things tyrants do on their rise to power is to disarm the citizenry. Such a move obviously wouldn't be explained as a preface to totalitarianism; instead, the government's actions would be couched in terms of its protecting the citizenry and making their lives better by reducing crime, etc. "We're from the government and we're hear to help you!"

Now as we approach the State of the Union Address, we hear there will be an empty seat in the House representing the victims of gun violence, like a missing jet in formation. In theory I have no objection. However, I think there ought to be a sign in the chair that says, "Chicago Murder Victims." There's a city that is controlled, absolutely run by Democrats, with some of the strictest gun laws in the nation, and it has a runaway gun violence problem. Interested in the stats for 2015?

Shot & Killed:	443
Shot & Wounded:	2,552
Total Shot:	2,995
Total Homicides:	501

Yet we never hear Democrats or this administration talk about how their new proposals for taking away my guns are going to solve the problem of gun violence in a city where nobody who's a law abiding citizen is supposed to be carrying a gun. (Actually, the state of things in Chicago is in a sort of limbo, as they wrestle with how to fight the Supreme Court's decision that their laws are unconstitutional.) So I think the empty seat in the House when Obama gets some more help and manages to cry some more tears (and he will, I'd bet on it) should say: "Chicago: 2,995 wounded, 443 killed. What are you doing about that, Mr. President?"

Until Obama can promise me without lying (which is to say he can't promise me) that his orders or liberals' new laws taking away my Second Amendment rights will absolutely protect me from criminals, who don't obey the law and will have guns anyway, then I will oppose anyone who thinks he's going to disarm me. It's basic self preservation.

Cry all you want, Mr. President, but you're not going to convince me you really care about gun violence any more than the rest of us. You simply think you can put the toothpaste back into the tube, and you can't. Since we can't un-invent guns, the only thing we can do is make sure that if the bad guys have them, the good guys do, too. You wouldn't want a policeman responding to a disturbance without a weapon. In this country, every person has a right to be his own protector in the face of violent threats. That's the way the Founders wrote it, and it's the way things ought to be.

Obama's Plan is Working

Back during the summer I wrote an email to, well, someone you'd know, telling him my guess as to the President's 7-point plan for Hillary:

1. Let the information about Hillary's email fiasco dribble out, a drop at a time.
2. Hold off the dogs of the FBI and the Justice Department telling them, "Wait for it, wait for it."
3. Keep Biden out of the presidential race while he builds up emotional sympathy and Democrats' romance with Hillary finally sours enough to dump her.
4. When the time is right, confront Hillary with an ultimatum: drop out of the race, or I'll let the dogs loose and you'll be indicted.
5. If Hillary drops out, Biden immediately announces his candidacy.
6. If Hillary tells Obama to go jump, Obama tells the Justice Department, "Now."
7. Either way, Hillary is toast and Biden is toasted as the new heir apparent to the Presidency.

Considering the report out today that Hillary and Obama have had it out over the rising tide of government investigation of her—which she blames him for (and rightly), I think the time is just about right. Expect to hear very shortly, within the month, that Hillary is out and Biden is in.[1]

Have you noticed that every time Hillary appears in public she smiles like a clown and applauds herself? In just a little bit, we'll see how happy-clappy she is. The clock is ticking down.

---

[1] I wrote this short article well before the primaries and the 2016 election. I think I'll just wait for my own book to come out to see if I was anywhere near right.

Is Obama Self-Evidently Anything?

I gave Chris Christie good marks for the CNN Debate on September 16, 2015, but he was not my favorite candidate among the stampede of Republicans wanting the White House. It surprised me, however, to hear his comments on Donald Trump's post-debate rally where some one (not a reporter) asked him what he would do about Muslim terrorists—the questioner said the President was a Muslim and not an American. Trump didn't chide the fellow or correct him. He brushed off the question quickly and generally and went to someone else.

The media loved it because it gave them something to hate. They immediately set about trying to pit candidates on both sides against Trump. An interviewer asked Chris Christie what he thought about the incident and while Christie didn't weigh in on what Trump should do now, he did say, if the same thing happened to him, "I would correct him. I'd say that the President's a Christian and he was born in this country. Those two things are self-evident."

I take issue with Christie most forcefully. There's nothing self-evident about Obama's religion. Granted, he is a member of Trinity United Church of Christ in Chicago, but if you know anything about that church you know it isn't very distinct as to its Christology. It is far more a political rallying place for Black-related current events than it is a lighthouse for the gospel of Jesus Christ. Its beliefs have been heavily shaped by Black Liberation Theology, a theological trend in which major tenets of Christianity are seen through a heavily colored filter of race, where Blacks in America are held to be oppressed constantly and systematically by Whites. The now infamous Jeremiah Wright, who was Obama's pastor, appeared to be constantly angry at Whites and America in general.

Black Liberation Theology in part arose out of the need of Black Christians to respond to the criticisms of Black Muslims (The Nation of Islam), who said that Blacks could not be Christians and loyal to the Black cause at the same time, because, as they said, racism was endemic to Christianity.

The Trinity United Church of Christ has a creed, and the term "Black" or "Blacks" appears seventeen times in it. The name of Christ, other than in the name of the church, appears *nowhere* in the creed, nor does the name Jesus. The mere fact that someone is a member of the Trinity United Church of Christ may be reason to call into question his identity as a biblical Christian.

All that aside, it is not self-evident that Obama is a Christian. He said at one point that he is a Christian, but that proves absolutely nothing, as evangelical preachers constantly try to get people to see. I understand that Obama reads devotionals regularly; that's good. He rarely attends church; that may be safer for him, but he doesn't let security issues keep him from going on late-night shows or playing golf.

What really casts Obama's Christianity into doubt is his affinity for Islam. There can be no serious denial of the assertion that President Obama has favored Muslims right and left during his term of office, while largely ignoring the rising tide of anti-Christian sentiment in this country. His steadfast avoidance of identifying Islamic terrorism as what it is when it strikes frequently, is a matter of great concern, and it points to a probable lack of desire to show antipathy toward a manifestation of the religion that he feels very close to.

It's understandable that Obama would have this affinity for Islam. His father, a Kenyan, had a Muslim background though he wasn't much of anything when he married Obama's mother in Hawaii. His mother wasn't much of anything, either, though she came from Christian parents. The President wrote of his mother that "she had a healthy skepticism of religion as an institution." Obama has apparently inherited that skepticism, and he is not much of anything religiously, either.

Judging from what has been made public, what religious ideas Obama has are confused, an amalgam of Muslim sentiments and affections drawn from his father's general heritage, with some general Christian ideas seen through racially polarized optics. The result is that he is sympathetic with Muslims while having a rather blasé view of Christianity—the evangelical sort, anyway. If he feels the need to defend anyone, it's not Christians but Muslims. He comes to their defense rather regularly, while the few statements I have ever heard him make about Christians seem to have been prodded out of him by advisers who have likely told him he needs to throw Christians a bone now and then.

Was it a slip of the tongue in 2008 when Obama told George Stephanopoulos that "John McCain has not talked about my Muslim faith"? In context, he certainly seems to have been referring to the fact that McCain had not said Obama was a Muslim, but I know if I had been saying what Obama was telling Stephanopoulos, I would have rearranged my words and made it clear that "my" and "Muslim faith" don't belong together in the same sentence. But then, I'm a very much a Christian and very adamant that I do not accept any of the tenets of Islam. I don't believe one can say that about Barack Obama.

I doubt, too, that I would ever be caught saying that the sound of minarets calling Muslims to prayer at sunset is "one of the prettiest sounds in the world." He said that when he was running for president, and he also recited the opening to the Islamic call to prayer in what has been described as a first-rate Arabic accent. I've heard the Muslim call to prayer in Jerusalem, and in the light of what's going on in the world today it's eerily menacing. I think if I were commenting on Muslim culture as Obama did I would have steered clear of being confused for a Muslim, but then I'm very much a Christian and very cautious about the impression I leave with people about my beliefs and associations. I don't think one can say that about Barack Obama.

I also doubt that I would refer to Jesus as "*a son* of God," as Obama did in 2012 at an Easter Prayer Breakfast. In prepared remarks he referred to "all that Christ endured—not just as a son of God, but as a human being." Muslims don't believe that Jesus was either "the" or "a" son of God, but a messenger. It's Mormons who sometimes refer to Jesus as *a son* of God. But so do many people who have the concept that various historical figures who have been mystics or generic spiritual leaders are "sons of God." Obama is apparently not committed to the belief that Jesus was and is the unique Son of God, God the Son, the only Savior. If I had been in Obama's position at that breakfast and had said Jesus was "a son of God," and had heard myself, I would have corrected myself immediately. If I had been informed of my gaffe later, I would have corrected myself as soon as I could. But then, I'm a committed Christian and very concerned about expressing my faith biblically and not being misleading. I don't think one can say that about Barack Obama.

Do I think Obama is a Muslim? No. Nor would being a Muslim disqualify him for the Presidency, though I doubt he would have been elected if he had actually been a Muslim and had been known to be such. That's not the point of this continuing national debate. What people wish they could do is nail him down to some defensible identification, and there's the rub. I don't think he's a genuine anything, whether Muslim or Christian. Christianity is easy to feign for the general public, by casual claims, by the use of quasi Christian phrases, or by just occasionally going to church. It's harder to convince devoted Christians of genuine Christian faith, however, because they notice the absence of the marks of believers.

If anything is "self-evident," as Chris Christie said, it's that Obama cannot make a defensible claim to being an orthodox Christian. What is self-evident is that Obama possesses religious ideas that align in part with Christianity, in part with Islam, in part with generic Black spirituality, and in part with Liberation Theology. Mostly I think Obama is just a basic theist. He acquired his father's theological amorphism and his mother's skepticism, and there is no evidence that he has ever had a conversion experience to anything in particular.

As to whether Obama is self-evidently an American citizen, I still think the jury is out on that debate. I'm a strong believer that where there is smoke there is usually fire, and there's plenty of smoke here, far more than exists to prove that aliens crashed at Area 51. I don't believe that Hillary Clinton is innocent of conducting classified communication using her private email server simply because she has given us some of her emails and said, "See?" In the same way I don't believe Obama's giving us a birth certificate from Hawaii—after refusing to do so for suspiciously too long—proves that he was born there. I think the evidence that has been adduced or produced pointing to his Kenyan origins deserves official scrutiny in a public way, but I doubt it will get such treatment. However, in a day and time when Congress holds hearings on the length of frog hairs, I think it makes sense to say, Okay, hold a hearing on Obama's country of origin, and let's be done with it, one way or the other. It won't happen. For that reason, there will always be doubt.

The bottom line is that it isn't self-evident that Obama is a Christian or a natural-born American.

These issues, however, are less important to me than that Obama is a socialist. Now *that* is self-evident.

Impeach Obama

Mark Twain once said, "Everybody talks about the weather, but nobody does anything about it." I feel that way about the rising discontent about Barack Hussein Obama.

Initially, it was only Republicans, Libertarians, and independents who objected to Obama's becoming the president of the United States. He was liberal. He was possibly Marxist. He was certainly anti-capitalist. He was a closet emperor. Unfortunately, objectors were outnumbered by the blind, who simply heard a message of hope and change and pulled the lever (or pushed a computer button) for the man. Now that he's out of the closet on not only his desire to be emperor but his dangerous brand of socialism slash liberalism, significant numbers of your ordinary, everyday Democrats realize that Obama is threatening the future of America. More and more people have decided that the only "hope" they have now is that we can "change" presidents soon.

So the airwaves, or the cable wires and satellite transmissions, are rife with the complaints of more and more Americans about the political weather in Washington, particularly the dangerous White House front moving over the country. Unfortunately, nobody is doing anything about it.

I believe Obama should be impeached.

I know, the chances of that happening are slim, but the reasons for it are solid. Obama has acted numerous times outside the constitutional limits of his office, through his so-called recess appointments and his executive orders, if not the actions of the IRS in trying to squelch conservatives. Obama's chief legislative initiative, Obamacare, while ruled constitutional by the Supreme Court, isn't, no matter what they say, but while he could not be impeached on that count since SCOTUS has given him a pass on it, he could be impeached for issuing executive orders every other week altering the Affordable Care Act unilaterally so as to excuse this group or that from the law's execution.

Of course, I would like to impeach him simply for being the most arrogant person I have ever seen in public office,[2] but I realize that wouldn't be considered an impeachable offense. What it should have been, however, was sufficient reason for people not to have elected

---

[2]This article was written before Donald Trump became a candidate for president, but also before the November, 2016, elections. I muse as I write this whether Obama's arrogance will be surpassed.

Obama in the first place.

That, I suppose, is the most curious and troubling thing about this whole Obama presidency. How could the majority of the electorate not have seen through this man from the beginning? What superficial, distorted, misguided, anti-American sentiments led people to vote for Obama? Certainly a good portion of those votes came from people who were or hoped to be on the public dole.

It does little good for me to say, as many people have, that they deserve what they get for having elected Barack Hussein Obama to the White House, because the sad fact is that we will *all* get what only those who voted for him deserve.

I love some of the bumper stickers that throw Obama's—and all his voters'—slogan back in their faces:

"Forget Hope and Change: I'll settle for Competence."

"Hope and Change (crossed out): Bait and Switch"

"I'll keep my Guns, Religion and Freedom: You keep the Change."

(Picture of Reagan) "Remember Real Hope and Change?"

(Picture of Bush) "Miss Me Yet?"

"How's that Hope and Change workin' out for ya?"

It doesn't make me feel better, however, to come up with some new zinger, some persuasive observation about Obama, because nobody who is in a position to do anything about him seems to be trying. Lindsay Graham is up there in the Senate saying that this or that won't stand, but it still stands. Talk! Boehner (gone now) barked about this and that, but the House of Representatives mostly gets together and talks! I'm just one of the little people out in the sticks who can't do anything about the government that is eating our lunch, tapping our phones, taxing us to death, taxing us after death, and otherwise generally taking control of our lives. The only thing I can do besides talk is vote, and I do. The fools and the blind simply outnumber me.

We've had a lot of men in the White House who have done illegal, immoral, unethical, un-Constitutional things, but Obama is on track to set the record for the most destructive presidency ever. It amazes me that he still has a cheerleading section that defends him no matter how miserable his policies and actions are going to make their children and grandchildren, if not them.

I wish someone who doesn't have blinders on, who isn't fooled by him, who isn't prejudiced for him, isn't giddy to make America into an echo of the dead Soviet Union, would do something about him.

Impeach Obama!

President's Policy on Press Criticism

(Note: This policy paper was recently unearthed, so to speak,
in a collection of uncatalogued documents at the White House.[3])

From the Desk of President Franklin Delano Roosevelt
Date: October 1, 1939

My Fellow Americans and my Friends,

I speak to you tonight to lay out what shall be the policy of the United States as regards public statements of this administration about the government of Germany and its leader, Adolph Hitler. It shall be the policy of this Administration to maintain the highest respect for the government of the German people, and in particular Chancellor Adolph Hitler.

Some of our friends in various European nations have expressed concern over actions taken by the German government vis a vis Poland a few days ago. Specifically, critics in Poland have characterized the German visit as an encroachment. The United States shall consider the actions of Germany as an investment in the future well being of Poland, and shall regard Chancellor Hitler with optimism. The U.S. is confident that Hitler will be able to demonstrate to the world the beneficence of his actions.

I note with great sadness the tendency of the press in our fellow democracies of Europe to call Chancellor Hitler a dictator or worse, and I wish you to know that this president respects the Chancellor and views him with high regard.

This Administration wishes its policy to extend to the fifth estate, the estimable press of the great cities of the United States. Under the First Amendment, while it is technically the right of any newspaper publisher to engage in criticism of political leaders, it is understandable that on the world stage the leaders of countries whose present political circumstances are precarious, would justifiably resent the attempt of the foreign press to impugn their motives or condemn their actions. We may reasonably expect, therefore, that a critical press would share the

---

[3]Readers may need to review their Oxford, Webster's or other dictionary for the meaning of "satire." What would happen if Roosevelt had adopted the sort of hands-off approach to international events that Obama has?

blame for any reprisals that foreign leaders might take against the armed forces of the United States.

Therefore, it shall be the policy of this Administration to pursue dialogue with the press in this country to seek agreements on the reasonable quelling of American criticism of Hitler. The safety of our troops at home and those few stationed abroad depends in part on the good will of Hitler and other leaders such as Benito Mussolini in Italy and Emperor Hirohito in Japan. I am certain that if Americans will join me in congenial expressions of mutual good will with these great nations of the world, we will all live together in peace.

While we acknowledge that, in parts of the world, governments regard themselves as in a state of war with each other, we need not use their language or adopt their aggressive stances toward respectable world leaders. If there is war, it is their war.

I hope the United States will keep out of this war. I believe that it will. And I give you assurance and reassurance that every effort of your Government will be directed toward that end.[4]

---

[4]This ending paragraph appeared in Roosevelt's Fireside Chat on September 3, 1939. Hitler had invaded Poland on September 1, 1939. Strangely, this document represents a Fireside Chat Roosevelt never gave. I will inquire as to why, but I am doubtful that an answer will be forthcoming.

Trump and the 2016 Election

The Difference Between Egotistical Narcissists

When campaigning for the 2016 Presidential Election cranked up and Donald Trump decided to get into the race, I said immediately that I didn't support him. We already had an egotistical narcissist in the White House: why should we replace him with another?

Now near the middle of March, the Republican field has narrowed to four candidates: John Kasich, Marco Rubio, Ted Cruz and Donald Trump, in order of their pledged delegates, least to most. Some people say Trump is pretty much assured the nomination, but I'm not certain that's true. Multiple scenarios are possible whereby one of the other three, or someone else, could be the final candidate, as a result of a contested convention.

Trump supporters can be heard saying at this point that if Trump goes into the convention with a substantial delegate lead, though not the number needed for the nomination on the first ballot, they think it will be dirty politics if he isn't eventually selected. By expressing this sort of opinion these Trump supporters give away their basic ignorance of the way the political parties work.

We don't have direct popular election of the president in this country. Neither do we have a direct nomination of candidates. We have a two party system. Anyone who is a member of one of the two parties can run for the office. The parties have primaries in each of the states, with some states having a caucus form instead. Even among the primary states delegates are chosen differently. Some give all the delegates to the candidate who gets the most votes, while others apportion delegates among the candidates getting a percentage of the vote over a certain threshold.

What's important to realize about the national convention of either party is that the country at large does not control the parties: the parties control the parties. They are private organizations with members, and the members make the rules. To assert, as many of Trump's supporters do, that Trump should be nominated irrespective of party rules and procedures is a reflection of not only ignorance but also obstinacy. "I don't care how the system works; I want my way."

I think it's very likely that the Republican National Convention will be contested. Marco Rubio or John Kasich may drop out within a short time, either because one of them suffers embarrassing losses where he should have won or because he listens to reason and decides to let the non-Trump voters partly consolidate behind the number two candidate, Ted Cruz. Theoretically, Cruz could have the lead among three candidates going into the convention. Obviously if it comes down to two, one of them will have enough for the nomination. In a contested convention, or heaven forbid a brokered one, Donald Trump may lose, or he may win. A lot can happen between now and then. Things are in constant flux.[5]

As I began by saying, however, if it comes down to Donald Trump's being the nominee, I still feel the same about him: I'd rather not put another egotistical narcissist in the White House. We have an arrogant emperor there now.

However—and this is a very, very big however—if the race comes down to Trump on the Republican side, it really doesn't matter who is the Democratic nominee. As I have said and will say again shortly, anyone with an "R" in front of his name. Electing Hillary Clinton or Bernie Sanders will complete the demolition of this country.

So where does that leave the matter of putting another arrogant president in power? I think it comes down to the striking difference between Trump and the President we now have. The difference between Trump and Obama is that Trump is an egotistical narcissist who believes that America is the greatest country in the world and should remain so, while Obama is an egotistical narcissist who believes that America is too big for its britches and needs to be taken down a peg or two. He's been trying to do it for more than seven years. Trump pledges to reverse that trend.

Trump is definitely not the candidate I hoped would be in the lead in mid March, 2016. I still hope he will be displaced by Ted Cruz. But if he isn't, it isn't the end of the world or the country. However, it will be, if the Republican candidate, whoever he is, doesn't beat the Democrat. In view of that, any Republican who helps the Democrat win by failing to vote will be a traitor to the cause.

---

[5]Of course, by the time this book went to press, one of those fluxes took place, Cruz dropped out, and Trump garnered the support of enough delegates to secure the nomination outright.

Anybody With an "R" After His Name

- If I can't go to the prom with the prettiest girl in school, I'll go with the ugliest one instead.

- If I can't go to heaven on my terms, I'll go to hell to spite God.

- If I can't have the big juicy steak I've been craving all day, I'll eat worms.

- If the Republican Party nominates somebody other than the candidate I like, I'll vote for Hillary.

They're all the same thing. I defy you to find any flaw in the logic. Moreover, I defy you to argue logically that it makes any sense to vote for Hillary if Trump or Cruz or Rubio, for instance, does not win the Republican nomination.

If you would have voted Republican but you plan to "protest" the nomination of Trump by voting for a Democrat, you're either proving that you are absolutely stupid or you're showing everyone that you have no principles at all. There is next to no similarity between Trump and Clinton, even less between Cruz or Rubio and Clinton, and, if the Democrat were to be Bernie, there's vast crevasse between any Republican in the race and Sanders.

So why would anyone who previously wanted to vote for a Republican in this election vote instead for Hillary or someone even worse if the "wrong" candidate gets the Republican nod? To protest the nominee? Do you really think anyone would get the message? Do you really think anyone would be affected by your protest?

Just as bad as pushing the "Hillary button" on the voting machine is not showing up to vote at all. That would be like saying, "If I can't go to heaven on my terms when I die, I'll not go anywhere at all." Sorry, but you don't have that choice. If you don't choose heaven on God's terms, you've chosen to go the other direction. There's nothing more clear in the Bible than that.

Same with voting. If you don't vote, you're voting for the opponent of the one you would have voted for. You must realize that 9 million Republicans who didn't vote in the last presidential election decided the election in favor of Barack Obama.

That's why I say, Anyone with an "R" after his name. That's not the thing you had in mind in the middle of 2015 when there were nearly twenty candidates; it's not even the thing you had in mind at the dawn of 2016; and it's not the kind of ambivalence you inject into the campaign of one of the remaining half dozen, or three, or even two candidates. Run the preliminary races as if you were running the final one; strive to have your favorite nominated. But when one of them wins the nomination, *get behind him, whoever he is.* In this election year, the only choice that makes sense at all to people who want to save the nation from plummeting over the edge of a political cliff—with little likelihood of ever recovering a Constitutional and moral government—is to choose the Republican.

There's very little difference in the principles that define Rubio and Cruz. Trump, for all his personality flaws, still has plans and principles that differ markedly from any Democrat. The other "R" candidates have little chance to be nominated, but among them even Kasich would be much, much better to lead this nation than Hillary Clinton.

Take your head out of the sand: this country is going to go down the tubes if we have another eight years of liberal Democrat leadership. For certain, we're looking at the death of the First and Second Amendments, the virtual dissolution of our borders, voting rights for illegal aliens, surrender of U.S. sovereignty to world courts and other world organizations, the concession of laws and land to Islamic states, the growth of communism in the world, and many other things that true Americans find unthinkable.

In other words, if you vote "D" instead of "R" this fall, or you don't vote at all, you may not personally be going to hell, but you're certainly voting for the country to go there.

Will Trump Finally Fail?

Ever since Donald Trump entered the race for the Republican Party's nomination for president, Party establishment people as well as most Democrats have repeatedly claimed that Trump won't win the nomination—even can't win the nomination.[6] They're adamant that he isn't a serious candidate, or if he's personally serious, he isn't fundamentally serious because he isn't substantive (their assessment).

In other words, opponents of Donald Trump are urgent to believe that there's no way he could be president,[7] because they are afraid of the possibility. Never mind that he's running away with the polls and has been since nearly the beginning of the race.

Obviously the race is far from over, however. The Republican Convention is just about exactly seven months away. A lot can take place in that time. But what has happened in the previous year? Trump talked about running for a while before announcing; he officially threw his hat in the ring six months ago. He has been the frontrunner most of the time since. Further, he has made a number of highly controversial statements that his opponents have repeatedly said would ruin him, and which conversely have boosted Trump's support. At a loss to understand the phenomenon, political pundits of all stripes have been analyzing and over-analyzing Trump's popularity, putting out a wide variety of plausible (mostly) explanations.

David Merritt, who advised three Republican campaigns and is now with Luntz Global Partners, wrote an article attempting to explain why, in the face of his overwhelming poll dominance, Donald Trump is not the frontrunner. Merritt doesn't bother wasting time trying to explain how Trump will fall in the polls. Essentially, Merritt just tells us that the polls most referred to have it all wrong. In doing so, Merritt reveals, probably inadvertently, why his own organization's "polling" data (Luntz does focus group polling) was possibly grossly wrong.

Merritt tells us first that in April, 2015, the Luntz organization polled

---

[6]While this article was written in December, 2015, this book is being compiled in early June, 2016. Everyone but Trump suspended his campaign or dropped out of the race altogether. Donald Trump recently acquired the number of delegates needed for nomination on the first ballot.

[7]With Trump the only remaining, active candidate, actor George Clooney said derisively on May 14, "Look, Donald Trump is *not* going to be president."

1,200 likely Republican voters in the four states that would have the first primaries. That was two months before Trump officially became a candidate. Merritt's point in referring to the poll was to point out how things have changed in eight months. The poll in April largely showed that Trump would not get prevailing support for the nomination, and obviously there is great fear now among some who were certain that he wouldn't, that he will.

Right off the bat, however, the April poll was deficient, because it didn't include independents, who I suspect will turn out in unprecedented droves this time for both primaries and the general election. Many independents these days tell us they're in-between parties because up until now the establishment candidates in both parties have been routinely breaking promises they made when campaigning, or not promising to do anything about things that deeply concern the grassroots citizenry. A poll that seeks to understand Trump's popularity without asking these no-party people, who *will* vote in primaries, is going to be a defective poll from the start. As a baseline for making his observations now, the poll Merritt refers to shouldn't have been trusted thoroughly in April, 2015.

Further, the questions the Luntz group asked these not-quite-so-representative Republicans may have skewed the answers. I don't have a copy of the actual poll, but Merritt's article about it strongly justifies inferences as to what the questions were.

For instance, Merritt says the polled group wanted "a moderate governor with a proven track record of results." That wouldn't have been a phrase people just made up; it would have been a choice from a multiple choice question. Clearly, "a moderate governor" refers to one of two specific candidates in the field. In fact, the polled Republicans wanted a governor over a senator, a moderate over a strong conservative, someone who had balanced budgets (which would be a governor) and had cut taxes (which, in spite of the lofty self-assessments of senators, would be a governor). The last thing they wanted was "a very successful self-made businessman." Obviously the 1,200 people polled were in favor of Jeb Bush, and sniffed at Trump.

Does anyone think that even in April, 2015 the people who would vote in the Republican primary were strongly in favor of Jeb Bush? Jeb's numbers have never, ever been that good, and there's no way that any of Merritt's reasoning could explain how Jeb was really in first place, despite it all.

Well, Merritt's point in the article was to say that things have changed a lot since April. Donald Trump announced his candidacy and immediately began to rise to the top of the standings and hasn't lost his place. He hasn't even been threatened.

In spite of all this history, Merritt writes to tell us all why Trump will not be the candidate.

Let me first say that he may be right.[8] As I said, a lot could happen in the next eleven months—who knows that Trump will still be in the lead? Even if he is, who knows what machinations may take place within the party at the convention?

So it could happen that Trump will take a turn for the worse. But why is Merritt so certain that he will, that Republicans will suddenly sweep in another direction and drop Trump? It's as if Merritt sees Trump's followers en masse like a flock of starlings moving mindlessly in murmuration, shifting in the wind toward another candidate. Why would they do it?

Merritt thinks they will because consistent polling shows that Americans want (there's that phrase, again, "Americans want;" see my chapter on "What Americans Want") someone who can solve problems, not just rail at them, someone with serious solutions. Time and again Trump's critics have blasted him as a candidate who isn't serious, with "solutions" that aren't serious, or aren't practical. Merritt thinks that Republicans, even those who now are responsible for Trump's lead in the polls, will see the light and turn to someone else.

Who? Cruz or Rubio? Someone as yet waiting in the wings? Why? Merritt simply reviews for his readers the positions of Cruz and Rubio and argues that they make sense and that they're eminently supportable. For that reason and that reason alone, Merritt claims, "That's why the true frontrunner is not Donald Trump."

To bolster his opinion, Merritt points to a poll (I know, I'm tired of polls, too) in which 71% of voters—not just Republicans, but all voters—say that rounding up and deporting all illegal immigrants (the generally reported view of Donald Trump) is unrealistic, and most say it's impossible.

What is going to force significant numbers of Trump's supporters to finally rectify practical sense with their emotional attachment to him?

---

[8]At compilation time, Trump has secured the nomination (without shenanigans) but now we're hearing talk of a contested *election,* not merely a contested convention, where a third party candidate keeps anyone from a majority of electoral college votes and the election moves into the House of Representatives. Some people really, *really* don't want Trump to be Pres.

Merritt doesn't say. He just assumes it will happen.

Let me say at this point that I like Ted Cruz, and I like Marco Rubio pretty well, too. I see Cruz pulling steadily forward in popular support. Perhaps the campaign has been, and will continue to be, more like the race between the tortoise and the hare than like a 100-yard dash. Maybe the candidate who makes steady progress will win, while the one who dashed to the front at the start will lose steam. I don't know. But I don't think it will have anything to do with Trump's supporters waking up from some kind of dream and admitting they've been stupid. Nor do I think that many of his supporters don't actually intend to show up to vote.

If someone displaces Trump for first place among Republicans, I think it will be because another candidate shows himself superior to Trump in ideas to accomplish the same broad goals he has espoused, and who can ignite the same kind of fire in the hearts of Americans who want their country back from freedom-destroying, gun-confiscating, abortion-worshiping, tax-raising, Muslim-favoring, terrorist-enabling, country-dishonoring, Constitution-violating liberals. The phenomenon of Donald Trump is the direct result of the Presidency of Barack Obama. The candidate to best him, if not Trump himself, would have to be one who is equal to Trump in vowing to reverse the failure and treachery of Obama, while being better than Trump in his plans to accomplish these goals.

Frankly, as I have written elsewhere, the candidate who likely will get my vote will promise to undo, with a stroke of the pen, nearly every executive order issued by the current president. I only wish we could write that president out of our history. I'd like to forget he ever existed.

On the other hand, we remember the Alamo. And the Maine. And Pearl Harbor. And 9/11. They were awful events that remind us forever to do everything in our power to never let them happen again.

Homosexuality

Do Homosexuals Wear Genes?

Homosexuals probably think the holy grail of their cause has been located. In November, 2015, a lab at UCLA (of course) announced a study telling the world that homosexuality may be linked to seven epigenomes, the chemistry that switches a portion of the human gene on or off. The biochemistry is quite complex. But to summarize it, using a map of the epigenome, these UCLA researchers were able to predict with a 70% success rate which one of twins in the study was a homosexual. Their theory is that the chemical marker, or switch, gets turned on by something, causing that person to become attracted to his own sex. The study included only male homosexuals.

Various British attendees to the conference where the UCLA lab announced its findings were mostly skeptical. Looking at the study, Darren Griffin, professor of genetics at the University of Kent, took issue with it, saying he believed the data show that multiple factors contribute to homosexuality, including life experiences. (Hmm, let me see: yep, that's what I've been saying for fifty years, and I'm not a scientist by profession; but Griffin is, and quite a qualified one. What, so not all scientists agree that homosexuality is genetically determined? Amazing!)

What I find more interesting about this recent study from UCLA (of course) is who did it. Remember the study out of Harvard that was debunked because it was conducted by homosexuals who configured the data to produce the desired result? Well, the head of this study out of UCLA (of course) is Dr. Tuck Ngun, a young buck just out of grad school, who describes himself this way in a published text: "I am a giant (gay) geek." No-o-o-o, no bias there.

Here's what the UCLA Center for Gender Based Biology says about Ngun in its official faculty description:

Tuck Ngun, Phd.

Tuck is a postdoctoral scholar in the lab whose main interest is in sex differences in the brain and behavior. He is currently investigating the biological basis of sexual orientation using twin pairs that are discordant for sexual orientation with Matteo Pellegrini's group. In addition, he is working on the genetics of gender identity in collaboration with Dr. Mark Keil, who is currently at the University of Michigan Medical School. Tuck was a graduate student in the lab. His dissertation work focused on the long-term effect of perinatal testosterone exposure on the brain and the role of sex chromosome complement and number on behavior and molecular phenotypes in the brain of a mouse model of Klinefelter Syndrome. Tuck graduated from the University of California, San Diego with a B.S. in Molecular Biology where he worked on elucidating the links between splicing and transcription.[9]

Did you get all that? Biologists just love to speak their own lingo. Let's see if I can decipher it for you. Tuck is just out of school and is trying to prove that homosexuals are genetically determined, so he can feel better about himself, because right now he is laden with guilt that he successfully hides beneath a veneer of giddy and carefree "gayness." (That part I just inferred.) He's gathered a test group of male twins, 37 pairs where one in each pair is homosexual, the other not, and 10 more where both are homosexual. He's trying to find proof that some biochemical influence triggered a change in the genes of the homosexuals, making them "gay." [For you newcomers, refer to my previous articles why I'm determined not to use the word "gay" to refer to homosexuals.]

I predict that what will happen is that the study will either prompt its prejudiced performers to reach logically flawed conclusions that will ring hollow with less compromised scientists, or it will fizzle because it can't go farther than making inductive guesses guided by preconceptions. In any event, the study will not change the facts. People are born heterosexual; a small minority become homosexual afterwards.

---

[9]"Former Team Members," U.C.L.A. Gender Center for Gender Based Biology, Available at *"https://gendercenter.genetics.ucla.edu/ former-team-members"*, the Internet.

Gayhoo

Yahoo might as well rename itself Gayhoo, because it's officially the most left wing, anti-Christian, anti-conservative, pro-homosexual "news" site out there in cyberspace. Time was when Yahoo was the go-to news site, the site that computer technicians automatically typed in when they wanted to test Internet connectivity, the site where newbies went to get their first Internet-based email accounts. It still may be, but now, it treats all visitors to news content absolutely loaded with the homosexual agenda.

This book features many articles about the homosexual quest for domination, but I don't pretend this book is a compendium of objective articles. Yahoo, however, does implicitly claim objectivity, since it purports to deliver the news, which by any common standard should at least approach objectivity. In fact, however, Yahoo news is highly biased—no, let me restate that: far from being merely biased, Yahoo is a division of the army of homosexuality's immoral imperialism.

Once a week or so I note how many pro-homosexual articles there are relative to other "news"—which often cannot really be called news. The balance of articles features anti-Christian pieces, anti-conservative political writings, and fluff—entertainment news for those who live their lives vicariously through tales of the rich and famous, and royalty.

This week I note that of the top fifty articles, ten of them are homosexual propaganda, often connecting to the anti-Christian theme, or showing how victorious homosexuals are in their ongoing quest of intimidating the political and social structure. Here are the headers for those ten:

Mississippi pastor trots out horse in wedding dress to protest gay marriage

Children Of LGBT Couples Share Their Experiences Growing Up

I Was Taught To Be Ashamed Of My Sexuality

Cure Homophobia With This One Weird Trick!

Judge refuses to lift stay, permit gay marriages in Texas

Alabama recalls vanity license plate with gay slur

When a Homophobic Group Asked for Stories of Strong Marriages, These Gay Couples Were Happy to Oblige

Bill would let Michigan doctors, EMTs refuse to treat gay patients

'Nobody Is Born Gay' Billboard Tells Drivers on I-95 in Virginia

Doorstep visits change attitudes on gay marriage

When 20% of the news headlines are self-evidently advocacy journalism for homosexuality when only 2-3% of the general population may be homosexuals, bias is nose-on-the-face obvious. I haven't heard or seen anywhere that Yahoo bills itself as a self-confessed champion of homosexuality, or, to the contrary, that it claims to have no bias at all, but clearly it has a mission in cyber-life.

I left a message on Yahoo one time in response to one of these articles, and an activist of the homosexual persuasion responded snidely that I shouldn't be reading Yahoo news if I were offended. The reader may wonder why at the time I went to Yahoo if I found its pro-homosexual content objectionable. Fair question. It does occasionally have genuine news that other sites don't have, or a different take on a current event. For instance, the same day I saw that 20% of Yahoo's articles were about homosexuality, I also saw an interesting piece on Apollo 17 I hadn't seen elsewhere. Eventually— perhaps soon—I'll abandon Yahoo for the very reason I've cited here.

The interesting sociological issue illustrated by all this is how corporations simply reflect the obsessions of their top dogs. I mean, why wouldn't they? Of course they do. I don't know if Yahoo started out with different dogs, but somewhere along the line they started running with a pack intent on tearing up the moral fabric of this country.

So, it's Gay-hoo from now on. I'm looking for a better news source.

No More Yahoo

I remember a story about a lady who recognized a newspaper publisher on a city street and stalked up to him to say, "Mr. Smith, I have stopped the paper!"

Smith looked alarmed. "What have you done?!" he asked. He clearly feared that she had harmed his presses somehow. The woman then explained that she had become so outraged at the editorial slant of the paper that she decided to cancel her subscription—"stop the paper."

Relieved, Smith said, "There are a hundred more who will buy my paper for every one of you." He waved her off dismissively and went on his way.

I don't have any illusions about the impact of my doing so, but I have "stopped Yahoo." I've cancelled my *yahoo.com* accounts. I won't visit the site anymore. I have had a Yahoo email address for almost as long as I have had Internet access, and I was accessing the Internet in the early days, even before browsers were invented. I have never had premium services with Yahoo, so it hasn't cost me anything. I have tied some online accounts to Yahoo, which I have now changed to another email address. I lose related features such as Flickr by cancelling, but I have to say goodbye to Yahoo. It's my only way to protest.

I wrote recently that Yahoo might as well call itself Gayhoo. Yahoo News, to be specific, is dominated by articles chronicling the march of the homosexual movement and promoting homosexual causes. The latter it does by presenting a flood of articles purporting to be news that are in fact the editorial opinions of Yahoo in support of homosexual practice, homosexual marriage, and the entire range of lesbian, bisexual, gay, transgender issues. Some days as many as half the articles purporting to be news are simply pro-homosexual diatribes.

Obviously, there's very little way an individual can affect the character of a major site like Yahoo. I did find a way to send a comment to the site administrators, but Yahoo and other sites like it are not interested in the personal reactions of Internet users. My two cents, if it even got into the email of anyone in charge at Yahoo, was no doubt dismissed entirely. No one up there at Yahoo is concerned about my finding it objectionable that they are championing the cause of homosexuality under the guise of being a news-site/search-engine.

Yahoo can do anything it wants, of course, and obviously they are doing so now. They have gone whole hog on the homosexual movement and, at least as far as the news end of their business is concerned, they have sacrificed any claim they may ever have had to objectivity. And clearly they don't care.

I don't know who runs Yahoo but I imagine they're dedicated homosexuals—dedicated to thrusting homosexual living in the faces of all viewing Americans and people all over the world, dedicated to promoting homosexual issues at all costs, dedicated to making homosexual practices seem more prevalent than they really are, dedicated to forcing the culture to normalize and even celebrate homosexuality, through the tyranny of the minority.

They won't convert me. They won't co-opt me. They won't intimidate me. As I say, "I've stopped Yahoo." Not that they noticed.

We Must Reverse the Supreme Court

Kentucky's Rowan County Clerk Kim Davis refused to issue marriage licenses to same sex couples after the June 26, 2015 decision of the U.S. Supreme Court in *Obergefell v. Hodges*. That decision effectively required states to allow homosexuals to marry. Kim Davis has refused to issue licenses in her county because of her Christian beliefs based on the Bible. A federal judge ordered her to comply and then put her in jail on September 3, 2015, for contempt of court when she refused. On September 8, she was released under new orders from the same court requiring her not to interfere with others in her office who might issue the licenses.

I know there are some pundits out there, to say nothing of presidential candidates, who think that the question of whether Kim Davis did the right thing is an open and shut case. I don't. It's like so much of life; it's a complex event involving a mixed bag of principles each of which has a strong argument for an action that differs radically from the other possibilities. I'd like to ruminate on those principles or issues for a moment.

I begin with the opinion, stated, rather interestingly, by people of opposing viewpoints on homosexual marriage. I've heard homosexual activists and those waiting to wed say vehemently that Davis and every other license issuing clerk and official in the country has to comply with the Supreme Court because it's now the law. On the other hand, some Republicans and some Christians who oppose same-sex marriage are willing to say they believe that Davis was wrong, because "she's a public official and she has to uphold the law." It's this basic idea that permitting same-sex marriage is now the law that I'd like to address.

We have multiple sources of law in this country, in three tiers.

The first tier: the supreme law of this land is the Constitution of the United States, and after that the constitutions of the individual states.

The second tier: the federal and state statutes, enacted by assemblies, houses, and senates across the country.

The third tier: decisions by courts of record: state circuit courts and appeals courts, state supreme courts, federal circuit courts and appeals courts, and the U.S. Supreme Court.

Of these three sources of law, only two are established by the votes of representatives of the people: the constitutions and the statutes. We elected people to go to congress and to go to the various legislatures of the states, and they established the constitutions, and ever since, they have been proposing, debating, and passing statutes. Of the courts we cannot say the same thing. States vary in how judges come to the bench, some being elected and many appointed. In the most important case, the case I'm concerned with here, the Supreme Court of the United States, the justices are appointed by the president, only being confirmed by the Senate.

The Constitution of the United States isn't thoroughly detailed in its description of the role of the Supreme Court. Mostly the Court has defined its own role. Historically, it has been the duty of that Court to hear cases where a question has been raised about the constitutionality of some law. SCOTUS's decision in *Marbury v. Madison* (1803) established the doctrine of judicial review, wherein the Court can declare either legislative or executive actions unconstitutional, effectively overturning them. However, there has been a minor trend for a long time to "legislate from the bench," as it is called; to make law rather than review it only. It's known popularly as judicial activism. Highly controversial decisions by the nine in black have frequently reignited the debate between judicial review and judicial activism. I side almost completely with those who believe that the courts should shun activism. We have legislatures and congress to make laws. We don't need the Supreme Court doing it, and the principal reason is that the court is not elected. The justices are not representatives of the people.

For that reason, I hold that in perilous times when the Court has made a decision that not only reflects an activist role but also reflects an abandonment of the core moral and spiritual principles that underlie the founding and building of this country, it is the civic duty of people of principle to stand against the Supreme Court, to protest its decision without letting up, and as circumstance may make possible, to defy that decision in order to focus the attention of the public, its legislatures, and its executive branches, on the grievous injustice of the justices.

Witness the decision of the Supreme Court in *Plessy v. Ferguson* (1896), upholding racial segregation in schools in a doctrine that came to be known as "separate but equal." By the middle of the 1900s there was so much outcry in the public about this doctrine and this practice—in the north and the south, by the way—that a case in Kansas rose to the Supreme Court level and was decided in *Brown v. Board of Education* (1954), overturning *Plessy v. Ferguson* in all of its language that supported segregation in any way. I don't know if anyone was put in jail for defying *Plessy*, but I know that a lot of Black people were put in jail for defying authorities who wanted to keep them *out* of lunch counters, *in* the back of buses, and *out* of public schools and colleges. It was people willing to defy the "law of the land," as folks call Supreme Court decisions, that finally got a terribly unjust law overturned by another instance of the Supreme Court that had better sense.

Let me remind you also of *Dred Scott v. Sandford* (1857), in which the Supremes opined in no less than a 7-2 vote that Negroes could not be citizens and could not sue in a federal court. President James Buchanan was deviously involved in trying to sway the Court to decide against Black slave Dred Scott so that the country could go on having slavery as an institution. The strongest kind of objections were lodged against this awful decision of the Supreme Court, within hours of its coming down. The Evening Journal of Albany, NY, said in an editorial the next day:

> The conspiracy is nearly completed. The Legislation of the Republic is in the hands of this handful of Slaveholders. The United States Senate assures it to them. The Executive power of the Government is theirs. ...The body which gives the supreme law of the land, has just acceded to their demands, and dared to declare that under the charter of the Nation, men of African descent are not citizens of the United States and can not be... that the inhabitants themselves of the [States] have no power to exclude human bondage from their midst—and that men of color can not be suitors for justice in the Courts of the United States! ...All who love Republican institutions and who hate Aristocracy, compact yourselves together for the struggle which threatens your liberty and will test your manhood![10]

Republican President Lincoln effectively nullified the Dred Scott decision through the Emancipation Proclamation, but the Court later tried to extend the unjust treatment of Negroes through the *Plessy v. Ferguson* decision. It took *Brown* and later the Civil Rights Act to correct the horrible decision of seven men, products of their environment but people capable of knowing and doing what is good, if only they had. Interestingly, the undoing of slavery in this country involved all three branches of government, upholding what the Constitution originally projected as the overarching principle by which Americans live: "all men are created equal."

---

[10]Benson, Lloyd (editor). "The Issue Forced Upon Us.". Secession Era Editorials Project. Furman University. Retrieved 2008-06-17.

There's an eerie similarity of these two cases to the one at hand today. Particularly in the *Dred Scott* decision, the Supreme Court declared what was manifestly unjust to be just, what was immoral to be moral, and what was abnormal to be normal. The President was complicit; in fact, he was out in front leading the charge. And people who saw clearly the terrible, awful injustice it was, the spiritual obscenity it was, and the moral outrage it was, had come to the point where they believed it was a virtual if not actual conspiracy among people of amoral bent, to normalize immoral behavior.

I believe we are looking at such a terribly unjust decision in *Obergefell v. Hodges*. I think the Court has been overstepping its proper bounds at an accelerated pace since the 1963 decision in *Roe v. Wade*. Its decision denying states the right to regulate marriage is over the top, in my admittedly not so humble opinion. It was desperately wrong and misguided, and it reflects the absence of not only good sense but fundamental morality in the minds and hearts of the justices who voted with the majority in the 5-4 decision. The Court effectively gave its imprimatur to the claims of the homosexual movement and thumbed its nose at the principles of most of the nation, which stands solidly in the tradition and religious conviction—across religious boundaries—of millennia of human history, believing that marriage is a heterosexual union.

This decision should be overturned, and quickly. God grant that it should not take sixty years, as it nearly did to undo *Plessy*. Congress must move to amend the Constitution to include a definition of marriage that restricts it to one man and one woman. Congress has done such things before. It imposed an income tax on the Union during the Civil War. Then in 1895 in *Pollack v. Farmer's Loan and Trust*, the Supreme Court declared a federal income tax unconstitutional. Under a growing desire by both parties for more government revenue, however, Congress passed the Sixteenth Amendment, directly stating that the federal government could tax income.

Admittedly, this was a decision I think went the wrong way. However, there is nothing immoral about an income tax. I don't like it, and I think it's essentially unconstitutional and is not in the best interest of the liberty of the people, but it's not immoral. The point is that Congress reversed the Supreme Court by adding to the Constitution.

The decision in *Obergefell* is different. It creates a new institution, homosexual marriage, which in mine and the beliefs of millions of Christian Americans and other Americans too, is immoral, because homosexual behavior is immoral. Disapproving of it will not eliminate it, just as disapproving of adultery will not eliminate it either, but we don't have to institutionalize it and give it the seal of our culture's approval. The decision of the Supreme Court *to do just that* is therefore destructive to the American culture, and it should be nullified in whatever way possible as soon as possible. Toward that end, we need more people willing to defy the decision.

Now, second, I'm not so certain that it's a slam dunk case that Kim Davis has a legal obligation to uphold the decision of the Supreme Court. Kim Davis is not an employee in the strictest sense of the word; she was elected to her post, in a governmental system that is neither a democracy nor an autocracy, but a republic. She is morally bound to abide by laws that proscribe certain behavior, such as theft, for instance; at the same time she is not obligated as a requirement of her position to abandon her moral and religious principles merely because five justices on the Supreme Court abandoned theirs (or never had them). Since the authority under which Kim Davis defends her actions—other than her spiritual authority—is the Constitution of the United States itself, her case is that the First Amendment trumps *Obergefell v. Hodges*. She is arguing that the Supreme Court is attempting to force her to act against her religious beliefs in the performance of her job.

I know there's another side to this, illustrated by those who pose a not-so-unrealistic scenario in which a Muslim clerk might refuse to license a couple where one was Muslim and the other was not: that would violate Sharia Law. It would take more space than I want to devote to this article to deal with that argument. What I want you to see about the case at hand is that merely weeks ago Davis was not being forced to go against her religion, and then suddenly she was. This wasn't a simple change in a form or a procedural routine. This was a night and day change confronting Davis, and a lot of other people out there who are watching all this closely, with a moral choice. Davis decided she could not comply in good conscience.

Opponents of Davis's refusal to comply think their argument is simple and obvious: Davis should resign if she can't go along. Others modify that to say the county should find her another job where she won't have a problem. Of course, she wasn't elected to another job; she was elected to be the the Clerk of Rowan County.

It's really not an easy situation to solve with a single sentence answer. However, I think Davis's decision was fairly simple for her, although it was momentous and involved an uncertain future. She decided to participate in civil disobedience: peaceful and principled disobedience to a law on the belief that it is unjust, and an acceptance of the consequences, in the hope of provoking public outcry against the injustice and a change in the public's mind and in the law.

I suspect we have only begun to see incidents of civil disobedience in this matter. I certainly hope so, because unless those in power come to their senses quickly, it will be up to those not in power to assert the will of the people to overturn those in power so as to restore justice to the government of the United States.

Getting Tired

I'm getting tired of writing about the homosexual assault on our country, our culture, and Christianity, but that's one of the major battlefields of the moral and ethical landscape these days. Would a platoon leader in a war say, "Guys, I'm getting tired of engaging the enemy. Let's have a cookout and then go home"? Would a baseball team that had led the game in the odd innings and been behind in the even ones suddenly say in the eighth, "We're tired of going to bat. Let's concede the game"? Would President Obama come to the White House after years of struggle with terrorist-harboring countries and say, "Let's stop calling them terrorists and fighting them, and let's just negotiate our demise"? Oh, wait, he has. Never mind.

Anyway, as I say, the war is nowhere near over and the only thing that retreating from the battlefield will accomplish is an effective surrender and our defeat. The homosexual agenda is the battle plan of homosexual activists and their willing accomplices in media and government. Considering that one of the major offensive tactics of the homosexual forces is the cowing of the populace and that this tactic has been extremely effective with the average American, who doesn't have any fixed set of morals, it has never been more vital for people who do have those morals to lock and load. The homosexuals have long supply lines and are becoming very proficient in guerrilla warfare as well as traditional troop movements. If we don't mount an offensive ourselves, they will soon overrun our positions.

Too many military allusions for you? Well, that's what this is: war. The objective of the homosexual forces is to achieve court decisions and legislation forcing Christians, whether individuals or as companies, to accommodate and celebrate homosexuality however homosexuals may choose to assert it. Anyone else, whether Christian (or Jewish) or not, who shares Christians' objection to homosexual behavior, is included among the homosexuals' enemies.

What makes the issue so important at this moment in history is that now is the time that homosexuals are feeling their oats, empowered by the decisions of a number of liberal courts. They smell blood in the water (mixing the military metaphor with the popular shark metaphor). They smell fear on cowed Americans, who are deathly afraid of being labelled as haters, discriminators, opponents of freedom. The homosexual army is an organized force with a mob mentality and it is not afraid of bending or breaking the truth, of violating the Constitution they claim to be trying to enforce, or of destroying the moral character of the nation that, unlike Iran, would not jail or behead them.

This little essay is a small mortar shot into the enemy camp. I feel certain that if a customer to a bake shop wanted a Jewish or Christian cake decorator to put, "There is no God," the Supreme Court itself would uphold the baker's refusal to take the order. It would still be a clear issue of First Amendment rights, and the Court would defend the baker's right to the exercise of his religion in expressing his support of the Ten Commandments. I think the Court would have to side with the baker because, at least so far, adulterers aren't a government-defined group capable of being discriminated against.

Not so with homosexuals anymore. They've now been included as a protected group, and that trumps God's law in the view of SCOTUS. Homosexuality is not addressed in the Ten Commandments, but it is in the Old Testament and more importantly, for the Christian, in the New Testament, in no uncertain terms. This is a moral and biblical issue. Attraction to the same sex may develop from the earliest years for a variety of reasons, but taking action and engaging in homosexual behavior is incontrovertibly a choice, and it's a morally wrong one. When the United States government starts denying religious persons the right to obey what they believe the Bible commands them to do (which, one could argue, SCOTUS has already begun doing), our days as a free country are numbered.

As I edit this piece today, the Jue 12, 2016, Orlando homosexual nightclub shooting has just taken place overnight. At least twenty people were shot dead by a man identified preliminarily as an Islamic terrorist, who wounded at least as many more and then was killed by SWAT teams who stormed the club. Let me be very clear that although I have used the military metaphor in this essay, any sane reader knows I am not advocating violence toward homosexuals.

In 2010 Sarah Palin devised a campaign graphic featuring crosshairs, such as would be seen through a rifle scope, as she "targeted" certain Democrats for defeat in upcoming elections. Democrat and other liberal opponents of Palin raised a stink about the crosshairs on the ridiculous notion that Palin advocated violence against Democrat political candidates. This was an outrageously stupid accusation then, and it would be absolute idiocy for anyone to cite this essay and accuse me of intending violence against homosexuals.

That said, I will use every other, moral and ethical means of fighting the homosexual agenda as long as I have breath.

On the Other Foot

The Organization to Promote Heterosexual Exclusivity is a growing group devoted to just what its name says. It exists to convince Americans to perpetuate heterosexuality as not only the main, but the only lifestyle in the nation, and eventually the world. The organization holds rallies, publishes articles, solicits members and funds, generates and requests speaking opportunities, disseminates materials and seizes opportunities to engage in public and private debate about the homosexual agenda. The organization, in a word, seeks to convince individuals, communities and government entities that heterosexuality is the orientation and lifestyle intended by God, self-evidently intended by nature, affirmed overwhelmingly by history, and benefitting families, children, the community and all humanity.

In a very unlikely place like Cleveland, Ohio, OPHE recently planned a rally and banquet to be held in a major hotel there, to be attended by more than a thousand invitees from around the city. The gathering would include a buffet dinner with a fancy cake for dessert. The cake was to be about six by six feet in size and ornately decorated with the organization's logo, which includes the words, "Heterosexuality - God's Plan for Humanity."

OPHE contacted Main Event Catering to cater the banquet. Main Event Catering is run by Phil Swisher and Bruce Koskiovsky. Adam Lott, the event coordinator for OPHE at first simply told Main Event that his organization wanted to engage their services for a banquet for about 1,000 people. "No problem," said Phil. "And a very large cake, about six feet square," said Lott. "Not a problem either," said Phil, "what's the date?" Adam Lott gave him the date, and Phil checked it. "No problem," he said, "we have that date open." Lott asked how much the reservation payment would be and when Phil told him, he agreed to remit it by any method Main Event required. Then Phil said, "Are you ready to set it up?"

Lott said he was, and gave him the organization name: "The Organization to Promote Heterosexual Exclusivity," he said. After a moment of silence on the other end of the phone, Adam started to give Phil the contact numbers, but Phil interrupted him.

"Uh, hang on a minute Mr. Lott. I have to check something first." He was gone about five minutes. When he returned, he faltered a bit and then said, "We're not going to be able to do that banquet for you after all."

Startled, Adam Lott asked him, "Why? The date is good, and you can handle the crowd and the food."

Phil paused slightly and then said, "I'm just going to be blunt with you, Mr. Lott. We won't be associated with an organization that promotes hate and discrimination against gays. We're a pro-gay business. My partner in business is my partner in life, and we're gay. We can't help you."

Wait a minute," said Lott. "We don't promote hate or discrimination. We promote heterosexuality. You obviously don't know anything about our organization."

"I don't need to," said Phil. "Your name says it all."

Taken aback, Adam said, "So let me get this straight—and no pun is intended—you're going to discriminate against us? You're going to deny us service because of the lawful purpose of our organization?"

"No. It's because you want to deny civil rights to gays."

"How do you know that? And even if it were true, which it isn't, don't you agree that in America we have a right to our opinion and belief?" said Lott. "Don't you believe in toleration?"

"Not if you're against gays," said Phil.

"If I understand the law as it now stands," said Lott, "you don't have the right to refuse to cater my banquet on the basis of your beliefs' being opposed to mine."

"I don't want to talk about it any more," said Phil, adding sarcastically, "We're sorry—but really, we're not. Goodbye." And he hung up the phone.[11]

---

[11]Readers of my columns will have suspected from the first paragraph that this story was fabricated. From whole cloth, in fact. But clearly it could happen, and probably it already has. If it hasn't, then it should, as soon as possible. And then we'll see if the Supreme Court sees what a mess it's made.

Heather Missed Having a Dad

Recently a woman named Heather Barwick, who was raised by a lesbian couple, "came out," but not in the sense that you think. She divulged to the world that in spite of the fact that she was reared in a home with two mommies, she doesn't approve of "gay marriage."

Now, there's a surprise. It's even more of a surprise when you learn from the article that detailed Barwick's story that she loves both of her "mothers" very much, and that her father, who used to be her natural mother's husband, "didn't come around anymore" (to see her, we presume). You might think Heather would have so sympathized with her two mommies that she would come to side with the lesbian cause all the way, and be antipathetic towards men in general, to boot. That's not the case.

In fact, Heather wrote a piece for *The Federalist* in which she said she doesn't support "gay marriage" because of the "nature of the same-sex relationship itself." She said, "Same-sex marriage and parenting withholds either a mother or father from a child while telling him or her that it doesn't matter. That it's all the same. But it's not... A lot of us, a lot of your kids, are hurting. My father's absence created a huge hole in me, and I ached every day for a dad. I loved my mom's partner, but another mom could never have replaced the father I lost."[12]

I'm not finished. What makes this even more interesting is that in her 20s Heather was an advocate for "gay marriage."[13]

Now, however, matured, married, and reassessing her early life, Heather understands that there's no substitute for a father, no matter how much a lesbian, second mother tries to fill the role. A man is a man. A woman is a woman. (We won't delve into the abnormal and extremely rare instances of hermaphrodites.) Only a man can be a father. Heather wishes she had had a dad.

As to the guy who used to be her dad, and is still her biological father, I don't have enough information to know exactly what happened with him, but two things in *The Federalist* suggest to me what's probably

---

[12]Heather Barwick, "Dear Gay Community: Your Kids are Hurting," (*TheFederalist.com,* 17 March 2015, The Internet).

[13]For those of you who don't understand why I put "gay marriage" in quotes, I almost always do because I'm quoting other people. I don't typically refer to "gays" as "gay" but as homosexuals.

true. The article says that her mother left her father to live with a woman as lesbians. Then the article, which Heather wrote, says that her father "wasn't a great guy" and "didn't bother coming around anymore." Well, duh.

With only that information, I wouldn't blame the father for not coming to visit his daughter in a home where his wife had become a lesbian and was cohabiting with another lesbian. Talk about an awkward situation. I can imagine with perfect understanding that he would be very angry, hurt, humiliated, and perhaps outraged on any number of bases, religious, moral, common sensical, etc.

Now, the article I read gave the responses of several people who run LGBT organizations and who advocate for "gay marriage." Without exception, they miss Heather's point. They act confused, as if they don't get Heather's main concern. A homosexual man who heads up the "Family Equality Council" and who himself is raising a daughter along with his "husband," says that Heather was certainly entitled to her feelings but he says that her father "chose not to be in the picture," and that Heather's opposition to "gay marriage" is a non-sequitur.

Similarly, Abigail Garner, author of a pro-"gay" book who also was raised by a same-sex couple, criticizes Heather for being illogical, claiming that Heather's real pain was from having been abandoned by her father, and that the answer to that pain is not to deny homosexuals the right to marry.

Neither of these critics gets it. Heather's father may well have absented himself in an extreme way, but I guarantee you that every heterosexual male who disapproves of homosexuality and homosexual "marriage," understands what Heather's father felt when his wife left him for a woman. Under those circumstances, all Heather is saying—and it makes *perfect* sense—is that substituting a woman for her father was not what she needed.

I can imagine all the lies Heather's real mommy may have told her about her father. I can guess that she distorted the nature of her marriage and attempted, perhaps without thinking about it consciously, to cast Heather's father in a bad light in order to cast herself and her new partner in a good light. And it worked, for a while, until Heather was old enough to realize that fathers are important, after all.

Faced with the embarrassing situation of a very public, very cogent, argument from the child of a same-sex couple, a child who comes out opposing "gay marriage," the ardent proponents of such abnormal behavior have no way to argue against the child's claim that she wishes she had had a real father. Instead, they act confused, construct straw men, knock those down, and resort to *argumentum ad hominem,* calling the child illogical and confused herself.

It's telling, isn't it?

If Twins Are Identical, Then Why...

Hold the presses, people. The homosexual lobby may have done themselves in, provided that rational people listen to what they've just told us in the news.

Scores of news services are running the story of Liam and August Easton-Calabria, identical twins living in Seattle, who have been members of a Boy Scout troop there. One of them will be dismissed from the Scouts when he turns 21, because he is homosexual. The other one is not.

Did you hear what I said?[14] One identical twin is homosexual, but the other one is not. Now, did you hear me?

Identical twins have the same DNA. Identical twins have the same DNA. Yes, I know I repeated myself. Did you hear me? Identical twins have the same DNA.

The prevailing theory among homosexuals, the one they want all of us to believe, the one they preach to us with passion, is that they did not choose to be homosexuals: they were born that way. Now do you hear what I'm saying?

The homosexual lobby, the LGBT crowd, the ministers of the homosexual religion, have been trying to prove to us for years that there is a "gay gene." They have funded studies to try to find the piece of genetic code that makes homosexuals homosexual. They ginned up a Harvard University study a few years ago that found some evidence of this idea, but the study was debunked when it was discovered that all the researchers were homosexual and that their methods were deeply flawed.

But focus on the genetics of the issue. If being homosexual were in the genetic code, then if you had that gene, you would be homosexual, no doubt about it. So what if you are one of two people who have the same genetic makeup? Identical twins have the same genes! If one of them is homosexual *by nature,* the other one must be, too.

Liam is homosexual. August is not. Did you hear me? One is, and one isn't. But they're identical twins. If the homosexuals' foundational principle were true, that we're born this way, then it would not be possible for Liam to be homosexual if August were not, or for August to be heterosexual if Liam were not.

---

[14]If you were being really attentive, you picked up on the contradiction lurking in the "news" in the previous article, "Do Homosexuals Wear Genes."

The defensive homosexual will say, "Oh, well, August will come out eventually." Notice that the homosexual will assume that August must be homosexual, not that Liam has made a mistake about his orientation.

The truth is that homosexuals are dead wrong. They are not born that way. They become that way by a process involving conditioning, influence, parenting or failure to parent, and choice. Some choices are foisted on them by others, and some they make themselves before they know what they're doing. The occasional one will have made the choice when he or she was old enough to know better, but chose homosexuality for any of several reasons reflecting a dysfunctional development.

One thing is certain: if it were in the genes, then identical twins would have to be both be heterosexual or homosexual. They couldn't be one of one kind and one of another.

Liam and August are not the only examples. I've known others personally. And the news now and then features additional examples.

Folks, the arguments and "reasoning" of the homosexual lobby just don't compute. Sexual orientation is not in your genes. It's in your head and heart.

Genes, Environment and Choice

In the previous article, I pointed out an important and extremely convincing observation I made from news at the time, namely that identical twins who are of different sexual orientation disprove quite conclusively the idea that homosexuality is genetically determined.

I never thought I was the only one to draw this conclusion, but at the time I had not heard of anyone else's having drawn it. I'm hearing recently, however, that several notable scientists who study these things have made the same observation.

Predictably, homosexual advocacy groups are getting angry at the logical conclusion that simply must be drawn from the data, and they are looking for their own experts to attempt to debunk the truth, particularly by obfuscation.

J. Michael Bailey is one of these so-called experts. Bailey is a Professor of Psychology at Northwestern University. From twenty-five years of study he thinks that "male sexual orientation is inborn," a phrase he uses purposefully to mean "resistant to change."

Interestingly, Bailey found that among male twins where one was homosexual, in 52% of cases, the other one was, too. Bailey says that means that "it can't be completely genetic," but, he says, it means there is "some moderate genetic influence."

Bailey's conclusion utilizes seriously flawed logic. It's an example of *non sequitur,* a logical no no: the conclusion is not supported by he premises.

Bailey goes on to opine that "genetic influence can be thought of as something that pushes one a certain way, but doesn't push them all the way there." He likens the "genetic influence" to a genetic predisposition to some diseases, which does not "determine these things" absolutely. However, Bailey objects to the obvious conclusion that if one were predisposed to homosexuality but not destined to it, then influence and choice are still involved in someone's actually becoming homosexual. No, he says, "a trait can be completely inborn without being completely genetic. And I think male sexual orientation is a case in hand."[15]

As someone who identifies himself as a behavioral geneticist, Bailey needs to go back to school. There is no other physiological means for a person to have an "inborn" trait except genetics. Where does Bailey

---

[15]Dr. J. Michael Bailey, an interview *(LGBTScience.org,* the Internet, accessed 11 December 2014).

think this "inborn" trait comes from? He's grasping at straws by making up some other engine of heredity.

Bailey, however, is firmly prejudiced against the idea that parental and social influence have anything to do with homosexuality. He rejects out of hand the idea that "having a distant father or an overbearing mother" has anything to do with it. He says "we have lots of evidence to the contrary." Unfortunately for Dr. Bailey, we have a lot of evidence for the proposition, as well.

The weakness of Bailey's hasty conclusion in this regard is probably due to his failure to consider the extremely wide variety of dysfunctionality in families and cultural surroundings,combined with the ability or inability to resist external influence, and the will to do so.

One of Bailey's other positions on the subject that undermines his own conclusions is his opinion that while men are innately hetero- or homosexual, "female sexuality is more malleable, perhaps more responsive to environmental inputs, and social causation." In other words, he thinks women who may have inherited a tendency toward homosexuality are more likely to go that way in life.

It seems apparent that Bailey's conclusion is the result of his simply observing the modern trendiness of lesbianism. Girls have always gotten away with a level of overt, physical affection and behavior that would have resulted in raised eyebrows if observed between men. In today's culture, lesbianism is practically "cool." Bailey has absolutely no biological data to support his different conclusions for male and female homosexuality. Clearly, his source data is sociological, or as he says, "environmental."

Bailey seems urgent to support the contention of the homosexual community that being homosexual is definitely not a choice, that you are instead born homosexual. However, Bailey can't help but admit some things that directly militate against the homosexual line. In an interview, he was asked by a pro-homosexual writer to define "environmental." The interviewer wanted Bailey to go on the record as not supporting "anti-gay activists" who "easily distort" the word. Here's what Bailey answered:

"When I talk about environment... all I mean is something that is not genetic." While it might include family experiences, "it could also be whatever happened to you in the womb... illnesses... things you might have eaten." He's dancing around the question, trying not to say "choice."

Now, to be clear, I have never held that homosexuality was a matter of an adult choice coming out of the blue. I have always thought, based on a lifetime of evaluating evidence, that the full range of parental, moral, cultural, educational, religious and psychological factors that influence a child's life from birth onward, provide the atmosphere in which a person becomes homosexual, with a varying degree of personal choice involved. In view of the fact—*the fact*—that there is no biological evidence that homosexuality is genetically determined, it is always up to a person himself or herself to choose whether or not to *act* on impulses, no matter how ingrained those impulses seem to be.

We don't give criminals a pass because they grew up in a criminal family. Human beings willfully act on their impulses, in things that are either right or wrong. When there's no evidence to support the belief that homosexuality is "inborn," it's irrational to continue to believe it, even if admitting the truth implies a needful change of lifestyle.

Homosexuals in Jack Boots

Dean Obeidallah wrote an article recently for *The Daily Beast* titled "First They Came for the Gays."[16] He was opining that the Arizona legislature's law protecting the right of merchants in their state to refuse service to homosexuals if it violated their religious convictions, was a first step at rampant discrimination against women, other races, etc. Obeidallah took his title from the writing of Martin Niëmoller, a German Christian pastor who spoke out against Hitler and exhorted others to do so as well. In a speech published in 1947 Niëmoller said that it was the failure of good people in Germany to oppose Hitler that allowed him to roll to victory over all resistance. The exact quote is as follows:

> First they came for the Socialists, and I did not speak out—
> Because I was not a Socialist.
>
> Then they came for the Trade Unionists, and I did not speak out—
> Because I was not a Trade Unionist.
>
> Then they came for the Jews, and I did not speak out—
> Because I was not a Jew.
>
> Then they came for me—and there was no one left to speak for me.

Obeidallah, however, terribly twisted Niëmoller's warning. Mr. Obeidallah meant for his readers to think of those poor homosexuals as the eventual victims of the evil persecution of those awful Christians and their mindless, moralizing sympathizers. In point of fact, if there is any parallel between Niëmoller's observation and today's cultural situation in America, it's Christians and other morally oriented people who are being persecuted and marginalized. If anything, it's Christians that Homosexuals would like to do away with. It's Homosexuals who are the Nazis in this parallel.

Neimoller's point was that people of conscience who don't speak up

---

[16]Dean Obeidallah, "First, They Came for the Gays," *(TheDailyBeast. com,* The Internet, 24 February 2014).

in the face of evil are allowing evil to prevail completely, eliminating all opposition. In point of fact, it is Christians and all others who oppose homosexual behavior as well as homosexual 'marriage,' who are being systematically silenced and persistently persecuted. It is homosexuality that is marching in jackboots across the country, condemning all its opponents, intimidating its critics, and creating the climate of political correctness that convinces politicians that they will be reelected only if they champion immorality.

At the moment of this writing, the Arizona law is on the desk of the Governor awaiting either veto or signing.[17] Some of the most vocal critics of the law vociferously claim that the central injustice of it is found in the "fact," as they claim, that homosexuals are not so by choice but by birth. Indeed, this issue is at the heart of the entire matter. Homosexuals have leaped from the insubstantial argument of homosexuals themselves, using perhaps some of the long-debunked studies conducted by homosexuals, to make the unscientific conclusion that homosexuals are genetically determined to their same-sex attraction.

Unfortunately, the science is not on their side. There is not only no definitive scientific study showing that homosexuality is genetically predetermined, there is not even any important scientific study offering substantial evidence of that claim. Homosexual advocacy groups, who champion the cause of homosexual marriage, are on shaky ground when they argue that homosexuals are entitled to not only marriage but child rearing as well. When somebody does a definitive study of how many children raised from infancy by homosexual partners turn out to be homosexuals themselves, and that number is found to be startlingly high, will those who argue that homosexuality is genetically determined change their tune? I doubt it, but I don't doubt for a minute that if someone does the study, that's what they'll find.

As an addendum, if anyone reading this wonders why I keep using the word "homosexual" instead of "gay," it's really quite simple. I oppose the theft of a perfectly good English word meaning happy or carefree, to describe people who pervert the natural roles of the sexes.

---

[17]Arizona's SB-1062 was vetoed by Gov. Jan Brewer on February 26, 2014.

Miscellaneous Sexual Sickness

Bathroom Bills

In the crop of "bathroom bills" springing up here and there across the country, I wonder what it would take for legislators to be morally sensible instead of just politically correct. What if...

Jamie liked spying on girls in bathrooms and locker rooms. During his high school years he had developed various techniques for getting a peek, some of which were more satisfying than others. After he graduated, however, things got more difficult, with fewer opportunities. Jamie's hunger for the surreptitious view of fully or partly undressed female bodies did not abate. The challenge just got greater, and Jamie had always thought of himself as being up to a good challenge.

First he tried sneaking into women's bathrooms and installing little cameras he acquired from various Internet sources, but it was hard to conceal most of the devices he could afford. In one place or two he found ways to drill through walls for a pinhole view from an adjacent room, but that didn't go well, either.

Then the most amazing thing happened. His state passed a law guaranteeing the freedom of any person to use any bathroom he or she wanted. The law was aimed at equality for transgendered persons, but it was the open door Jamie had always wanted.

A fair skinned, light bearded boy with longish hair, Jamie had often thought he could pass for a girl if he tried, and walk right into a girl's room confidently. But he'd never tried it because he was too scared. But now—wow! It didn't matter if anybody was fairly certain he wasn't really a woman; he could go into a ladies' room anyway, on only the assertion that he was a woman trapped in a man's body. And he didn't really even have to assert that in the first place! All he had to do—and this seemed obvious—was to dress like a woman.

Jamie collected some women's clothes, and of course a purse and shoes. He also bought some underthings, though obviously he didn't plan to uncover himself and give himself away. He worked at brushing his already long-ish hair into a passably feminine style. Having watched his mother make up her face many times as a little boy, he thought he would be able to do a fair job at it, and he practiced for a week in secret. The worst thing he had to do was to take the sparse hair off his legs and arms, but he bit the bullet and did it.

Finally all procedures and plans came together and Jamie was ready to try out his new "identity." He picked a public restroom in a very busy place for his first entrance. He wanted to be sure there would be plenty of turnover—women coming and going rapidly enough that he could stay longer without raising suspicions.

His first venture didn't yield any dramatic results, but he passed muster. He didn't overdress—no sense in calling attention to himself. He just walked in, selected a stall with a slightly open door, obviously unoccupied, slipped inside, locked it, and waited. Shortly after he did, a woman entered the stall next to his. Jamie had no camera, no mirrors on his shoes, none of that. This was sort of a test run. After a half minute or so he figured he should exit, so he came out of the stall. He washed, touched up his hair, acknowledged other women who came and went, and finally left, himself. Success!

From this humble start, over the next few weeks Jamie became bolder and more inventive, finally carrying a pen camera in his purse. When he entered a stall, he placed his purse on the floor next to his shoe, with the pen clipped to the side of the purse and its camera already running. After spanning the coming and going of several women, Jamie finally left the bathroom himself, and when he got home he was thrilled with the results he had gotten on video. And nobody was ever the wiser.

Creative and inventive as he was, Jamie had no doubt that with a few more month's practice and the acquisition of a few more covert gadgets, he would be catching some pictures and video that would provide hours of satisfying viewing later, and perhaps would find their way to the Internet for the admiration of others.

It was funny, Jamie thought, how people in other states were proposing the same laws to accommodate the LGBT crowd (mostly the Ts) on the premise that they were eliminating discrimination against them. Jamie had no use for transgendered people. On that count he actually agreed with the conservative Christians: he thought transgenders were sick. Jamie was simply a generously sexed heterosexual; he just wanted to see women's bodies. Those politically correct legislators were playing right into his hands. Well, more power to them. He hoped they did the same thing in every state. His only worry was that there would be "conservative backlash" from the religious types and that the laws would be overturned. A few states had already tried passing laws going the other way, requiring people to use bathrooms matching their birth certificate gender, but it looked like the transgender lobby was going to win, since they were stirring up demonstrations and getting entertainers to boycott those states.

As long as the trend toward free access to any bathroom continued, the future was full of bright possibilities. As long as he could waltz into women's restrooms anywhere with no opposition and usually no question, he could figure out ways to maximize the opportunity that this newfound freedom offered.

And who knows? He might be able to get a job in a school![18]

---

[18]For those interested in doing a little research on why opposition to transgender access to bathrooms of their choice is not merely theoretical, try going to the following links, just for starters:

http://www.dailywire.com/news/3466/heres-infuriating-example-why-those-gender-am anda-prestigiacomo

http://www.king5.com/news/local/seattle/man-in-womens-locker-room-cites-gender-rul e/65533111

http://linkis.com/www.lifesitenews.com/12D80

http://www.dailywire.com/news/4844/transgender-advocates-say-men-dressed-women- will-amanda-prestigiacomo

http://www.dailywire.com/news/4522/man-drag-caught-macys-womens-restroom-secret ly-amanda-prestigiacomo

http://www.massresistance.org/docs/gen3/16a/bills-in-MA-legislature/upd/transgen der-bill/bathroom-danger.html

Dead Giveaway

If a man has transgender surgery and reappears in public as a woman, it's understandable that he would wear women's clothes. But why would he have a complete makeup job? Is that a necessary part of being a woman?

I'm serious, here. I think that the makeup that a surgically transgendered person wears is a giveaway. Maybe a dead giveaway. I think it points to a progression of events mired in dysfunctional living in that person's past that led him to crave being feminine, quite apart from any claim or presumption to actually being a female "inside."

During the 60s it became popular for girls to go without makeup of any kind. I came to maturity during those years and I really liked this trend. Frankly, I didn't enjoy the soapy taste of makeup when I kissed girls who used it. More fundamentally, though, I thought that makeup was basically a lie. It was a disguise. It was a contribution to a fictitious identity. To this day, I prefer to see women who don't wear makeup. What's the point—to them, I mean—I ask myself? Yet, I realize that many women are so conditioned to accept the idea that they aren't complete until they put on makeup—a false face—that they will not listen to reason and give it up.

You see, for most women who use makeup, their cosmetics turn them into the women they want themselves to be, the women they see themselves as, when they imagine their own looks. Nature doesn't ordinarily give women eyebrows that are thin and elegantly arced. Makeup does, though. Nature doesn't usually give a woman ruby red lips, and never the shades of pink and purple and even black that some women want, but lipstick does. Nature doesn't tint a woman's eyelids blue or green, or put sparkle on them, but a few minutes with makeup turns a natural woman into something she was never born to look like.

The made up female face, then, becomes *emblematic* of femininity, though of an artificial femininity that is not part of nature. A boy who by reason of the perverted, excessive, or dysfunctional influence of a woman or women in his life when he is young, comes to identify himself with them more than with his own gender, fixates on the *emblem* of femininity, the quintessential, made up, female visage. When his obsession with experiencing what it would be like to be a woman reaches the extreme stage at which he is willing to have his male organs removed and have the verisimilitude of female features created there and on his chest instead, the process is complete. Almost.

And here's where the giveaway comes. He insists that if he didn't have the genitals of a male but those of a female, and if he had breasts, he would finally be a woman.[19] But when he finally has them, it isn't enough. He has to make himself up, because he still doesn't see the woman he expects in the mirror. Since he can't change his looks entirely without plastic surgery, he is still going to see the face he was born with. But that face he then makes up, as did the women he idolized, the women he wanted to be, the woman or women who, possibly too long ago for him even to remember, implanted the idea in his little psyche that he would make a nice girl.

Even without going all the way, so to speak, to having sex change surgery ("gender reassignment surgery," for those of you who are politically correct), a guy who thinks he's a girl inside still gives away the fundamental mistake of his conclusion when he adopts makeup as part of his transformation. He falls into the trap of believing that he has to make up his face to be feminine. He focuses on the cultural *emblem* of the female gender rather than on anything inherently female. In fact, generally speaking anything that is merely associated with being a woman rather than actually characterizing womanhood itself, can be labeled merely an *emblem* of femininity. Female clothing is an example. There's no inherent gender requirement involved in wearing tops that button backwards (from a man's point of view) or zip up in the back, or donning pants that have no fly, or pulling on pantyhose. All these things are cultural *emblems* of femininity. The idea that one must do all these things to be a woman, when one is actually biologically a man, is proof in and of itself that desiring to be transgendered is something that comes from a process of social conditioning rather than some mistake of genetics.

I like my simple, original thought, however, because it's what turned the light on for me. It's the *makeup* that's the dead giveaway. Some very few persons in this world are actually born with genitalia of two sexes, confused or ineffectual parts resulting from chromosomal abnormalities. I truly sympathize with the hardships they undergo in life. However, the typical transgendered person is someone who was done a great disservice by people around him (or her) in childhood when they confused his development. But he then compounded his own problem

---

[19]This concept is a fiction, however. A man with the normal complement of male chromosomes will never become a woman, no matter what surgery he submits to or what hormones he takes.

by choosing to pursue a perversion of his purpose in life, perhaps unaware of the self-deception he was indulging and the illusion he was following.

Why our government is enabling and empowering these persons instead of discouraging the confusion of even more young people, is beyond me.

Race and Racism

What Are We All, Anyway?

The entertainment world is known for producing some really wacky opinions, many of them as leftist as Marx or as spacey as Kevin. Meryl Streep recently weighed in on criticism by some Blacks that they were under-represented—even not included at all—in nominations for some prestigious film awards. In fact, the Berlin International Film Festival had an all-White jury, which some critics said was inherently racially biased. Streep was reported widely as having said, as something of a defense of supposedly White bias, "We're all Africans really."

The larger context of her remarks changes their weight somewhat. When asked if she understood films from the Arab world and North Africa, Streep said, "There is a core of humanity that travels right through every culture, and after all we're all from Africa originally...We're all Africans, we're all Berliners." In that last sentence she was referring to John F. Kennedy's famous "Ich bin ein Berliner" speech." She could have added "I am Charlie [Hebdo]" for effect.

In making the comments, Streep was trying to contextualize earlier criticisms Blacks leveled at the Academy Awards, where no Black films were nominated. On that subject, I figured it was as simple a matter as there having been no films typified as "Black" films that were worthy of nomination; it would have been stupid of the Academy to jump back three quarters of a century and act racist, and they're not stupid. Anyway, Streep was trying to minimize the complaint by lumping us all into the category of Africans. Her point, if you go along with the evolutionist theory, is that since we all came "Out of Africa"—a Streep film, just in case you aren't up on your movie-going—we should all claim that ancestry.

Why don't we go back further? Since evolutionists say that the first humans were descended from apes, why not say we're all apes? For that matter, why aren't we all fish, or even amoebae?

I'm sure Native Americans wouldn't like that, or Hispanics or Irish pubgoers for that matter. It doesn't fit the narrative necessary for minorities and oppressed peoples—and those who like to think of themselves as oppressed—when they go looking for labels to attach to themselves. And Streep's remarks were controversial precisely because they don't fit the narrative of most Black Americans (okay, African-Americans), who would like to remain a distinct group, not mixed in with Europeans, so they can continue to set themselves apart from Whites and every other group as well, for whatever advantages they see in such a cultural strategy.

Should we be able to identify ourselves as coming from one part of the world, as being of one race or another, without going back farther into the mists of the past and acknowledging our common human ancestry? I for one believe we should. However, many people use their ancestry or racial or cultural identity for selfish gain, or for claims of superiority. My roots are Scottish and English. Suppose I complained that the movie industry didn't make enough films about Scots. (It's been a long time since Braveheart.) Should they feel guilty and get busy pleasing me?

I wouldn't make such a complaint, of course, because I have no interest in using my Scottish heritage to set myself apart or put myself on some pedestal. And I'm not Scottish-American. I'm an American, plain and simple.

Frankly, I don't concede the point that we all came from Africa originally. I don't think the jury is anywhere near in on the origins of man, in spite of the case being made by the idea's promoters. They'll have to prove their case not only beyond reasonable doubt but beyond all doubt, and I don't think they'll do that in my lifetime.

Shame

It is to the shame of England that as early as 1554 British slave traders were stealing Africans from coastal countries and selling them throughout the world. Slavery had long been a practice in the British Isles, and until the Slave Trade Act in 1807 the English were key players in the immorality of slavery in the world.

It is to the shame of Africans in west coast nations of their continent, that some of them captured and sold people of their own race to traders from European nations. Africans had a long history of raiding each other's countries and villages and making slaves of their people.

It is to the shame of the American colonies that they allowed the purchase of slaves. Colonies from north to south imported slaves from British and other traders, closing their eyes not only to the denial of liberty and often the abuse that slavery represented once slaves came ashore here, but also to the unspeakable brutality and inhumanity of the acquisition and transportation of slaves to markets here and around the world.

It is to the shame of the framers of the Constitution that they did not settle the issue of slavery then and there, the issue that had already been hotly and emotionally debated in their time. It was another seventy-five years, and after an immensely costly war, that in 1863 Republican President Lincoln declared American slaves free.

It is to the shame of Americans, Southern and Northern, that the Black peoples of America were not accorded the freedom and opportunity they deserved. Particularly, it is to the shame of Southern states that they devised ways to deny Blacks access to society, to segregate them, and to suppress their right to vote.

It is to the shame of Democrats and Republicans alike that as late as the 1960s Black citizens continued to be second class. It is particularly to the shame of Democrats, across the South and in the North as well, that they resisted the adoption of laws guaranteeing American Blacks full civil rights. Republicans were the voting strength behind the Civil Rights Act of 1964, which a Democrat president placed before Congress.

It is to the shame of both the Southern and Northern states that the quest led by Martin Luther King, Jr., and others to firmly establish the equality of Blacks in America, was so ignorantly and brutally opposed by racists. The finger on the trigger of the weapon that killed King belonged to a wicked Northerner named James Earl Ray, born in

Illinois; however, the racism that spawned his kind of violence and hatred existed throughout the nation.

It is to the shame of Democrat presidents and their party that they championed what they called "The Great Society," the centerpiece of which was a giant welfare program, with the ostensible purpose of lifting vast numbers of people out of poverty, but which, predictably, had the fairly rapid effect of enslaving Blacks again. A generation of largely Black Americans came to depend upon government for their sustenance, as Welfare provided a strong disincentive to work. Welfare programs have continued to grow to an enormous size such that today, thirty-five percent of Americans are on welfare. It is to the shame of America that Congress has largely underwritten the concept that money must be confiscated from those who work, to support those who won't.

It is to the shame of many Black Americans that they have not continued the quest of their slain champion for a colorblind society, but have instead sought to institutionalize their minority status for the purpose of preferred treatment, conceiving of themselves as perpetual victims. It is to the shame of many Blacks in America that they have reared successive generations of their children to believe that the government owes them a living. Emancipation and Civil Rights now won, Blacks must learn the lesson that confronted the ancient Hebrews: it is one thing to take the slave out of Egypt, but quite another to get Egypt out of the slave.

It is to the shame of American youth of the 1960s and 1970s that as part of their revolution of "peace and love" they bequeathed to this country a culture in which sex became recreation not requiring marriage, and that as a result, along with the predictable consequences of Welfare, in the Black community more than 72% of children are born to unmarried couples, and that in most cases there is no father even around. It is to the shame of those Black biological fathers that they do not care that their children are growing up with an even lesser concept of human dignity, morality, civic responsibility and respect for authority than their parents' generation have.

Finally, it is to the shame of the first Black President that he has, by his partisan and prejudicial statements and actions, promoted an increased racial divide in this country. Many Whites who voted for the President did so with the hope that he would promote racial healing in the nation. Instead, he has exacerbated racial tensions.

As we mark another Martin Luther King, Jr., Day in America in 2015, we should stand silent, not celebratory. We have much work to do if we are ever to become a nation where citizens are not hyphenated, but simply Americans. For that day to come, all Americans must accept the challenge. Arguably, the greater challenge lies before Blacks.

A Curious Observation

In the town where I grew up in the 50s and 60s, to my knowledge there were no interracial couples. I first noticed White-Black couples at college in 1967. As I encountered more interracial dating and marriage, I was curious about a striking fact, that most of the couples I saw consisted of a Black man and a White woman. For years I didn't see a pairing the other way around. The observation was so persistent that I began to wonder about the apparent psychological component to the phenomenon.

Recently I accessed some statistics on interracial marriages and found that the 2009 U.S. census showed there were 354,000 Black male/White female and 196,000 White male/Black female marriages, a ratio of 1.8 to 1. This ratio has changed since 1981 when it was 3.7 to 1. More White men are marrying Black women now than they were in 1981. The 1981 figures were similarly different from 1970, when a Black female/White male marriage was even rarer. These statistics, of course, document only those interracial couples who are married, not those who are merely living together or dating. I suspect the dating numbers are significantly higher in the same direction. I hold to my observation that of interracial couples who are not married, the overwhelming majority feature a Black man and a White woman.

Moreover, my early observations led me to conclude that a disproportionate number of those Black male/White female relationships included a woman with red hair. That made me even more curious. Then I noticed that while some of the pairings feature blonde women, I rarely noticed a dark brown or black headed White woman paired with a Black man. Again, I haven't kept written records on these observations and to my knowledge there aren't any studies on the matter. However, I trust my cumulative recollection.

What is most curious to me about what I perceive to be the strong pattern in Black-White romantic relationships is how at odds that pattern is with the claim of many proponents of color blindness in interracial dating and marriage. If, as we might simplify their case, 'people should be able to date, cohabit with, and if they like, marry anyone they fall in love with,' then why do far more Black men fall in love with White women than White men with Black women? And if my subsidiary observations are also generally accurate, why do Black men who are romantically involved with White women more often get attached to red headed or, more recently, blonde women than dark haired ones?

Let me restate the question another way just so I won't be misunderstood. If interracial romances are simply about love and nothing more, shouldn't you expect that if you took a random sampling of all Black-White (heterosexual) romances you would find a roughly equal number of pairings of White men/Black women and Black men/White women? And if you find a significant disparity, wouldn't you assume that something was going on besides love striking like lightning out of the blue?

That's what I'm getting at: I think the reasons Whites and Blacks are attracted to each other romantically are more than the generic reasons anyone is attracted to anyone else apart from race—common interests, personality, talents, spiritual qualities, etc. Admittedly the initial reason a man is interested in a woman (or vice versa) may be nothing more than physical good looks. Some people might even subscribe to the idea that a person can fall in love at first sight without even meeting the other person, simply from the sight of him or her—in other words, fall in love on the basis of looks alone. (Love struck fans may actually believe they're in love with a TV or movie star they've never even seen in person.) To the contrary, however, one may certainly be stunned at the beauty of another and desire desperately to meet that person and to begin a relationship, but it's also conceivable that if a meeting takes place, nothing will come of it—looks make sparks, but no fire gets started. It's what begins happening when people meet that leads to love.

So: if love follows initial attraction, what attracts people to each other in the first place? Specifically, why do Black men more often find themselves attracted to White women than the other way around? What do they see that they like? What are they looking for?

I read recently a piece by a Black man who ruminated on the edge of this subject, not exactly on why Black men may be attracted to White women in the first place, but on why, when they are, they pick a certain type. He said that normally Black men—in his experience, anyway—like their women more curvy, thecurrently popular description of being plump. Most Black men, he said, don't like their women to be sticks. Think Kanye West and Kim Kardashian.

But then there's Black singer Seal and Heidi Klum, one of those skinny White models. But examples from the entertainment world may be unrepresentative; they're certainly biased strongly in another way. Type "celebrity interracial relationships" into Google Images and see what comes up. When I did it, 56% of the Black-White couples that displayed were White male/Black female. Hollywood trends the opposite way from the rest of the country. (You're not surprised, are you?)

I thought back to the first interracial couple I encountered at college. It was a big, Black football player and a plump White redhead. I saw them often, and I studied the pairing thoughtfully. There were certainly Black women on campus (one particularly cute one, as I recall), probably as many as there were Black men, so it wasn't for lack of prospects that this football player looked around at other possibilities. What attracted him to her? I never asked him, of course, but it may have included her sizable frame. He apparently didn't want diminutive arm candy but a proportionate match.

Eventually, I encountered a body of study by psychologists and sociologists who opine that many Black men are attracted to White women for what is probably an unconscious reason: recompense for a history of slavery or racial suppression. A century and a half ago and more, it was not uncommon for a White slave owner to take sexual liberties with a lithe Black slave, who bore the evidence nine months later. Apparently there are ways of documenting and backing up the conclusion that some Black men are trying to even the score. I haven't found out yet what differences exist in the psychological motivations or the sociological manifestations of them in places other than the U.S.

I think it would be unlikely that many Black men would admit that they were attracted to White women because they wanted payback for their great, great grandparents' slavery. In fact, I doubt this sort of motivation could be definitively documented in the first place, but those who study such things insist that there's an archetypal inclination of Blacks to seek reprisals for things that occurred long before their own lifetimes and that do not continue into the present, but of which they are powerfully aware through their upbringing and culturalization.

One of the most famous Black male/White female couples of modern times was O. J. Simpson and Nicole Brown Simpson. Ernest Baker of Gawker.com, a Black man who prefers White women himself, referenced the case of O. J. and opined (in my words) that O. J. pulled off the slap-back of the century.[20] After so many years when Black men were lynched for even thinking about sex with White women, O. J. not only married a beautiful blonde woman—the epitome of the White male dream—but also killed her and got away with it. Baker's theory

---

[20]Ernest Baker, "The Reality of Dating White Women When You're Black" *(Gawker.com,* The Internet, 3 Jun 2014).

assumes O. J. "did it," which is an unusual claim for a Black person since Blacks typically will say O. J. was wrongly charged while Whites think the other way around. However, Baker's point is the same as mine, and it comes from a Black man: some Black men take up with White women to stick it to the White race, whether they realize it or not.

A Black woman who bills herself only as Bronx Girl and is virulently anti-Republican, pro-homosexual marriage, in favor of Blacks changing their names to African-sounding ones—in short, extremely liberal—opined in her recent blog:

> The reason many successful black men opt to date and marry white women is because they were raised in a patriarchal society that constantly emasculates them, yet they still subscribe to said society's ideals. So when given the opportunity to achieve those goals, that is exactly what they do, from their car to their woman. Ultimately, white women are just another trophy in the case of their success.[21]

The opinions of Baker and Bronx Girl are representative of significant numbers of Blacks about this phenomenon of Black-White relationships that affects their race. In other words, as an old White guy, I'm not alone in theorizing that there's an underlying, partly or mostly unconscious, psychological reason for interracial dating and marriage that isn't necessarily reflective of admirable attitudes or beneficial reasons.

On the other hand, I'm not aware right away of any data that suggest that such pairings more often end in abuse than same-race relationships. O. J. doesn't seem to be representative. My musings on the subject for years have been prompted merely by the curiosity of my observations, especially when I think about my own inclinations. I am not attracted to Black women on the whole; I prefer the general features of the White race. The only Black women I have found attractive had significantly White features due to mixed parentage—think Halle Berry. I should think that Blacks, both men and women, would regularly find persons of their own race more attractive. That has nothing to do with racism,

---

[21]Bronx Girl, "Why Successful Black Men Date White Women" *(http://www.18karatreggae.com/2015/03/21/why-successful-black-men-date-white-women/*, The Internet, 21 Mar 2015).

only with the tendency all of us have to appreciate our own faces and features. That's why I wonder about the hidden psychology that may be involved in interracial relationships.

Especially when the girl so frequently has red hair. And does that have anything to do with Black women so often coloring their hair red? Hmm.

Trayvon Martin's Mother's Lie

Trayvon Martin's mother is on her own little lecture circuit. She spoke at Clemson University for Martin Luther King, Jr. Day in 2016, and while the report of the speech suggests that it was toned down on several fronts, in one of the most important respects—truth—she got it seriously wrong.

I realize I'm not as close to the circumstances as Ms. Martin was, but I'm as close as she could have been to the truth of what took place between her son and George Zimmerman, and apparently closer when it comes to understanding. Everybody in the nation was close to that event because of the ubiquitous and thorough news coverage. In fact, Ms. Martin may have willingly disbelieved the truth because of her prejudice toward her son.

What Ms. Martin said about the event, in which her son Trayvon was killed, was that he was just a boy walking home, talking to a girl on the phone. She said, "Somebody [meaning George Zimmerman] perceived my child as being a threat." Then, she said, "that someone" followed, stalked, chased and killed her son. Here's where Ms. Martin departs from the truth, and seriously so.

While Ms. Martin wants her audiences to believe her version, it's not true. The facts the court found when Zimmerman was tried on the charges revealed without any significant question that Zimmerman, who was a community watch representative, trailed (not stalked) Trayvon Martin because Martin did not seem to have a legitimate reason to be where he was and because Zimmerman suspected he was up to no good. Zimmerman, intending to be able to tell authorities the location of a suspicious person, made a call to report his activities. Before he ever approached Martin, Martin "made him," turned, and approached Zimmerman threateningly (that's the opposite of what Martin's mother is saying). Then Martin attacked Zimmerman, not the other way around. The resulting tussle almost resulted in Zimmerman's being killed, and would have, if it had not been for his having and using a legally concealed weapon to defend himself. Trayvon Martin was killed as a result. Zimmerman, who was doing his volunteer job, survived.

The nation, already mired in rising racial tensions, was plunged into open conflict, with vast numbers of Blacks glomming onto the cause of "Black Lives Matter," claiming that Zimmerman was a cold blooded murderer, and that poor little Trayvon Martin was just an innocent young man minding his own business. On the basis of that lie and a few other highly publicized stories about Black men dying that were thrust into high relief because they fit the "innocent Black victims" narrative, Ms. Martin now says that it's clear that "the nation's judicial system is broken." By that she means that the court that found Zimmerman not guilty intentionally let him off in order to protect a racist system.

Nothing could be further from the truth. The court looked at the evidence. The *evidence*. The rest of the nation got to see the evidence, too. The evidence, not a corrupt judicial system, cleared Zimmerman. It was a jury, by the way, that found Zimmerman not guilty, not a "judicial system." Apparently some of Trayvon's peers didn't agree with the idea that Trayvon was the real victim.

Hillary Clinton made a similar remark about "the system" recently, villifying the police as being guilty of "systemic racism." Her opinion is not supported by facts. Does she know what the word "systemic" means? Are there still racist attitudes here and there? Of course—on the part of Blacks as well as Whites, and some browns and yellows, too. But systemic? Go find any significant evidence of that.

Ms. Martin is probably enjoying a nice, enhanced standard of living from her invitations to speak. I don't suggest that she's cynically capitalizing on her own son's death; no, what I'm suggesting is that she's taking a lie to the bank. Perhaps she's simply unable to admit the truth because it would put a negative cast on her memory of her son. I sympathize with her, but I find her guilty, guilty of perpetuating a lie, and probably actually exacerbating the problem she claims she's trying to help solve.

Black Lives

When the trial of George Zimmerman on the charge of murdering Trayvon Martin concluded, Zimmerman was acquitted, and soon the nation began seeing the slogan, "Black Lives Matter." The chant began with the organization of a single chapter by that name in direct response to the Zimmerman trial. It now has numerous chapters around the nation. It bills itself as a movement. Wherever you hear that chant in organized protests, it is altogether probable that the BLM organization is involved.[22]

The slogan Black Lives Matter has become hotly contested, however, by many non-Blacks and some Blacks themselves. The objection being raised to the proliferating movement is that the slogan can be taken as being implicitly racist. The reasoning of the objection arises in the context of current events where some police have used deadly force against Black suspects and where some Blacks have executed police, clearly in retribution. The specific counter to Black Lives Matter is that All Lives Matter.

That assertion, however, has infuriated those who chant that Black lives matter. In essence, Blacks who support the BLM movement have asserted a sort of exclusive right to the phrase and demand that there be no variation on it.

I've heard dozens of conversations, particularly on news programs, about whether saying Black lives matter is racist (some would call it reverse racism) or whether saying all lives matter is showing disrespect to Blacks, etc. I don't think there can be any debate about whether, in fact, all lives matter, but that's not the substance of the disagreement between supporters of the BLM movement and its detractors. It's something much deeper than a single slogan.

To understand the protectiveness its supporters have for their slogan, we have to look at the premises of the BLM movement. Some of them are food for thought, but some of them are not only questionable but are imminently disputable.

Primary source material for the concepts that lie at the base of the BLM movement is the website of the Black Lives Matter core chapter, founded by Patrisse Cullors, Opal Tometi, and Alicia Garza. First among an explanation of the principles they espouse is the assertion that

---

[22]All references in this article to BLM come from the website *http://blacklivesmatter.com.*

George Zimmerman murdered Trayvon Martin. In other words, they do not respect the decision of the jury in the fair trial of Zimmerman.

I've always found it odd that Blacks in general think that O. J. Simpson really was not guilty of murdering Nicole Simpson, but they're sure that George Zimmerman was guilty of murdering Trayvon Martin. It's difficult for me to conclude anything but that the majority Black opinion is racially motivated in both cases. In the case of Zimmerman, however, to have based the BLM movement on a wholesale rejection of the process of justice in his trial shows a decidedly racist presumption that Blacks are routinely denied justice in the courts of this nation.

It's a presumption that simply cannot be backed up with facts and cannot be successfully argued on the merits. Are there occasions when it is true? Of course: just as many cases by proportion as when Whites are convicted when they are innocent or acquitted when they are guilty. Juries do get it wrong now and then, as do judges. The days of institutional racism, however, are largely over.

Not according to the BLM movement, however. The BLM website openly declares that the movement is a tactic to rebuild the Black Liberation Movement. It is important to realize that the Black Liberation Movement is the more general movement in which the Black Liberation Army of the 1960s operated, and that its tenets: included anti-capitalism, anti-imperialism, anti-racism, and anti-sexism; promoted socialism and class-struggle (a Marxist concept); and implicitly supported acts of violence to achieve these goals. While the reader may think that being anti-racist is not so bad (and it isn't, of course), anti-capitalism is by definition anti-American, and anti-imperialism means more than simply being against America's asserting its power over other sovereign countries: it means isolationism and non-interference, even at the expense of American security.

What the BLM movement regards as racism is not what the average person might think. Racism by definition is simply the philosophy that one race is superior to another, and by extension it includes institutions that arise to express and maintain this philosophy. Any objective reading of U.S. history shows that what has happened in the past sixty years in this country has brought about the substantial dissolution of institutional racism. What BLM holds, however, is that any disparity in the social, economic, or political position of Blacks in America with that of non-Blacks (principally Whites) is the fault of continuing racism among Whites, never the fault of Blacks themselves.

For instance, another of the BLM principles is that "Black people are intentionally left powerless at the hands of the state" (direct quote from the BLM website). To believe this with any justification demands that one be able to produce substantial evidence of it, and I contend that such evidence is not available. One or two disputable incidents such as the Zimmerman trial do not substantiate the claim. It is, in fact, an emotional claim not backed up by facts.

In a list of charges that BLM lays to the blame of the (White controlled) state is the assertion that "Black poverty and genocide is [sic] state violence." The casual accusation of genocide alerts the reasonable person to question the legitimacy of any other portion of the claim. Deaths of Black persons in this country are due to multiple causes—the same ones that take White lives by disease and accident, but also Black-on-Black violence, which is rampant in some areas, such as major cities. Chicago, for instance, has an epidemic of Blacks killing Blacks. BLM supporters are strangely silent about this major portion of Black deaths. Yet a few—a very few—Blacks killed by a very few police officers, not all of whom are White, are front page stories supposedly proving that the state is attempting to commit genocide against Blacks. This is simply not the case, and if it were in fact a case in a court of law, even a court where a jury was racially balanced, it could not and would not be proven but would be dismissed as unsupportable.

Another BLM assertion is that "2.8 million Black people are locked in cages in this country" and that this, too, is "state violence." No evidence, however—none—can be offered as proof that Blacks are systematically convicted of crimes they did not commit. Everybody is familiar with a story or two now and then where DNA proves some convict to have been put in jail when he/she didn't commit the crime he was charged with, but those wrongly convicted persons are not solely Black. There simply is no evidence that the somewhat disproportionate Black prison population is due to anything more than a somewhat disproportionate Black crime rate. Yet the BLM movement apparently is not attempting to analyze the reason for a high crime rate among Blacks; in fact, they ignore the fact itself. It doesn't fit their narrative that Blacks are the victims of White racism.

The Black Lives Matter movement (BLM) claims on its official website that "Black women [bear] the burden of a relentless assault on our children and our families," and that this "is state violence." They offer no explanation of just what this assault is. Apparently they expect people to simply accept the proposition that the state of some Black women, which one may surmise is their subsisting on public assistance, being housed and paid welfare for themselves and each of their progeny, is de facto proof of government suppression of them and their lives. The claim is nonsensical, but it is what the BLM founders think.

Further, and even more reprehensible, is BLM's accusation that "a hetero-patriarchal society" imposes a burden on homosexuals and transsexuals. How so? From their rhetoric is it obvious that the BLM movement endorses "queer and trans folks," to use their language, which is a position not shared by quite a few people, White, Black and other races alike. The objection is morally, historically or culturally based, not racially. A moral outlook that holds that heterosexuality is the norm and all variants are abnormal does not somehow equate to "state violence."

BLM goes further to opine that "500,000 Black people in the US are undocumented immigrants and relegated to the shadows." To the extent that there is a persistent majority cultural opinion that illegal immigration should be stopped, being in "the shadows" is hardly evidence of state violence or any other act of injustice. It is illegal aliens who are breaking the law and weakening the economy by putting a drain on public assistance, among other things. Do BLM supporters propose that immigration should be unlimited and that anyone arriving inside U.S. borders should be granted citizenship automatically? The position is illogical, unreasonable, and outrageous.

The movement makes a number of other claims, some of which do not even need contradiction because of their irrationality. But it should be said that the movement also affirms some principles that are sensible and should be agreed to by all. For instance:

"We affirm our contributions to this society, our humanity, and our resilience in the face of deadly oppression." Anyone familiar with Black history must agree that Blacks have been resilliant, and anyone with a broad based education knows that Blacks have made substantial contributions to American society and culture.

But then BLM continues its extremist stances with the generalization that "war is state violence." While war is violent, "state violence" in BLM's usage does not mean simply actions by armies. Would BLM attempt to assert that the U.S.'s involvement in World War II was "state violence?" Does BLM not countenance armed national response to protect this homeland or others? In context, "state violence" to BLM means actions by governmental entities to suppress a minority or restrict its rights.

Back to sensible tenets, BLM states that "when Black people get free, everybody gets free." This is a moral truth that challenges everyone. Freedom is more than the absence of chains. Slaveholders more than a century ago were not truly free, because they enslaved others: Whites who owned Blacks were not morally free, because they were enslaved to a corrupt mentality. The same goes for Whites who fostered racism and segregation after the Civil War and well into the 20th century. It is also quite arguable that those Whites who today still espouse racist views are not morally free. It is not true, however, that this racism is rampant in America anymore, much less ensconced in its government.

Where the BLM movement goes wrong in this regard, however, is in its assertion that Blacks need a "strategy and action centered around Blackness without other non-Black communities of color, or White folks for that matter, needing to find a place and a way to center themselves within it."[23] This appears to mean two things: First, it seems to indicate that Blacks, particularly BLM supporters, do not want their movement coopted by Whites insisting that "all lives matter" should be substituted for their slogan. Second, it suggests strongly that what BLM wants is not the equality and inclusion characterized by Martin Luther King, Jr., as color blindness, but rather a heightened position of separateness based on being part of the Black race. Oddly enough, it would be accurate to describe this notion as "separate but equal," which of course was the theory of White segregationists. In other words, BLM promotes Black racism. They wouldn't agree, but the evidence is against them.

Yet the movement attempts to turn the tables on Whites who want to say, "All lives matter," by stating, "If we are committed to a world where all lives matter, we are called to support the very movement that inspired and activated so many more. That means supporting and acknowledging Black lives." Curiously, this is basically true, but what it suggests is that Whites should join hands with Blacks in chanting "Black lives matter" without regard for the implicit agreement with the BLM movement and its other tenets that such an action would imply.

For most of my adult life I have found it wise to know what a group stands for—all of it—before I join it in any of its activities. To side with some group in a single proposition with which I might agree when I don't know what else the group believes is to run the risk of "being in bed" with that group on many things with which I decidedly do not

---

[23]BLM movement supporters should study the success of the Civil Rights Movement, in which significant numbers of Whites participated, some of them suffering the same attacks as Blacks who marched and demonstrated. Bernie Sanders was one of those White people who joined with Blacks in non-violent efforts to bring change.

agree. This is true in theology, in politics, and in this current blaze of cultural revolution being promoted by BLM.

One of the saddest and most revealing assertions of BLM is the contention that "hetero-patriarchy and anti-Black racism within our movement is …killing our potential to build power for transformative social change." By that, BLM means that Blacks who don't agree with them, who believe instead that the more beneficial stand and lifestyle is to work for color blindness, are somehow traitors to their race. This is a repetition of the conflicting views of Martin Luther King, Jr. and Malcolm X, all over again. Martin wanted "all God's children" to be able to sing, "Free at last," and did not insist that his dream be achieved by Whites joining in a quest for the celebration of blackness. Malcolm sharply disagreed, standing for a racial quest not for equality but for "Black power." There is little difference in this latter philosophy and that of BLM.

Finally, by implying that only the BLM philosophy has the "potential to build power for transformative social change," the movement is promoting a future in which racial groups will always be at odds with each other about race. They speak passionately about "our collective futures," meaning the future of all Blacks, not all persons. They do not want to "water down unity" in the movement.

This is what "Black Lives Matter" means. It's why I for one cannot cheer them on when they begin the chant.

The Muddled Mess
of Ferguson and New York

After 2014's most significant set of news stories, namely the Ferguson and New York grand jury decisions following two deaths at the hands of policemen, I initially held back on writing about them. I talked about these situations with family and close friends, but for the most part I let the matter brew a while. Then I read an article written by, and attached to an email by, a friend of mine in which he unleashed his furor over the Ferguson, Missouri, events in particular. A few days later he told me he hoped I had not read the article and to disregard it. People close to him were alarmed that he had let the dogs out.

Ignoring him, I read the article anyway, and I agreed he had pulled out all the stops; however, I didn't disagree with anything he said. I may have been making mental notes all along, however, to exercise self control about the whole matter, considering how volatile it is.

At any rate, the time has come for me to opine. I would like to lead off with the blunt statement that the shooting of Michael Brown in Ferguson, Missouri, had nothing to do with race.

I would like to follow that statement with the equally blunt assertion that the accidental death of Eric Garner in New York had nothing to do with race, either.

Neither incident featured any action or statement that had racial content or overtones. In the absence of any such events, the only way you can conclude that either situation was at all about race is to assume first that any time a Black person is killed by a White person, it's about race. Such a premise is absolutely unsupportable in general, and is absolutely unsupportable in either of these two cases.

I defy anyone to argue successfully to the contrary.

The argument I anticipate I would hear in contradiction is what the court would call irrelevant and what logicians would invalidate for any number of reasons: the unwarranted assumption fallacy; a confirmation bias; shifting the burden of proof; false attribution; fallacy of contribution; inductive fallacy; and hasty generalization, to name a few. Look up these logical fallacies if you need to.

I don't for a moment deny that there is racism left in the country and in some pockets that racism is more deeply rooted than in others. What has happened in Ferguson and New York, however, in response to the deaths of those two Black men under very different circumstances, is not rooted in a rational evaluation of the incidents. It was rather merely precipitated by them. The incidents gave people a sufficient excuse to react out of previously amassed anger. In Missouri, in particular, it was an excuse to commit crimes for no other reasons than to act out violence and to profit personally by stealing.

The focus of the two events began, of course, with the deaths themselves. The public engaged itself in furious debate about what happened and who was to blame, and people tended to choose sides on the issues depending on whose story they had heard and what account fit their prejudices. Once grand juries were empaneled in each case, the focus shifted to whether or not these groups of people would indict the respective policemen with some crime. First in Ferguson and then in New York, the grand juries declined to indict the cops. Those decisions provoked the waiting rioters and demonstrators.

In general, we could say fairly that those protesting the grand jury decisions were largely Black and that they believe the grand juries sided with Whites out of racial discrimination. I never heard any credible criticism of the Ferguson grand jury, in particular; I never heard anyone give a substantial evaluation of the evidence the grand jury considered and who then arrived at a different conclusion. Instead, the accusations are general, sweeping, and grossly illogical.

I've heard people calling for a nationwide review of the grand jury system on the grounds that people called to serve on a grand jury don't know much about what they're doing. For that matter, the same criticism could be leveled at regular juries. In point of fact, however, juries of all kinds are given instructions about their job. What they do, however, is not all that complex. The job of a grand jury, for instance, is to make a common sense determination as to whether or not there is probable cause to believe that a person committed a specific crime. When a judge takes a warrant application, that's all he does. He looks at the allegations of a crime first, to see if a crime was committed; then he looks at the evidence against the accused person and makes a judgment about whether or not that person *probably* did it. That's pretty much it. It's up to a trial jury to determine a person guilty or not guilty based on proof beyond reasonable doubt.

When a grand jury looks at absolutely *all* the evidence, it differs from you and me in that most of us know only what we saw on the television. Even those who might have been at the scene of an event usually have a very limited perspective. From the standpoint of imminent reasonableness alone, we ought to hold the decision of a grand jury above our own. Unless there is some clear and convincing evidence that a particular grand jury was not impartial, we should not toss their decision aside as if we know better.

I don't know what the answer is to the malignant unrest in the culture that displayed itself in Missouri and New York, which are just two examples of brewing racial tension.[24] I do know that what demonstrators, rioters and looters have done in the name of justice, ironically, has served only to widen the gap. So much has been said, so many lies have been perpetuated, so many aggravating offenses have been committed, so many accusations hurled, so many agitators interested in self-aggrandizement have muddied the waters of reasoned discussion, that we may not be able to reach any civil agreement about anything significant that was involved in the Ferguson or New York events.

---

[24]The death of Freddie Gray in Baltimore after being apprehended by four police officers took place after this article was written.

Call Me Something Else

I am not white. You may have a picture of me, I know, but I assure you, I'm not white. In the sunshine my skin color averages RGB values of 247, 189, 147. White is 255, 255, 255. I'm nowhere near white.

I'm tired of being referred to as a color I'm not. It's been going on for a long time. I'm conscious of the fact that some people of my race have been glad to distinguish themselves from people of other races by adopting a simplistic term to describe their skin color. However, it is a terribly inaccurate term.

Further, "White" doesn't communicate any useful information, and in fact, it carries the implication of a valuation that I reject.

A better historical term would be Caucasian, though that term has been abandoned by anthropologists to describe my race. It used to be that the world divided neatly, though mistakenly, into three races: Caucasoid, Negroid, and Mongoloid. Mongoloids understandably didn't want to continue to be called by a term we also used to describe a birth defect, and Negros abandoned with great hostility their race's moniker. Caucasians haven't complained, but without notice they have come to be called Whites, a term that has been around for a long, long time, but has not acquired any increased legitimacy or accuracy simply for having stuck.

It's time for my race to change its name. How about "European-American?" No, I hate hyphenated American names. "Pink" is out, though as an RGB hue, I'm nearer to pink than to white. However, pink has its own attached prejudices. Let's either go back to Caucasian, or find something else to call ourselves.

There's added reason to change our race's identification in the fact that it is used in a pejorative way by many people who belong to what (currently, anyway) is referred to the Black race. (Blacks, as you know, were previously Afro-American, Negro before that). African American, a term encompassing that race only in the United States, is not really a racial description. In fact, it is used with outrageous inappropriateness to describe "Black" persons in America who did not come from Africa.

British actor Benedict Cumberbatch recently apologized for using the word "Colored" on U.S. television to describe non-White actors. Never mind that his remarks were critical of the lack of diversity on British TV; he was still castigated for using the term. Along with "Negro," "Colored" became a supremely derogatory term sometime in the late 60s.

Blacks took control of their own nomenclature somewhere during the Civil Rights Era, changing their title by both their own usage and by intimidating the increasingly politically correct White media and government culture. We were to call them whatever they felt like in the era of the moment.

Now, it's time for me to reject "White." It's insulting. I'm offended by it. I want you to stop saying it. Now!

Politics and Liberals

What War on Women?

After the first Republican "debate", which wasn't, of the campaign for the presidential election in 2016, I had several thoughts.

First was how remarkably similar all ten candidates making the "main" debate were. Yes, they had some differences, but they were all on the same page, or if the book were open, they were on one of the two pages it was open to. The Democrats by contrast were over toward the left of the book, and by Democrats I mean Hillary. Bernie Sanders isn't really a Democrat, just a socialist who tacks "D" onto his name. Wait, that's what Hillary is, too. Oh, well.

Second, I thought Donald Trump announced just how "Republican" he is, or isn't, by telling us yet again that if the Republican Party didn't nominate him, he would probably take his ball and go home, or rather, he would try to field a third team and still play the game. In politics, you can play with three teams, but it always defeats the team the rebel parts from, and the rebel never wins himself. The third party tactic, while serving the ego of the third party, guarantees that the real opposition wins. Can't Trump see that? Can you say, "Ross Perot"?

Third, "What war on women?" FOX's Megan Kelly, of all persons, posed a question to Donald Trump, mentioning some of Trump's remarks and asking him, "How will you answer the charge from Hillary Clinton who is likely to be the Democratic nominee that you are part of the war on women?" Trump went around and around in a very Trump-like fashion, but what he should have said was, "*What* war on women?" *Breitbart.com* remarked within hours that Kelly had legitimized the "war on women" accusation of Democrats. Whether or not she meant to do that, Trump missed a wonderful opportunity to ridicule the idea that there is any such war.

There isn't.

When conservatives stand against abortion as a method of birth control, that's not a war on women: it's a war on the slaughter of innocent human beings.

When conservatives stand for a Christian business's right to provide a health care plan for its employees that does not include coverage for abortions, that's not a war on women: it's a resistance to government denial of the First Amendment right to the free exercise of religion.

When conservatives call for de-funding Planned Parenthood because it is mostly just a provider of abortion on demand, that's not a war on women: it's a campaign to keep any more innocent blood off the hands of the U.S. Government.

Nobody is carrying on a war against women.

As I say, Trump missed a wonderful opportunity. Let no one mistake my remarks, however, to be implicit endorsement of Trump. Whatever credit he gets for being plain spoken and tapping into the frustrations of the common man, I have a real concern about replacing one phenomenally arrogant president with another one.

That said, the "war on women" subject is likely to reappear in the summer of 2016 after the candidates of the two parties have been officially decided. My guess is that Hillary will accuse Trump of waging such a war, hoping he will take the bait. I repeat, Trump should say simply, "What war?" It's a figment of the twisted Democrat mind.

Champions of African Americans?

Where do Democrats get the idea that they are the chief if not the sole defenders of the rights and prosperity of African Americans?[25] A look at the plain facts of history mocks the Democrat Party's present day boast.

All Democrats honor Thomas Jefferson as their party's philosophical founder. Jefferson articulated the philosophy of "equal rights for all, special privileges for none." Yet Jefferson had slaves and was an apologist and defender of the institution of slavery.

Andrew Jackson, of twenty-dollar-bill fame,[26] along with his political friends was the founder of the Democrat party proper. He also owned hundreds of slaves during his lifetime, whom he paid, housed well, and also whipped and hunted down if they tried to escape his plantation.

Stephen Douglas, famed for his debates with Abraham Lincoln, said of Democrats, "Our people are white people, our state is a white state, and we mean to preserve the race pure without any mixture with the negro."[27]

In the 1870s the head of the Democrat Party, James Jones, longed publicly for the days of slavery. During the tumultuous elections of 1876, Democrat Ben Tillman, a South Carolinian later to be governor and then senator from that state, led Red Shirts in terrorizing Blacks who intended to vote. He later helped found Clemson University and after he was elected governor of South Carolina he stated that he would be willing to lead a lynch mob.

Democrats in the mid to late 1800s were class warriors for White privilege, demeaning if not demonizing Blacks in bold public stances.

---

[25]I use the term "African Americans" with frustration at the evolving names that members of their race collectively choose for themselves. In my youth, Martin Luther King, Jr., referred to his own race as Negroes. His contemporaries of the same race who had opposing strategies to accomplish racial equality chose to refer to themselves as Black, while Afro-American was popular on college campuses. African-American arose somewhere around the 80s to replace all other terms. I suspect it will be something else before long.

[26]Perhaps not for long, since the Treasury Department is planning to replace Jackson with Harriet Tubman.

[27]John Gerring, *Party Ideologies in America,* 1888-1996 (Cambridge University Press, Cambridge, UK, 2001), 163.

They vowed to defend White Americans against the incursion of Black Americans, and employed ugly stereotypes in their campaigns stirring up fears of rape and other atrocities by Black men.

In the Midwest and Southern U.S. during the first half of the 1900s, the Democrat Party milked the racist and segregationist sentiments of the citizenry for their political preeminence. The deep South in particular was Democrat territory, where Republicans were seen as the party that might threaten White supremacy.

Even in 1964 when Congress passed the Civil Rights Act, the position of Democrats was reminiscent of their party's legacy. Of 244 Democrats in the House, only 153 voted for the Act, while of 181 Republicans 166 voted for it. That's 80% of Republicans to only 63% of Democrats. Over in the Senate, 46 out of 67 Democrats voted to strike down all segregation laws, or 69%, while 27 out of 33 Republicans, or 82%, supported the equal rights of all Americans.

In 1965, Congress passed the Voting Rights Act, and the previous year's numbers were echoed. In the House, the bill passed by 333 to 85. Democrats were 221 for and 61 against, for 78.4%, while Republicans were 112 for to 24 against, or 82.3%. Of 94 Senate Democrats voting, only 77 of them supported the Act, or 81.91%. Fifteen of them abstained. Among Republicans, however, of 32 voting, all but 2 voted aye, for 93.75%. Only 2 Republicans abstained. In short, far more Republicans by percentage voted to recognize and protect African-American rights to vote than Democrats.

Once Congress, with a double-whammy, decided that Blacks and all other citizens of the United States would have equal rights, the Democrat Party, always quick to construct and load the bandwagon of the populist cause, recast itself as the party of not only downtrodden Whites, but now the champion of long-oppressed Blacks. They attempted a rewrite of history to make themselves, at least in the mind of present day people who know little of American history, the friends of Blacks in this country. The rewrite worked, as Blacks now turn out in overwhelming droves to vote for Democrats.

Why? When history before 1965 shows that Democrats were always behind Republicans in standing for the rights of all races? And why, when the history of the country in the fifty short years from 1965 to today shows dramatically that in spite of the Democrats' constant promises to lift Blacks out of the poverty and inequity they see as the residual effects of slavery and segregation, they have not shown any great success. Indeed, they still hold themselves out to be the great Black hope. But consider this: a Democrat president signed the Civil

Rights Act; a Democrat president led the country after the debacle of the Vietnam War; a White Democrat president known popularly as the first "Black" president took the nation through the 90s; and a Black Democrat president has had the helm for seven years; yet Democrats still claim that Blacks are disenfranchised and need liberating. What, in heaven's name, have they been doing all this time?

One wonders if they simply promise Blacks the moon, knowing it's permanently on back-order, all for acquiring Black support, election to election. I don't wonder anymore. I know.

Why Romney Lost

It was 2012 when Romney ran against Obama for president, so it may seem a little late to you now, but I'll offer this analysis as to why Romney didn't win.

Long after his loss to Obama, Mitt Romney was on a podcast with David Axelrod, the guy who ran both of Obama's campaigns. Romney, a Republican, waxed sentimental about the good old days when everyone watched the same three TV stations and read the same newspapers to get their news. According to Romney, those were the days when there was only one set of facts. Mitt said, "We had three networks that we watched for the evening news; we mostly got newspapers… So we got the same facts whether or not we agreed on them." He implied that now we have more than one set of facts—versions of facts, if you will. Now, he said, we have all the cable news stations and blogs galore, and people watch and listen to what they already agree with, so that they don't get exposed to other opinions.

The problem with what Romney said is that his premise is not true. Mitt blames the Internet and cable for the division in America. The fact is… wait, let me say this with emphasis:

The division in America gave birth to the diverse views on cable and the Internet, not the other way around.

It's sort of a question of which came first, the chicken or the egg. In this case, it's pretty easy to see which came first. The division came first. The media exploded in opinion-related diversity precisely because the political, social, cultural and moral divide was widening. Cable and then Internet came along at just the right time to make it possible for people whose views were rarely reflected in print or broadcast to be read and heard.

The 60s can be identified as the major era during which this division grew cancerously. Republicans and Democrats, who had been relatively minimally separated in philosophies of governance during the WW2 era and mutually distracted by the prosperity of the 50s, were increasingly divided by the Civil Rights Movement, the Feminist Movement, and the Vietnam War. Culturally, the establishment, by its sluggishness in responding to the nation's growing discontent with the status quo in these and other issues, prompted the radical movement among the baby boomer generation. It was that movement, and the conflict it produced and continues to produce that brought about the vast divide.

To see one of the clearest indications of that vast divide, just look at sexual mores. Fifty years ago most of society regarded homosexuality as an aberration, a psychological illness, or serious immorality. Today, homosexuality is not only accepted widely, but celebrated by cultural elites.

Or take cohabitation. Fifty years ago "shacking up" was shameful. Today, it's all but officially an expected step between dating and marriage. As for marriage, fewer people are getting married—shacking up is enough for them, since society hardly criticizes it anymore, much less condemns it. Similarly, having children out of wedlock is no longer even an embarrassment, much less considered as wrong. A generation has turned all these issues 180 degrees.

Political issues have also done an about face. John F. Kennedy, a Democrat, lowered tax rates to raise revenue; no self-respecting Democrat would propose anything but raising tax rates these days. In the 60s the Democrats opposed the Civil Rights Movement in greater numbers than Republicans. In the 50s, Democrats were the ruling party in the South and were synonymous with conservatism. These days, Democrats see themselves as the chief benefactors of all minorities, and they are the quintessential liberals. JFK would not have been at home in his own party today.

Democrats and Republicans have been getting farther and farther apart in philosophy since the 60s. When cable TV came along, at first the Democrats, who were already establishing themselves as the darlings of print and TV news because they were becoming more and more liberal, held sway over the dissemination of news through CNN. But conservatives, more and more identified with the Republican Party, entered the fray with FOX. Let the games begin. The Internet then burgeoned with opportunities for both corporate and personal expression. And with nearly everyone having cell phones with cameras, raw news was available more widely than ever before.

Mitt Romney longs for the old days of unified news sources because he believes he got all the facts, when what we all got was the *selected* facts that fit the editorial purposes of the left-leaning media. The rest of the facts they downplayed, disguised, or completely ignored. Romney and a lot of other people can't accept the idea that the mainstream media filtered the facts through the fine mesh of editorial bias.

Romney is dead wrong about his assessment that Americans get two sets of facts these days where once there was only one. The facts are still the same; it's just that we aren't told what to think of them by just one, collaborative front of progressives and liberals. Now we have two major viewpoints and many minor ones, all interpreting the facts differently. In what Romney fondly remembers as the good old days, the news and the government largely colluded in presenting liberalism as the natural, normal, rational, logical view of the facts.

Their monopoly on the news is no more. Perhaps the news and editorial scene today is much more chaotic, and maybe people who don't care to keep on exposing themselves to opinions that make them crazy when they hear them do limit themselves to news outlets whose editorial bent is to their liking. But the upside is that we aren't slaves to a news collective that cannot or will not police itself in order to become and remain objective. I really don't remember when it ever was.

The divide between liberals and conservatives (to oversimplify the contrast in our culture) produced the divide in media, not the other way around. Romney longs for the good old days because he was and is part of the Republican establishment whose roots are still in the old-guard generation—even in the younger characters who still carry on under old-guard principles. So here's why Romney lost in 2012: he was not a conservative, no matter what he said. His remark about the news was prima facie evidence of his non-conservative sentiment. He was, and is, an establishment politician, part of the old-boy network, not interested in turning the country back to founding principles. Conservative Republicans knew he wasn't, no matter what anybody said. That's why four million or so Republicans didn't turn out to vote for him, and that's why he lost.

That leaves the issue of why millions of Republicans were absolute idiots by refusing to vote. They apparently thought that pulling the lever or pressing the button for Romney would taint them morally. Stupid. All it did was guarantee Obama would win, which he did. Instead of voting for the lesser of two evils, they stayed home, and the greater evil stayed in the White House, where he could fundamentally transform America, as he promised/threatened.

Republicans have a chance to learn from the 2012 election as they approach the one in 2016. They can learn that it's time, finally time, to put up a truly conservative candidate, who will win. They can learn that if the candidate they really want doesn't get nominated, they only cut the throats of the nation if they don't support him anyway. Translation: Republicans who don't want Donald Trump to be the Republican nominee had better make their minds up right now to support him if he gets the nomination, because the alternative, Hillary Clinton, to say nothing of Bernie Sanders, is unthinkable. Truly unthinkable.

Does Anybody Really Know What the American People Want?

A car salesman in my area who owns several dealerships advertises on all the television stations here plus some cable-only channels, such that every time you turn on the TV, he's in your face. I fantasize about going to whichever lot he's attending that day and walking into his showroom office with a bullhorn, repeating the nauseating phrases he shouts over the television night and day, sometimes three or four commercials in a row.

I thought I couldn't be irritated by anything on television more than this fellow, but I'm beginning to think that anyone and everyone who claims to speak for "the American people" vies for the position. Almost exclusively it's a political posturing phrase, where a candidate or other activist for a partisan position claims that he or she is promoting what "the American people" want.

In doing a little research for this column I came across a blogger who seemed to think that the principal offenders in claiming the support of "the American People" are Republicans. Frankly, I've heard the sweeping generalization out of the mouths of both major parties in equal amounts, and independents, too. In fact, independents, because of their desire to appeal to dissidents, are especially prone to claiming that most Americans are tired of the elephants and donkeys and want to go rogue.

Business Insider tells us the American people don't want budget cuts. *In These Times* says the American people want to tax the rich more heavily. *The Lubbock Avalanche-Journal* says the American people want to move to the right. *Read Write* claims the American people want to be the greenest country in the world. Barack Obama says the American people think gays should be treated like any other persons. Rush Limbaugh says the American people aren't concerned about making illegal aliens citizens. Ronald Reagan said the American people wanted arms control. George Bush said the American people want solutions and not empty party bickering. Mitch McConnell says the American people want things done in the political center, things that both sides can agree on. McConnell also broadly says "We know what the American people want." President Obama says the American people agree with him.

Harry Reid says the American people love government, and want Democrats and Republicans to work together. Newt Gingrich says the

American people believe corruption is widespread in government. *The American Thinker* says the American people believe that the size of government is one of the top issues facing the country. Nancy Pelosi says the American people want a progressive economic agenda.

Joe Biden said a significant majority of the American people believe that the country is not moving in the right direction. Martin Mawyer says exactly the same thing and means the opposite of what Biden said. Marco Rubio says the American people believe in immigration.

Perhaps the most significant statement about what the American people believe or want was that of William Casey, Director of the CIA. In 1981 he said, "We'll know our disinformation program is complete when everything the American people believe is false."

I suspect that quite often, Americans claim that Americans believe or want this or that because they have been led to believe it by someone they respect or follow, or someone who has either legitimately persuaded them to believe it, or manipulated them emotionally or politically to believe it. In other words, I suspect that many people who claim to know what the American people believe and want are basically credulous.

American psychologist B. F. Skinner articulated a concept that became quite popular in the field, oversimplified as: people believe what they do because they have been conditioned to believe it. The foil to this concept has been humorously stated: Skinner believes that people believe what they do because of conditioning only because he was conditioned to believe this. But the root principle is useful even if it is only general. Democrats who tell us the American people love government say it mostly because they were conditioned by their Democrat upbringing and indoctrination, and those who indoctrinated them were themselves indoctrinated. Aside from a few crossovers now and then, political party tends to run in the blood.

To be fair, Republicans who tell us the American people want the government to operate in the political center have been indoctrinated by a Republican establishment, which was in turn indoctrinated by the previous Republican establishment.

The only way to find out what the American people really want or believe is to poll them. Many organizations exist to do just that; however, some of those who poll are biased. The basic problems are in how their samples are chosen and, more significantly, the selection and phrasing of the questions asked.

I am suspicious of any news network that does a poll, simply because it has been shown to my satisfaction that no news organization is overwhelmingly objective. NBC, ABC and CBS are biased toward political liberalism. CNN is even more biased in that direction. FOX News is biased toward Republicans, and I say that as one who watches FOX more than any other news network. *The New York Times* is in the tank for almost any Democrat, while the *Wall Street Journal* is often right leaning. When any of these "news" sources does a poll, I take it with a grain of salt. Sometimes a whole shaker.

Even Gallup, the pollsters who used to be the go-to guys for what Americans think, has been shown to have taken polls with preconceptions that produced biased results. Its 2012 polling showed Romney ahead of Obama on the day before the election, was not just a wrong result but a biased result by definition. Shortly after that colossal goof the organization announced it was going to overhaul its methodology.

Not everyone who claims to know the mind or will of Americans has been duped, of course. Some people are deliberately trying to deceive us into believing that if we don't believe something, it's because we aren't in touch with the majority (ergo, the "correct") opinion. These are the politicians, of every bent, who are always trying to load us all on their bandwagons by claiming they are merely reflecting the will and mind of the vast majority of Americans. If we want to be true Americans, we'll think like "the American people" think.

This strategy only works with people who are substantially malleable, suggestible, or downright gullible. Those of us who are not politically naive, not historically uninformed, and not cultural lemmings cannot be deceived by casual appeals to what the American people believe or want. We recognize when we are being told what we supposedly want when it isn't, and we are not convinced to accept the opposing belief. The targets of all these appeals to American sentiment are the uninformed and uninvolved citizens, and the independent voters, whose favor both major parties curry in every election.

The claim to know what the American people want, however, has grown tiresome. As a speech phrase it is trite and immediately subject to dispute. Fifty-one percent of the voters does not constitute "what the American people want." Arguably even sixty-six percent wouldn't. I might think of using the phrase if I believed that eighty-five or ninety percent were in unanimity, but there's really very little in this country on which most people agree. In some things, that's a troubling reality. In others, it's the way things ought to be.

If I Ruled the World

Watching the Republican Debates on FoxNews a few days before the Iowa Caucuses, I couldn't help but think of the song, "If I Ruled the World." I don't mean the rap version by Kurtis Blow, which generally wished the world peace and love but also expressed Blow's sensual desires: "If I ruled the world, I'd love all the girls; I'd love 'em, love 'em, baby!" And I don't mean the newer version by NAS, which mostly wishes for the license to smoke marijuana, be rich and have sex without responsibility.

No, I'm talking about the Tony Bennett version, written by Cyril Ornadel and Leslie Bricusse, which wishes that "every heart would have a new song to sing and we'd sing of the joy every morning would bring." Bennett crooned that "If I ruled the world every man would be as free as a bird, every voice would be a voice to be heard …Every man would say the world was his friend; There'd be happiness that no man could end… If the day ever dawned when I ruled the world."

The song came to mind because, in spite of the fact that we'd all love for the world's problems to be solved, or even the nation's, there's not a candidate on any stage of either party who can do it. Donald Trump continually boasts that we're going to make America great again, and I honestly think that's possible, but the picture the candidates as a whole give us is that everything that's wrong can be fixed, including uniting all Republicans or even uniting all of America. While I try to be an optimist, I tend towards being a realist. And I'm a bit of a student of history, as well, and it teaches us that every four years the candidates promise us the moon, if they ruled the world, or at least our portion of it in America. And every time we elect a different president, realism sets in and the new president fails to be able to keep most of his promises.

President Obama has kept some of his, unfortunately, and failed at some others, thankfully. He has gotten the nation into unprecedented debt, dramatically reduced our international leadership, perilously weakened our national security, violated our Constitution right and left, and made attempts to disarm the citizenry.

Now that it's election time again, the opposition party has fielded numerous candidates all vying for the privilege to be in charge. Their priorities are telling. Jeb Bush said during the debate that his first priority was to fix the VA. (I wonder what his second priority is? Or his twenty-fifth? "Priority" doesn't need "first" with it, because it means "first thing." But I digress.) Jeb was merely trying to incorporate the nearly single-issue candidacy of Jim Gilmore, former Governor of Virginia, into his own campaign. Ted Cruz has said that if he were elected the first thing he would do would be to issue an executive order nullifying every executive order signed by Obama (or every one that did an end run around Congress or violated the Constitution). Marco Rubio said in so many words that he would put his priority on utterly defeating ISIS. Depending on the forum, the candidates bring one or the other of their issues to the fore and pledge to solve the problem. Of late (well after the debate) Ben Carson ran an ad that touted his surgical record and claimed that he "will heal the nation." Good luck with that.

I liked a lot of what I heard in the pre-Iowa debate, but I still haven't made up my mind. I have family members who are deeply committed to a particular candidate, and he's a good one (which may mean that I'm not going to vote for the only Republican "she" in the race, but she's not bad, herself); however, I don't have to vote yet, so I don't have to decide yet. I'm more interested at the moment in proposing what I would do if I ruled the world.

1. I would declare war on radical Muslim extremists and any other kind of extremist who might glom onto their cause, and I'd do my best to get Congress to declare war on them, too. Terrorism today sends apocalyptic shivvers up my theological spine, and while I'm eager to see Christ return, I'm still in favor of trying to defeat the vile enemies of Christ who are trying to precipitate their own form of the last days. I agree with Cruz and Rubio: wipe them out.

2. Cut the size of the Federal government by one third in the first four years I ruled the world (or the U.S. at least). I'd love to cut it by two thirds and keep on going, but as I say, I'm a realist. Actually, a realist probably wouldn't think that I could cut it by a third, either, but that's where my optimism kicks in. Present a budget to Congress that simply defunds things that don't need to be in the purview of the Federal Government in the first place, beginning with the IRS.

3. Build a wall separating Mexico from the U.S. for real. We can send a man to the moon, but we can't keep Mexicans from scaling a wall? As for illegal immigrants, of whatever origin, in the U.S., we should find them and deport them. I realize there are between 11 and 12 million of them at present, and that we don't know where many of them are and that we don't have the resources to mount a high pressure campaign to find them. But when we do identify one, we shouldn't be soft and sentimental. Out he goes.

4. Make Congress subject to every law they pass for the general population.

5. Issue an executive order cancelling nearly every executive order issued by Obama, including all the ones that tinkered with the Affordable Care Act that he proposed to begin with and then found unworkable. His orders exempting this and changing that were unconstitutional, but the government has obeyed them as if they weren't. What happened to statesmanship? Is there none left? Will all the lemmings in Washington just march right after Obama into the sea of totalitarianism?

6. Present legislation to Congress overturning what portions of Obamacare that weren't rendered ineffective by cancelling his executive orders. Convene a task force to study for one month what should be put in place, if anything, to replace Obamacare, and present the recommendations of that task force, if palatable, to me and to Congress.

That's enough for the first six months. I know, I know, it sounds impossible. But we like to celebrate the impossible, don't we? And who would have predicted that the very existence of the United States of America was possible in the world prior to, oh, say 1600, to say nothing of 1776. This is a nation where the impossible has come true.

The adorers of John F. Kennedy liked to call the America of their dreams "Camelot." Alan J. Lerner's lyrics were just as unrealistically idealistic as were Tony Bennett's dreamily crooned wishes:

A law was made a distant moon ago here:
July and August cannot be too hot.
And there's a legal limit to the snow here
In Camelot.
The winter is forbidden till December
And exits March the second on the dot.
By order, summer lingers through September
In Camelot.
Camelot! Camelot!
I know it sounds a bit bizarre,
But in Camelot, Camelot
That's how conditions are.[28]

But we're not talking about changing the climate—that's what liberals are blathering on about, in the face of the fact that the mean global temperature hasn't changed in eighteen years. No, I'm talking

[28]Source: *http://lyrics-a-plenty.com/c/camelot.lyrics.php*

about objectives that actually can be accomplished. While it may seem to be as unrealistic to think of reducing the size of government as it would be to control the amount of snow, it is, it *is* possible. And while Obama seems to have run roughshod over the Constitution leaving his objectors fallen in his path, it is, it *is* possible to repeal it and turn things around. If I didn't believe that, I would give up. But as South Carolina's State Motto says, "Dum Spiro Spero"—While I Breathe, I Hope.

I don't have what it takes to be the President, much less to rule the world. But I can dream, can't I. Hey, I think that was a song...

Blame for 9/11

One of Donald Trump's bold pronouncements as he vied for the Republican nomination for the Presidency was that he might have been able to prevent 9/11. His claim began as an off-the-cuff remark in response to Chris Wallace in an interview. Wallace was asking him about some of Jeb Bush's remarks, specifically that his brother George had kept the nation safe. Trump suggested that the claim about President Bush was not entirely true, since 9/11 took place "during his reign." Never mind for the minute that the term "reign" is inappropriate for our American system of governance. Trump explained his summary assessment by saying that if he had been in charge, his tough policies on immigration might well have kept the 9/11 hijackers out of the country, thus preventing the attacks that took down the Twin Towers.

The horrendous events of 9/11 are a sensitive issue when it comes to blame and recrimination, especially in light of the truly insane idea that the United States Government carried out the attacks itself, and the equally insane radical Muslim concept that the U.S. deserved to be attacked and that the terrorists who did it were righteous. Let's be clear, here: 9/11 is to be blamed on those who planned and carried out the attacks, out of their evil beliefs and vile hatred. That said, Donald Trump did not blame 9/11 on George Bush; he implied, however, that a level of responsibility for the vulnerability of our country belongs on Bush.

Trump didn't go far enough back, however. We should go back into the presidency of Bill Clinton (as much as I hate to do that) and say that long before 9/11, the U.S. should have been cracking down on terrorism worldwide. The attack on the U.S.S. Cole in 2000 should have been the last, last straw. Really the first World Trade Center bombing in 1993 should have been the first last straw. President Clinton should have launched the War on Terror then. If any U.S. president should be held responsible in a major way for the extent of terrorism's success in the world, it's Bill Clinton. If, when the first bombing of the World Trade Center took place, President Clinton had declared war on terrorism, we probably would not have seen any sort of 9/11 attack. We should have been marshaling forces here and around the world searching out terrorist rat holes and wiping them out, ever since the early 90s.

In spite of my antipathy for everything Clinton, however, I'm going to give him a slight break. He still bears some responsibility, but he was simply part of the culture of the sleeping giant. There was sufficient intelligence available to tell the U.S. there was a substantial danger of attack by terrorists. There was plenty of evidence—and had been since the emergence of the Palestinian Liberation Organization—that worldwide terrorism was on the rise and that America in particular would be its ultimate target. The problem was that we were unwilling to believe, really believe, that it would happen.

When the surprise attack of Japan on Pearl Harbor took place in 1941, Japanese officers were celebrating the news when a sober Admiral Isoroku Yamamoto put the entire event into its prophetic perspective. He said, "We have awakened a sleeping giant."[29] On 9/11, sixty years after Pearl Harbor, the American giant was again awakened, which means we had been sleeping again. At least in the sense that Americans thought terrorism was something that only the Middle East really needed to worry about, and, oh well, maybe Lockerbie Scotland, and maybe Munich during the '72 Olympics, and maybe—wait: the growing exceptions should have shown us a long, long time ago that terrorism was a growing international threat. Nor was it anything like what Obama likes to call it these days: "random acts of violence." It's precisely this kind of naivete, or worse, strategic obfuscation, that has enabled terrorism to rise and threaten civilization itself, because this attitude of denial resulted in our leaders' failure to take action.

We cannot lay the blame for 9/11 or today's continuing terrorist incidents at the doorstep of any single president only, or any CIA or FBI director, or any other individual alone. It would make as much sense to do that as it would be to blame FDR for Pearl Harbor. We know now that he had intelligence information that certainly indicated Japan was a growing threat, but FDR was a human being capable of disbelief just as we are, capable of denying the possible or the probable just as we are, and able to convince himself that while something could happen, surely it wouldn't right then. But it did.

Donald Trump, for all his controversial remarks, continued to gain popularity among Republicans and Independents, and his opinion that Bush should take some responsibility for the terror that fell upon America during his watch (not his reign) did not destroy Trump's lead.

---

[29]Critics in the past few years have insisted that Yamommoto never said this. If critics had their way, I suppose few people would be discovered to have said anything at all. You can quote me on that, but it won't do any good. In fifty years, there will be no evidence that I said it.

Trump needed to be reminded that hindsight is 20/20; it's easy to boast about what one woulda coulda done. Nevertheless, the 2015-2016 campaign shouldn't have been a referendum, even ever so briefly, on a President who, when terrorists struck, did his best to see that America woke up. George W. Bush deserves America's continuing thanks for his leadership through that tumultuous time. Our challenge, certainly the challenge of every President, is to stay awake and do the hard things necessary to protect the nation. It should not take another 9/11 to motivate us to defeat the demonic enemy that has designs on world dominion.

Not What She Said

At this writing, Baltimore is in flames, both symbolically and actually, as the result of protests over an incident in which a Black crime suspect who was placed in a police van subsequently died of a severed spinal cord, exact cause unknown. After the funeral, mobs gathered in the streets of Baltimore and began getting out of control immediately. Some news organizations suspect that "professional" riot organizers (for lack of an official term) fomented the protests.

In the wake of the first day of rioting, Baltimore mayor Stephanie Rawlings-Blake gave a press conference. She came under fire immediately after her remarks on April 25, where she commented on how the city was trying to respond to the protests going on in the streets. Here's a transcript of what she said that got so much press for days afterward:

"I made it very clear that I worked with the police and instructed them to do everything that they could to make sure that the protesters were able to exercise their right to free speech. It's a very delicate balancing act. Because while we try to make sure that they were protected from the cars and other things that were going on, we also gave those who wished to destroy space to do that as well. And we worked very hard to keep that balance and to put ourselves in the best position to deescalate."

I heard the recording of her remarks, having not heard any comments about them first, and I immediately sensed what she was saying. Let's be honest: the mayor is not very articulate, and she could have said what she said more clearly if she had been better prepared and also had had some help putting together her remarks. Nevertheless, she was out there promptly, trying to exercise some leadership, which is more than you can say for Barack Obama, who was silent for days. Anyway, this is what the mayor meant by what she said:

"We were trying to make sure people were permitted to protest, and by not clamping down on them, we risked some destructive actions, which was, in fact, what happened." That's what she said: I'm certain of it. I have spent my career reading people and attempting valiantly to be fair and to avoid inaccurate judgment. I believe without hesitation that Mayor Rawlings-Blake did *not* say that she had directed police to stand back and let people burn things.

Yet, that's exactly what most conservative pundits claimed she said. Local hosts on conservative radio ridiculed and lambasted the mayor for going on record approving of the violence in Baltimore. Rush Limbaugh raked her over the coals for it. Fox News commentators climbed on the bandwagon. I don't watch the Democrat Media, so I don't know how they interpreted the mayor, but it seemed as if everyone else condemned her.

I'm a conservative (surprised?), but this isn't about being conservative: it's about interpreting someone's words properly. And not only did I hear what she said and take her meaning from a combination of her words, intonation, and circumstances, but I offer this additional logic for holding that the mayor didn't mean what her critics are saying she did: what sane mayor would go before the press during a time of rioting and admit that she deliberately granted the rioters the opportunity to set her city on fire and destroy property? It simply doesn't make sense that she would say such a thing, even if she might secretly have felt that it was about time Blacks stuck it to Whites and got some payback. I don't think she thinks that, however, and even if she did, the rioters weren't being highly discriminating in whose property they were destroying. They never are.

Bottom line, I take issue with my conservative fellows who were hasty in finding outrage where none was intended. There are enough genuine outrages to be upset about in this Baltimore situation without inventing one with the words of the city's inarticulate mayor.

Okay, Let's Just Repeal the Bill of Rights

The horrific 2015 shooting in Charleston's Emanuel AME Church prompted the President to say that at some point Americans must talk about getting guns under control. Those who want to change the status quo with regard to the law (*all* of us want mass shootings to stop) want us to "have this debate." Just like the race situation, where some national leaders tell us "we need to have this debate," those who want gun laws to be tighter or who wish there simply weren't a Second Amendment to the Constitution would like for us to discuss guns nationally.

Well, if you think you agree with that idea, then it isn't just the Second Amendment that needs to be abolished or severely amended; it's most of the other Amendments in the Bill of Rights as well. How many of the following do you agree with? Use the check boxes.

☐ First, we need to change the First Amendment. Hate speech has gotten so bad in America, so many crimes are prompted by hate speech, so much needed change is not taking place because of the opposition of people who are backward and religious and prejudiced and full of hate, that we need to limit the right of free speech. Not only do we need to prohibit someone's shouting "Fire!" in a crowded theater, we need to keep people from standing on street corners and marching near abortion clinics and spewing their hate speech there. Anyone who protests existing law and settled public policy should be quieted. It's for our own good. There's too much difference of opinion in this country. People are too divided. The only way for us to come together for the sake of our future is for the government to put a lid on this rampant ranting and raving by people who don't like change or who don't like the President or whatever.

☐ The Fourth Amendment also needs to be changed. When we look at America, we have to admit that crime is so terrible and that criminals are getting away with things so easily, that government simply must have the right to speed up and empower the search for evidence and the apprehension of criminals. The courts long ago made a serious mistake in disallowing evidence simply because it had been obtained without a warrant. Police do a good job, but if they think someone perpetrated a crime, they have to go to a judge somewhere, who doesn't know much about police work, and get a warrant. Police should be able to search a suspect's house and car and person if they want, because we know that many perpetrators get away with drugs or weapons in their pockets, cars and houses, or have a chance to ditch evidence before they can be caught with it. Who knows how many cases have been lost against criminals because the State had to go through hoops to get evidence or had to prove its case without evidence they knew was there but just couldn't prove to the satisfaction of some know-nothing, skeptical judge.

☐   And how about the Fifth Amendment? Just because somebody skated on a charge once shouldn't mean that if new evidence comes up later for the same crime, they should go scot free. There's no telling how many people we have walking around free who were found "not guilty" for some lame reason by juries that were manipulated by slimy lawyers, but who are guilty nonetheless, and now they will never pay for their crimes. The jury's verdict shouldn't be the last word. Not only the defense, but the State should be able to appeal the verdict, and try a person again until a jury gets it right.

☐   While we're on the subject of slimy lawyers, we need to stop providing free lawyers for people who have been living off the rest of us by stealing our stuff, and then don't have money to hire a lawyer when we finally catch them and put them on trial. They can represent themselves. The Sixth Amendment needs to go, or at least the part that guarantees people lawyers at public expense—that's you and me. Lawyers who represent people who obviously are guilty of the crimes they're charged with (like all these people who committed mass murders in the past few years, for example) are mostly attorneys from the bottom of the barrel who would use any tactic to trick a jury into allowing murderers or even terrorists to go free. Let the criminals represent themselves. If they lose, they lose. We win.

☐   The Tenth Amendment needs to be repealed altogether, and a host of new Federal laws put into effect. The argument of "States' Rights" during the Civil War and since should have convinced us that the only reason to limit the power of the Federal government is to enable racist states to remain rebellious and to prevent the true unification of the country. Strong, Federal law is necessary to control the wayward States and put us on a path to a golden future.

If you agree with me on the above, please photocopy this article, check the boxes beside the paragraphs you approve of, and then present them to officials on your way *out* of the country.

Why Liberals Say They're Liberal

Taylor Batten, the Editorial Page Editor of *The Charlotte Observer*, recently asked readers of the *Observer* to ask him questions on Honest Day, April 30. (Who came up with that, I wonder?) One of them asked him why the newspaper supports such liberal agenda?

Batten gave an answer, defending his being a liberal.[30] I think it's a wonderful example of liberal hypocrisy, and that it reveals the prejudices and categorization of which liberals are liberally guilty. What follows are the responses of Batten, in italics, and my comments after each one.

We believe that everyone is created equal.

Conservatives do, too. For instance, we believe that Blacks and Whites were created equal, and that neither White nor Black deserves to be given preference by government.

We believe that children should not bear responsibility for the sins of their parents.

So do conservatives. For instance, we don't think White people whose parents may have been part of the race problem or whose great great grandparents may have owned slaves (of which very, very few did) shouldn't be blamed for the disadvantage that some Blacks think they're still working under in the 21st century.

We believe that prevention is a heck of a lot cheaper than a cure.

Guess what: so do conservatives. For instance, we think preventing poverty by working for a living is cheaper than trying to cure poverty by pouring public funds (read, Taxes) on it, which doesn't work.

We believe people should not be treated as lesser citizens, with fewer rights, because of whom they love...

Guess what: we conservatives do as well. In fact, we think Christians should not have their rights under the First Amendment abridged simply because they love Jesus Christ. (I know, Batten meant he agrees with letting homosexuals get married. However, "rights" must be defined somewhere, and it generally is, in the Constitution of the United States. We conservatives simply don't believe in defining new rights and

---

[30]Taylor Batten, "Honest answer to a reader's question" *(http://www.charlotteobserver.com/opinion/opn-columns-blogs/taylor-batten/article21108579.html,* The Internet, 16 May 2016).

assigning them to persons whose behavior is immoral and unnatural.)

We believe discrimination is wrong in every instance.

First of all, really? Discrimination is a broad word. It means to make distinctions. Sometimes that's quite necessary. Suppose the issue were whether or not a government agency should hire a pedophile to work in its day care center. Should the agency discriminate? Absolutely.

Of course, if you're going to talk about the usual descriptors— religion, race, ethnicity, gender—we conservatives agree there should be no discrimination. Oh, but I suspect the editor is talking specifically about sex (as opposed to gender), meaning whether a person is a homosexual, transsexual, transgendered person, or some other variation on the M/F spectrum now being explored by those living on the edge. Interestingly enough, most conservatives still agree with the editor, as long as he's not talking about forcing people to change their religious or other moral beliefs and to adopt the position of the "gay" community that homosexual behavior is not in any way immoral.

And while we're at it, let's turn the question back on the good editor of the *Observer:* do you really believe that Christians should not be the targets of discrimination? Or just liberal Christians? How about people who believe in the Second Amendment?

We believe that police officers should act professionally, under incredibly difficult circumstances, regardless of a suspect's race.

So do conservatives. The problem with the editor's expressed opinion is that given the tenor of things right now in the nation, he appears to be buying into the "Hands up, don't shoot" concept of recent incidents involving police. The incident in Ferguson, MO, is claimed to have inspired the phrase, but the report that the Black, gentle giant put his hands up and pleaded not to be shot is a lie: it never happened. Likewise, the generalization that cops all over the country are killing Blacks right and left is a lie. There's more media focus on the use of service weapons by police, and thus more publicity of such incidents, but there's no actual troubling trend developing.

Where does the editor get the idea that everyone else but liberals is guilty of encouraging racism among cops?

We believe taxes should be kept as low as possible while still providing a sound safety net for the neediest, a robust education for all, decent health care for the elderly and the destitute, and other basics.

We do, too. A safety net should be for people falling through no fault of their own. We already provide education for all (what's the editor campaigning for?). We also provide health care for the elderly, etc. The editor is implying the construction and then destruction of a straw man.

We believe politicians of any party should keep their promises, avoid the appearance of personal gain from the public trust, and look out for the general welfare, not that of any one special interest.

So do conservatives. In particular, we think Hillary Clinton should be defeated in disgrace for a history of ill-gotten gain, and some of us think that President Obama should be impeached for not serving the public interest in his destructive policies. He must hold some kind of record for broken promises and failure to look out for the general welfare.

We believe there are peace-loving Muslims.

So do we conservatives. We also believe they should disavow their terrorist brethren, which they mostly do not.

We believe in the separation of church and state.

We do too. We also believe, however, that the phrase (which is not in the Constitution) does *not* mean to keep Christians out of government or to keep Christians who *are* in government *quiet*. The Constitution says, "Congress shall make no law respecting an establishment of religion, or prohibiting the free exercise thereof…" Government should neither compel people to be religious nor keep them from being so. The problem in our country just now is that government is waging a growing war on church, trying to put gags in Christians' mouths, forcing Christians to acknowledge if not even celebrate forms of immorality defined as such in the scriptures for three thousand years, etc. Really committed liberals actually believe the founders should never have uttered the word "God" or "Creator" in their writings, especially the ones that begin with "We the people."

We believe if you're a fan of a politician solely because he has a 'D' or an 'R' after his name, then you're not paying attention.

Which explains what? —that liberal newspapers and broadcasters are almost never fans of the "R's," only if the "R" is a moderate? Methinks the good editor is being disingenuous, and that he doesn't really practice what he preaches.

We believe we have only one planet, and we should protect it for our grandchildren.

Me, too, and I'm a conservative. But we have to start with facts, not fiction. The eco-liberal manifesto is full of unscientific, hippie mythology about the earth, which political liberals by and large have swallowed whole. Heck, some of them helped write the manifesto. Then they expect the country to go along with a mindless transition to socialism in order to "cure" the "global threats" posed by capitalism and democracy. What good would it do us if, even granting hypothetically the validity of the global warming exaggeration, we bequeathed a cooler earth to our great grandchildren only to subject them to totalitarianism that then robbed them of their liberties and erased the American dream?

Liberals tend to be some of the most subtly arrogant people in the world. They have the notion that their opinions are merely rational, that their values are demanded by common wisdom, and that it's everyone else who is prejudiced, racist, discriminatory, uncompassionate, and anything else negative that you can think of.

They're wrong.

Liar, Liar

There are just some faces that when I see them I cannot summon any feelings of trust or belief. One of them is Obama's. He lifts that arrogant nose and lies straight into the camera, and he's done it so much that it would be foolish of me to believe almost anything he says.

Another of those untrustworthy faces belongs to Obama's Secretary of State, the laughable Lurch, John Kerry. You know, the one who was in Vietnam. The one who made a name for himself protesting and throwing away war medals. I find it abominable that Kerry has become SecState, an indication of the anti-American sentiment of the President himself. Worse, Kerry reflects the fundamental dishonesty of his boss.

In front of the House Appropriations Committee on February 25, 2015, Secretary of Prevarication John Kerry said, "This is counterintuitive but it's true: Our citizens, our world today is actually, despite ISIL, despite the visible killings that you see and how horrific they are, we are actually living in a period of less daily threat to Americans and to people in the world than normally— less deaths, less violent deaths today than through the last century."

I ask you: why in the world should we believe him?

If you're going to say a thing like, "This is counterintuitive but it's true," you had better follow it up with some hard facts to prove it.

In other words, if you say you know your claim doesn't make any sense, you'd better be able to cite hard data why I should believe you anyway.

How, on the other hand, would you be able to prove the truth of such an assertion? You would have to have a standard by which to measure "daily threat." What exactly would that be? Kerry specifically described his word "threat" with the idea of "less deaths" (which, for us grammarians would be "fewer deaths") and "less violent deaths." Do you mean to say that if we took figures for Americans who died as the result of any kind of homicide in the decade of the 50s, for instance, or even the 80s, and compared them to homicides from 2001-2010, we would find that there are fewer murders these days than fifty years ago?

Well, let's look at some hard data, Mr. Kerry. The FBI keeps that sort of thing around, you know.

The average homicide rate for the 50s was 4.48 per 100,000 persons. In the first decade of the 2000s, it was 5.55. Looks like to me that 2001-2010 was more violent, not less, than the 50s.

If you select the very violent 70s, the rate does go up to about nine people per hundred thousand. Maybe Kerry was thinking about his salad and protest days.

But Kerry wasn't really talking about street crime. He meant to be implying that the sense Americans have these days that we are under the threat of anti-American violence, terrorist violence, is not well founded. On what basis can he even pretend that we are more safe today than we were twenty years ago, or thirty or forty? How many terrorist events conducted by foreign groups or their converts here, were there on American soil, in the 20th century, before the first World Trade Center bombing in 1993?

You can find a few, notably a bombing tied to communists in 1920, and a 1975 bombing by a Puerto Rican group. Until 1993, however, escalating attacks were on foreign soil.

Since that time, however, we have had: the 1995 bombing of the Murrah Building in Oklahoma City (168 people killed); the 1997 Empire State Building shooting on the Observation Deck (1 killed); 9/11 (2,992 people killed); the 2001 anthrax attacks; the 2002 Beltway sniper shootings, jihad related; the 2006 Chapel Hill SUV attack; the 2008 San Diego courthouse bombing; the Little Rock killings (2) in 2009; a New York bomb attempt in 2010 (foiled); the 2011 Spokane bomb attempt (foiled); the Boston Marathon bombing in 2013 (3 killed, 260 injured); the Fort Hood shootings in 2009; and the 2015 Capitol terror attack (foiled). I've left out some lesser known events.

You would think that John Kerry would have checked his facts before he flapped his gums in front of the Appropriations Committee and claimed that we're a lot safer here in America nowadays from foreign terrorists than we were back during the bad old days (before the Obama Administration).

As John Belushi famously said, however, "But no-o-o-o!" Kerry didn't do that. He simply counted on his prestigious position for credibility, or the tendency of likeminded political sycophants to believe him, or simply the truism attributed to Joseph Goebbels, that if you repeat a lie often enough, people will believe it, and you will even come to believe it yourself.

Christianity and Its Enemies

You God Haters: Why?

Throughout my life I have found it difficult to understand why the most vicious critics of Christianity and the Bible have been as contemptuous as they are. In my morning perusal of news I often come upon articles online that have something to do with religion, and in the comments section below, the conversation quickly degenerates to the most excessive, hateful, sometimes vile ridicule of Christians, churches, and God himself.

One of the recent threads of text I was reading included comments from a fellow who tossed in some dismissive remarks about the Apostle Paul's having "invented" Jesus Christ. Acquainted as I am with the opinion of some scholars that Pauline theology represented a distinctly different strain of thinking about Jesus than what is reflected in the Gospels, I thought to myself that this online writer's opinion took that scholarly theory to an entirely different level. I began thinking how to refute this idea, and my thoughts expanded to considering the question I've posed above: why do some people hate Christianity, God, anyone who believes in God, and the very idea of believing in God or in a Savior?

Don't get ahead of me, here—some of my readers will, I'm sure. Don't think I don't know the answer to my own question.

Start at the beginning of the Christian's theology and look at the message of Genesis. The Bible says that "in the beginning God created the heavens and the earth." What's so terrible, so worthy of hate and detestation in that? The Bible declares in its first sentence that there is a God. I know that atheists differ in their view, but by no means are all atheists filled with hate for Christians. What is it about Genesis 1:1 that makes some people hate God? Moreover, the verse says that this God created everything that exists. Even if you're a radical evolutionist, you could adopt Genesis 1:1's message as the answer to the question that even astrophysicists cannot answer: what made the Big Bang bang? Plenty of astrophysicists and scientists of every stripe are theists, too, if not full bore Christians. Why hate the Christian belief in God and creation? It's strange.

Consider then the Hebrew sojourn in Egypt, the rise of Moses, and the ten plagues that convinced Pharaoh to free the Hebrews to go to Canaan. The vilest critics lampoon the entire event and deny any of it ever happened. They do this ostensibly because official Egyptian history doesn't record it. Yet they make their arguments on this basis in the face of the fact that ancient empires, in particular, frequently produced historical accounts that assiduously avoided any record of defeat, making out their leaders and armies as constantly victorious and their national story as heroic and glorious. Jewish history as recorded in the Bible, in fact, while not alone in including self-effacing accounts, is not in the mainstream of self-serving records.

What is so hate-provoking about a historical writing that records the testimony of hundreds, thousands, or hundreds of thousands of people who witnessed miraculous events? I've occasionally asked someone who has a particularly vicious disgust for stories of miracles if he would call his mother a damnable liar if she had told him that in her youth she had seen a known cripple healed as a result of prayer? If he had no other reason to think his mother mad as a hatter, would the God-hater think his mother a fool?

Moving on to the life of Jesus himself (the very reality of whose existence some God haters deny), what prompts some people to ridicule the account of the resurrection and to call anyone a fool to believe it? Some critics, I know, dismiss the authenticity and historicity of the Gospels, but they do so out of hand, not because there is any competent scholarship to do so. Trained historians who are not already hopelessly biased by a preexisting hatred of religion of any sort do not make such rash statements dismissing the validity of the gospel accounts.

Moreover, biblical scholarship has improved with every passing century and even decade, while anthropological studies continue to confirm accounts of the Bible. What we have in the Gospels, while clearly theological treatises, is also a compendium of kernels of history, describing the birth, life, work, message, death, and yes, resurrection of Jesus of Nazareth. Of this last event, the resurrection, there simply is no rational reason for dismissing its truth. The accounts of the synoptic Gospels and John are strikingly consistent, and one of the greatest arguments for the historicity of the resurrection is that if it had not actually taken place, the disciples who had been thoroughly defeated by Jesus' crucifixion would not have been so transformed that they could change the world—which they began doing fifty days after the Passover when Jesus had died.

But the haters of Christ and Christianity will have none of this sensible thinking. To them, Christians are fools, ignoramuses, rubes and gullible bumpkins, and the Bible is a pack of lies.

Why?

Now, you second guessers can answer the question. I could go on citing passage after passage in the Bible and arguing for the reasonableness of the theology taught, the history recounted, the principles illustrated. It would be all for naught, however, because those who detest Christians and Christ, those who hate the Bible and believers, those who ridicule religion, do so *not* because they have a convincing argument—because they don't. Rather, they hate the truth, because it brings guilt and conviction to their hearts. Their hearts, the very core of their lives, are deceived and depraved by sin, the spiritual infection of all humanity, and they have rejected all things biblical and all things Christian rather than confess the truth and face up to their spiritual need.

Isaiah, Jesus and Paul all put it this way, that although seeing, they don't see, and though hearing, they don't hear, lest in understanding they might actually respond and be changed (Mk 4:12).

It's that change of heart and life, that admission of sin against God and need of forgiveness and true life, that people don't want to go through. They fear it the same way a wounded animal often will not accept the helping hand of a compassionate human being. They fear it the same way an addict doesn't want anyone to confront him and help him get free, only to give him money so he can get another fix.

It's still exasperating for me to read the venomous diatribes of those who vilify me and my fellow Christians, and who most viciously slander Christ himself. Jesus, however, warned his followers realistically, "If the world hate you, ye know that it hated me before it hated you. ...If they have persecuted me, they will also persecute you ...all these things will they do unto you for my name's sake, because they know not him that sent me" (Jn 15:18ff).

Some reader of this article may spew out fresh venom against me. I just have to keep remembering that he's not making sense: he's just telling me his heart is black and lost, and in need of the very God he is trying his best to deny.

Cheap Miracles

Many years ago I read a little story about two men who were comparing their experiences riding in horse carriages. If I remember correctly one of them was a professor at Princeton University and the other was the school's president. This was back before the twentieth century when Princeton was still a school with a Christian character. (Few people remember that the college was begun by Presbyterians who wanted to perpetuate their faith through college trained young people). Anyway the identities don't matter. The story went that the professor arrived at the college one day with a breathless tale of his narrow escape from death on the road to the school.

He told the college president, "I have had the most harrowing experience. My horse bolted and began running away with the carriage. I was nearly thrown out several times. As you know, the road runs near a steep cliff. At the last moment, I was able to get the animal under control before going over the precipice! It was a miracle, sir!

The president looked at his faculty friend and replied, "Why sir, I can tell you a greater miracle than that! I have ridden that same road hundreds of times, and not once, not once mind you, has my horse ever been frightened, nor has my carriage ever sped out of control, nor have I ever been nearly thrown from it, and never have I been almost tossed over the cliff to my death! What do you think of that?

The point of the story, of course, was that God sometimes rescues and other times merely prevents. The point is also that whether or not something is a miracle is often a matter of perspective.

I don't know what circles you live in, but frequently I hear people attribute some welcome event in their lives to a miracle of God. I hear it from some people more than others, and that isn't necessarily a compliment. To them almost any wonderful event is a miracle. It matters little that human beings had anything to do with the wonderful event, such as skillful surgeons. No, the non-recurrence of cancer after its excision by a wonderful surgeon was a miracle.

You can contrast that approach to miracles with the perspective of the total non-believer, for whom nothing is a miracle, even if he can't begin to explain how some amazing event happened. Someone who had a tumor on an MRI two months ago and has no trace of one now, when no one did anything but pray, is not a miracle to the non-believer, just a coincidence, or perhaps fakery. If it happened more than a lifetime ago (such as in the Bible), then the report was a lie or a myth (a lie).

There are no miracles because there is no God, would be the non-believer's take on it, or if there is a god, he/she is not really involved in life in what would be described as supernatural activity.

In the middle, of course, are a great many other people for whom miracles are possible, and some happened a long time ago, and perhaps some happen nowadays, but only rarely. The middle group is happy to concede that miracles reported in the Bible took place, that at least some of the more famous reports of miracles in the past two thousand years are true, and that people today are occasionally healed by God in response to prayer with no other intervention, which would qualify as miracles.

I'm somewhere in this middle group, I'm afraid. I say "afraid" only because I know that some people condemn a middle-of-the-road stance: "You get knocked down by traffic from both sides," said Margaret Thatcher. "There's nothing in the middle of the road but a yellow stripe and dead armadillos," said Jim Hightower. "The middle of the road is the worst place to drive," opined Robert Frost. The critics are addressing the middle of the road as a metaphor for compromise, however, and my position is no compromise. In my opinion, it's the result of properly interpreting the evidence and avoiding irrational extremes. I'm convinced that both the non-believer's rejection of the miraculous and the hyper-believer's thinking that miracles utterly surround us are both irrational.

In the news recently was a report that the Catholic church had confirmed a second miracle by Mother Teresa. In 2008 the family of a man in Brazil prayed to Mother Teresa (who died in 1997) to heal him of a viral brain infection. The man got well, and the Catholic church counts the event as a miracle to the dead Mother Teresa's credit. It was the last hurdle to her being declared a Saint by the Roman Church.

In my book, the notion of anyone but God's taking credit for a miracle is antithetical to the very concept, so there's that; but on top of that is the problem I have with both the general credulity of Roman Catholics, who are known for their superstition, and my rejection of the idea that anyone but God (Father, Son and Spirit) may be addressed in prayer. I take issue with Catholics on this and many other points, and I'm in good company, since Martin Luther and every Protestant since him has been at odds with the Catholic church on a great deal.

However, at least the Roman Catholic Church is checking out reports of miracles before it accepts them as genuine. In the Protestant traditions, no one I know of is actively checking out the truth of miracle stories. In fact, there are so many claims of miracles that no one could keep track of them anyway, much less attempt either to verify or debunk them.

Christians who see a miracle behind every surprising, mysterious, or especially welcome event are often folks with a modicum of education and a paucity of knowledge even of their own religion. However, my greatest problem with prolific reports of miracles is not merely disappointment in the ignorance of many Christians. Rather it's the related, two-pronged problem that (1) their credulousness provides ammunition to critics of Christianity, who are all too willing to charge all Christians with being gullible fools; and (2) the loss of meaning that the word "miracle" should communicate to the world.

The first of those two prongs doesn't need much discussion. Christianity has always invited ridicule when its adherents have attributed science to the work of the devil and any welcome coincidence to the miraculous hand of God. This is not to say that God isn't to be credited for his general grace at work in the world and for his being the source of "every good thing," as James said (Jas 1:17). Nor is it to cast any doubt at all on God's providential involvement in wonderful events in people's lives. All I mean to say is that Christians' haphazard claims of miracles are an open invitation for non-believers to reject the Christian faith as being the religion of the ignorant and gullible.

The second prong is the point I've been aiming at since the top of this article. The word "miracle" has a meaning, a denotation. Used casually it can mean almost anything wonderful, opportune, highly coincidental or not immediately explicable. However, we really shouldn't use the word in those circumstances. We should save it for times when it means what it means.

Definitions of "miracle," depending on where you look up the word, may include common and errant usage, but so do most other words in dictionaries these days, which is why I'm finding dictionaries less and less useful. The first listing under any dictionary entry, however, is usually the most important.

A miracle is:

"a surprising and welcome event that is not explicable by natural or scientific laws and is therefore considered to be the work of a divine agency" - Oxford Dictionary.

"an unusual or wonderful event that is believed to be caused by the power of God; an extraordinary event manifesting divine intervention in human affairs" - Merriam-Webster.

"an effect or extraordinary event in the physical world that surpasses all known human or natural powers and is ascribed to a supernatural cause" - Dictionary.com

"an event that is contrary to the established laws of nature and attributed to a supernatural cause" - The Free Dictionary

You get the gist, I'm sure. An event that is truly miraculous is one that cannot be explained as the result of natural processes or which, by its circumstances, timing, or effects gives commanding evidence of the direct intervention of God in the natural world. Refusing to attribute to God what God clearly has done is the essence of atheism, but declaring any welcome event to be a miracle makes the concept of supernatural intervention meaningless. If everything's a miracle, nothing really is.

Yet it's all too common for Christians—even those who aren't particularly credulous—to toss around the word "miracle" casually —Babies, many of us say, are God's little miracles. This would extend to baby deer and all sorts of cute animals, but I doubt we'd be readily willing to call the birth of snakes to be one of God's miracles. Folks, childbirth, no matter what the species, is the way of the world. It's part of God's creation, but it's part of what we call the natural world. Save the word "miracle" for events where God intervenes in his own world to do something different, something outside the flow of events that would have taken place anyway.

A man being interviewed by a reporter during coverage of an immense apartment building fire said that it was a miracle that no one had been killed. I'm sure it was amazing to him. I'm sure everyone was thankful that no one lost his life. But no one offered the slightest evidence to show that people were about to lose their lives but that a supernatural event took place sparing them and that no one can explain what happened. In other words, there were no miracles.

A woman told her prayer group that her father was a walking miracle. Forty years ago he had been diagnosed with a problem for which doctors had limited solutions, involving surgery from which many people died. Twenty years ago, however, solutions were much improved and more people survived. Nowadays, the condition was easily treated by a minimally invasive technique, and almost everyone went on to live well and die from something unrelated. The woman's father had undergone the modern procedure and was just fine. "It's a miracle," she said.

It was nothing of the sort. A man's broken part was fixed by a doctor, using techniques invented by other doctors and perfected by still other doctors. Should God be thanked for the doctors, for man's ability to learn how to fix the human body, and for the very fact that something good happened for a concerned family? Of course! Thank God in everything. Just don't overstate the facts. It cheapens the concept of the miraculous for us to find miracles every day in what are actually quite explicable matters, even if those events amaze us.

By the same token, we should be willing to call a miracle a miracle when one really takes place. I don't know about the fellow in Brazil with the brain virus. I don't trust the fact checkers in the Catholic Church; after all, they've told us from time to time that paintings and statues of Mary bleed from the eyes. I'm sorry, that's just nuts.

However, I think we should be unafraid to pray for miracles and then willing to recognize them if they occur. A young woman I knew back in the mid 70s had a brain tumor. Doctors suspected it and then did scans, which showed a well defined, classical image of a cancerous mass, positioned so as to be inoperable. She went home to think and pray about it. She told the details to her church, and they began to pray for her. She was one of the church's most spiritual, most godly, most Christlike people. The church prayed repeatedly and devotedly. In two month's time, the woman returned to the doctor for another scan to see where things stood. He nearly fainted when he saw nothing remarkable about the scan; there was no tumor, none. He was a Christian, and after he checked and double checked all the evidence, he joined the woman and her church in declaring publicly that a miracle had taken place. God and nothing else had healed this woman.

Some people, extreme as they are in their disbelief, are still willing to lampoon Christians for believing in miracles at all, or in God himself. There will always be such fools.

All I'm saying is that we ought not to give the critics of Christianity unnecessary ammunition with which to impeach our veracity. We need all the credibility we can get in this world of skepticism. Ultimately, the gospel is a message that seems foolish to the world and that is believed only when God does a work of repentance and faith in the heart. Even so, we work against ourselves and against God if we reinforce people's disbelief by proclaiming supernatural intervention where natural forces are clearly at work—even though the entire natural world owes its existence and functioning to the genius of the creator God.

Foreign Worship

Frankly, I'm picky about church. I'll be the first to admit that what constitutes a worthy and productive worship service for me these days has narrowed since I was a youth or college student. In my young adult life church services were substantially the same from place to place I moved, and they were mostly satisfying in structure and content. Nowadays, however, it's difficult for me to feel at home in a church due to the many and significant changes that have taken place in the culture and, therefore, in worship.

When I say "changes" I'm referring not mostly to theological changes, because in my denomination, while there have been theological battles, the bulk of the churches are in the same place in the doctrinal spectrum. Many of them display a troubling lack of theological depth, but that's another article for another time.

No, what I'm talking about are the elements of worship and their form, that make up a sort of *worship language,* if you will. The worship language of the mainstream of Congregational Protestant churches in the U.S. was basically the same for a century or more when the 60s came along and influenced a generation of youth (including me) with strikingly different music adaptable to worship, as well as a casualness that began insinuating itself into church life. I myself participated in some "folk worship" services during my college years, in a church that welcomed college students and developing trends. (I realized only later that the church was theologically liberal). But the greatly different music and style of those services was not adopted as a new approach for the whole church all the time, and it didn't significantly change the church's way of doing things, at least right away.

Over the next twenty years, however, throughout American culture the so called contemporary worship trend took hold, changing the worship styles of most churches in most denominations. (Interestingly, even "contemporary" isn't so contemporary anymore, and churches that march on toward ever more radically different worship have been calling their most recent version of things "modern" since about the turn of the millennium. There are some large churches that have a traditional worship service, a contemporary service, and a modern service.)

This stylistic revolution was one factor that prompted the theological struggles of many Protestant denominations. Other factors were the Neopentecostal (Charismatic) movement, and the burgeoning of classic liberalism that came to the U.S. from Germany at the turn of the 20th century. It took that latter element half a century to mature and deeply infect the seminaries—and thus the pastors and leaders—of all the major denominations. In the froth and then wake of the denominational upheaval of the 70s through the 90s, the prominent "First" churches and other major congregations already riding a crest of liberal theology aligned themselves with new associations for mutual support. They also hoped to avoid having to associate with the bulk of their denominations' worshipers, who were bobbing merrily in the roiling surf of contemporary worship—what my father used to call "a hootenanny." This contemporary worship trend produced what I have termed a different *worship language*. If you speak this language, you will enjoy and experience worship in those churches. If you do not, you won't.

Some people who find themselves not liking the contemporary trend in worship aren't exactly certain why—they just don't. When confronted with the fact that some of them like pop music, they can't explain why they don't like contemporary worship music that sounds just like pop music. When asked to explain why they don't like choruses that use the same words over and over, when they do like some secular music that repeats phrases the same way, they can't tell you. What they object to, even if they can't explain it, is the different worship language now commonly used in churches everywhere—a combination of motions, appearance, words, music and beat that communicates the ideas of worship and leads the worshiper into an experience of God.

Contemporary worship in its most thorough form is a foreign language to me, but not like French (which stymied me in college), or Spanish, which I wish I'd studied instead. Nor is it foreign like physics is foreign to a third grade math student. And it's more than just a different dialect, like Atlanta vs. Brooklyn. It's the language of symbols and style. If you understand and are moved by it, those who "speak" it will be able to lead you in worship. If you don't understand the language, it will simply grate on you and irritate you. You will feel left out and you won't feel like going back.

For all the fact that I grew up in the 60s and love classic Rock music (and Classical—I'm a contradiction), I am not moved by this new contemporary worship language. For all the fact that I actually wrote some of the music used in those folk worship services back in the late 60s, I don't really thrill to what dominates most contemporary church music today. I like my rock music in the car or at home, not at church. I like concerts and appreciate musicians who are fully emotionally involved in their singing, but I don't care to see people emoting all over the stage at church. It just doesn't speak to me. Or maybe it does but I don't like what it says.

I'm not sure what to do about it, either. I could stop going to church altogether, but that's not a good solution, given my beliefs and commitment to God. Earlier in my life I was semi-serious about getting together with a few like-minded people and starting a church that would speak my worship language, but I don't think I have the energy to do that anymore. Mostly I'm just enduring the difference as it widens and leaves me behind. Eventually I'll die and have no trouble worshiping where I'll be—thank the Lord.

Many people who have written on the subject of contemporary worship have epitomized the difference between traditional and contemporary churches as one of "praise and worship," which is a code phrase for, 'you traditional worshipers don't really praise God.' Just how contemporary worship enthusiasts conclude that I don't know, but they do. I suppose they had negative experiences in churches where they perceived the calm, controlled, often formal manner of the leaders and congregation as lifeless, repressed and restrictive. They're wrong. But I've given up on convincing them of that.

It's true that the main thing that characterizes contemporary worship is the kind of music it employs, but many other things typify the worship of congregations that have adopted the contemporary and casual style. I'm talking about churches that have been in existence for a long time and were once traditional. A host of churches have arisen since 1970 or so that have never been anything but contemporary. These churches experience no tensions between traditional and contemporary styles because they have no history of anything but contemporary worship. No revolution has taken place; no transition has been undergone; no leaders have foisted new fangled worship on old time religion. So I'm not talking about those congregations. I don't visit any of them because I know from the get go I would feel painfully out of place.

Classified under one of two categories, here are the things that bug me about contemporary church worship:

Too Casual for Me

Clapping

Oh, I know the Bible says, "O clap your hands…" (Ps. 47:1), etc. But the ancient Hebrews did not have a culture of movies and concerts where applause was praise directed to human beings who gave good performances. Applause in church is almost impossible to interpret in any other way, despite the protestations of those who clap. The proof is that they clap enthusiastically for really great performances, while horrible renderings will get scattered or tentative applause. Oh, and they are beside themselves in clapping for little children. It's not for God. Sorry.

"Good Morning!"

Where did this come from, this incessant, repetitive greeting, not just by the first one to get up but by every person after him/her who gets up and participates from the platform. And then the congregation, which is just an audience at this point, feels it has to respond with, "Good morning!" as if we were in a 1st grade class saying, "Good morning, dear teacher," in sing songy rhythm. Cut it out!

Chaotic Greeting Times

I know people like to socialize, but there really isn't a good enough reason to interrupt worship for the purpose of wandering around the auditorium saying "Hi" and forcing introductions upon visitors. I've been in churches where this goes on for two or three minutes, though the average may be more like half that. Instruments play zippy little songs while the most adventurous members cross the auditorium just to prove they're friendly. If there happened to have been any sense at all of reverence and worshipfulness created so far in the service, it has just been shot to... well, it's been ruined. It's the pastor's fault. If he didn't plan it, it wouldn't happen. What does he think this barely controlled chaos is accomplishing that couldn't be done after the last "amen?"

Beyond Casual Dress

The present generation of children and young adults hardly knows what's meant by "Sunday best" nowadays. I've had this discussion with various people on the other side of it and I can't get anywhere. My belief is that while we might have a range of meetings from casual to formal, there should be a high and holy time of worship where casual dress is just not acceptable. I know, I know, there are some people who don't have the money to own nice clothes. Very few. Some of these folks might tell you they can't afford at least an $80.00 suit (J.C. Penney sells some), yet they sport $600.00 cell phones and don't have a problem spending extra money on lottery tickets, popular sneakers and a lot of fast food, which is more expensive than cooking at home.

That aside, I'm talking about people who wear jeans and T-shirts to Sunday morning church when they have something nicer. I've asked some people who try to make a case for casual worship attire, "Would you wear those things to a wedding?" Some would, at least to some weddings. I'm talking about typical cases, however. I stand my ground. Dress is too casual in church. I think it shows we don't have the same respect for God as we do for other people where more formal dress is expected.

Too Problematic for Me

Canned Music

Canned music is what my father and his generation called recorded accompaniment. Looking back, I realize that canned music began in my father's time. The earliest tape recorders were reel-to-reel deals that could be pumped into the new-fangled P.A. systems, but canned music began to come into its own when cassettes displaced L.P.s.

There have always been a few cases where accompanists couldn't handle a piece of music and the desire or need to use it justified a taped version. I'm not talking about that. I'm talking about the constant, regular, systematic use of recorded music, especially what is being played on Christian radio. I have two substantive objections to this.

First is that the insistence on using the music of contemporary Christian artists, with or without vocals, creates and then reinforces the concept of the performance-nature of worship. You could talk unto you're blue in the face but you won't convince me that what Christian artists do at their concerts is more worship leadership than a performance. What they do in the studio is the same thing, and probably more. And no, I have nothing against a good performance; in fact, I think that people who sing and play in church should do their best, and the better their best is the better I like it.

What canned contemporary Christian radio music does is more than that, however. Exceptions prove the rule: the music of recording artists,, stripped of vocals and used in church as basically karaoke creates a mood that is inseparable from what performing artists create in their concerts: it focuses more attention on the performer than on God, and it succeeds mostly because hearers replay in their heads their last hearing of the music on the radio or at a concert. It therefore detracts from worship.

The second thing is that the dominant use of canned music subtly and persistently decreases the importance of local accompanists. The number of competent pianists and organists today in churches is getting smaller, if my observation is correct. In part, this is simply a decreasing emphasis on these musical talents in schools and churches. Fewer people take music lessons, I think. But this trend has been worsened by the cult of contemporary worship music. Fewer people become competent musicians, these few rise to star status, and people out in the hinterlands just sing to their music. I generalize.

I'll admit that I've heard a piece of music slaughtered by an accompanist and wished the soloist had used a CD instead (my own last solo outing was such an event, for goodness sake!) but that's the price of remaining authentic and "live." There's much to be said for your musicians being there, being involved, and trying to be sensitive to the spirit of worship. Musicians in a can can't do that.

Singing Styles

Going along with the canned music is another detrimental feature of what I have already (controversially, I'm sure) called the cult of contemporary worship music. It's the style of singing that features a lot of ecstatically closed eyes, screwed up faces, and imitative hand and arm gestures. And the singing itself is done into a microphone that's held like an ice cream cone to the mouth. This may be in part because the singer doesn't know how to sing in the first place and couldn't be heard past the second row without electronic amplification. (The inability to sing isn't limited to contemporary performers, of course.)

This imitation of a singer's style, or of the general style of contemporary music, is fakery. It pushes genuine spirituality into the background and further exalts the emotionalism (mostly ginned up) of the performer. Rarely have I watched such a display and felt authentic worship.

To be fair, some singers in traditional settings look like cardboard cutouts and convey scant feeling in their presentations. Anybody who sings should study the matter and develop the ability to convey both the sense and the emotion of the lyrics. Somewhere between wooden renderings on the one hand and caricatured emotionalism on the other, is the genuine expression of spirituality that facilitates worship.

Children Sent Out

I included this gripe not because it's particularly associated with a contemporary style of worship but because it is, in fact, done contemporarily. Children's sermons are much older than the contemporary worship trend, but some churches have gotten into sending their children out of the service. The lovingly expelled class sometimes includes kids up to twelve. I think this is a dangerous trend for the future of churches in general.

I was never sent out to children's church, because there wasn't one. I was brought to, taught to behave in, and gently allowed to learn what happened in, "big church." At the age of seven, during such a church service I surrendered my life to Jesus Christ and was baptized. It wouldn't have happened in children's church. Yet churches these days have the idea that kids need their own pastors, their own church services, everything. On Wednesdays, in churches that have prayer services then, kids regularly have their own events.

I've asked the question of pastors and others for years: Just why would you expect kids to get the urge to go to prayer meeting, once they've gotten to the point where they should graduate to "big church?" Why would they? They've been treated differently all along. It's no wonder youth aren't following the faith of their fathers and mothers: they weren't exposed to it when it would have affected them most.

Orchestras

All of us aspire to something greater and higher in some realm of life. I'm not surprised that churches want little orchestras. Sometimes they aren't bad. I've heard some good ones, usually in larger churches in larger cities. Often, however, they're just the J.V., the second string stragglers who didn't make the community band, and the results sound exactly like you'd expect from wannabees. I was in one church this past year that has a single violinist, adding his acceptably produced sounds to the piano and organ throughout the service. Apparently there's no one else in the church who plays anything confidently enough to join him. Maybe I should have been thankful.

I almost didn't include "orchestras" because if the church can mount an acceptably good one—which at the least means one that is enough in tune that no one is distracted by sour notes—more power to it.

The rule should probably be something like that old adage about teachers—you know, "Those that can, do; those that can't, teach." Maybe the church rule on orchestras should be, "Those that can't, shouldn't."

Praise Teams

The little voice over one shoulder tells me, 'Tread softly, Robert,' while the one on the other shoulder says, 'Let 'em have it.'

The idea of having a smaller ensemble than a choir to come up and do a number is not new, and it's not inherently bad. What I don't like is the idea that an ensemble of, say, eight people, all of whom sing into ice cream cones on stage, is a must for real worship. It's a trend, one that's been going on for thirty years or more, but it's just that, trendy. And again, it invites the performance idea, much more than a standard choir, even much more than having soloists, duets, trios and quartets present music time to time.

It's the idea that the praise team should be a fixture that transforms it. I haven't worked on articulating the idea enough to communicate exactly what I feel about it, but given time I'm sure I could. It just strikes me negatively more than positively.

Hymn Word Changes

People have been tinkering with the hymns. I've been in liberal churches that have bowdlerized hymn texts and I've loudly sung the original words when I got to the relevant passages.

If you know the word "bowdlerize," you might associate it only with editing out profanity. Here's how one dictionary defines it, however: "to remove material that is considered improper or offensive from (a text or account), especially with the result that it becomes weaker or less effective." The tinkerers take out gender specific words, especially references to God, and also substitute simpler words for some wonderful terms that poets originally included, and that we should continue to use. For instance, "But purer and higher and greater will be / Our wonder, our transport, when Jesus we see!" Instead of "transport," some substitute "rapture," "gladness" or "victory." Why? Don't we know what "transport" means? Can't we sense that in context it means to be taken to another, glorious place? What's the matter with us if we have to dumb down a classic hymn?

Video Projectors

The original idea of video projectors was to get people's eyes up and out of hymnbooks. Then the hymnbooks disappeared. Never mind if some people wanted to sing parts and needed the music. Then everything else started getting put up on the screen. Announcements (still mostly pre-service); apparently people can't read their bulletins anymore. Sermon outlines play during preaching; I think I'd resent people watching the screen instead of me. Why is the preacher there at all? Why not just video his preaching and show it? In fact, why video himself? Why not just have a Minister of Video Worship who puts together a new video or two every week, containing the outline and key points, interspersed with B-roll that keeps viewers entertained?

The trend is tightly tied to the generations that have arisen since the advent of video cameras and digital projectors. I realize that young adults and teens in particular get a lot of their news and entertainment from videos, and in and of itself that isn't necessarily bad. I also realize that videos are ubiquitous and that we can't un-invent them, nor would I want to. But just because a thing is ubiquitous doesn't mean it has to be used in every area of life. In some things, videos are counterproductive.

We watch enough TV at home, folks. We see enough movies. We don't need everything we do to have a video screen, either as the whole enchilada or just as a side dish. Sometime, we just need to get away from the video. We used to, in church. I want us to, again.

Absence of Public Reading of Scripture

Whether by a minister only or by everyone, in unison or responsively, we need to read the Bible in worship. That's largely disappeared. The preacher reads the text his message is based on (if any—that's another subject), but the congregation mostly doesn't read or hear read to them any significant portion of scripture. From the first, the scripture was a vital part of worship. Think about it: how do we define the Bible? It's God's word. God's written word to us. Don't you think it makes sense to include a time in worship when we stop and focus on this one thing: what does God say to us?

The bottom line is that I think all the elements of worship should be included, omitted, revised, polished, adjusted, focused, edited, and constantly evaluated, for how much they do or do not enhance genuine, authentic worship. When we start doing things, or start doing them in ways, that detract from worship, distract the worshiper, or take our attention off God, we're hurting only ourselves. It sometimes takes a generation of time to realize what we've done.

Bloody Moons

John Hagee, pastor of a megachurch in San Antonio, and well known televangelist/telepreacher, wrote a book not too long ago in which he proclaimed significant events in *heilsgeschichte*. (He didn't use that word.) When he published *Four Blood Moons* in October 2013 the world had yet to see the latest series of lunar eclipses that conclude tomorrow in a spectacular event combining a total eclipse and the moon's being at perigee. For you non astronomy enthusiasts, that's when the moon is at its closest point to the earth (because of its elliptical orbit of our planet). I probably won't get to see this eclipse tomorrow, not because the world is going to end (which I don't know of, one way or the other), but because we're expecting bad weather locally and I don't want to travel several hundred miles to get out from under clouds. They'll show the event on TV lots and lots, I'm sure—if there still is TV.

Anyway, back to Hagee. He has made church headlines now and then over one thing or another, most recently for holding to a dual covenant theory—the concept that Gentiles are saved through Jesus Christ while Jews are saved through the Old Covenant Law. Hagee's book *Four Blood Moons* devolves from Acts 2:19-20, which says, "And I will show wonders in Heaven above and signs in the Earth beneath; the sun shall be turned into darkness and the moon into blood before the coming of the great and awesome day of the Lord." Hagee then identifies the four lunar eclipses occurring about six months apart that began in the spring of 2014. The April 15, 2014 eclipse took place during the Jewish Passover. The Oct. 8, 2014 eclipse occurred during the Feast of Tabernacles. Passover on April 4, 2015 saw another "blood moon," and the lunar eclipse of Sept. 28, 2015, tomorrow night, during another Feast of the Tabernacles. Once these lunar events have taken place, according to Hagee we should expect some globally significant happenings involving Israel. Exactly what, he doesn't say. One is left to speculate that he probably means anything up to and including the beginning of the tribulation, the second coming of Christ, etc.[31]

The fact that these full moons and eclipses take place on Jewish holidays is nothing out of the ordinary. The Old Testament feasts were deliberately assigned to phases of the moon. And, of course, eclipses of the moon by definition occur when the moon is full—it couldn't be

---

[31]That was September 28, 2015. So far, no identifiable, prophesied events have taken place in the wake of the lunar eclipses.

otherwise, astronomically speaking. So just pointing to the fact that four eclipses take place when Jewish feasts are happening is not worthy of any special note, whether you're a pre-millennialist, post-millennialist, mid-tribulation pre-millennialist or any other kind of eschatological -ist, or a follower of John Hagee, or one of his critics. It doesn't matter.

Qualified astronomers point out to us that there's nothing unusual about four lunar eclipses in two years since the average is more than two per year anyway, and not all of them are total. The spring eclipse this year was partial. What makes this particular tetrad interesting, however, is that the last of the four, which will be a total eclipse rather than just partial, takes place, as I said, when the moon is at perigee. That's something that won't happen again for quite a while. Whether or not this combination of events signals anything on the theological front in this world, I don't know. I assert as well that John Hagee doesn't know.

What's interesting for America about the eclipse on September 28, 2015, is that it will be total from Oregon to South Carolina. I could go down to the southwest corner of my county and see it dead center. But again, the clouds may obscure it altogether.

Again, back to Hagee. I'll grant the fact that some tetrads (series of four lunar eclipses) have taken place at interesting times that involved Jews. Hagee points to a tetrad in 1493, when Jews were being expelled from Spain; to 1949, after the state of Israel was founded; to 1967 during the Six-Day War, and to this year's—tomorrow night's!—total eclipse, the significance of which has yet to be identified by Hagee. Iran may bomb the Knesset, for all I know. Or, the Jews may bomb Tehran—even better. (Bomb, bomb, bomb / bomb, bomb Iran. —Has a nice beat; you can dance to it.)

Don't get me wrong: I'd be happy for this to be the dawn of the millennial reign of Christ, whatever eschatology is correct. It suits me to be done with the present corruption of the world. I'd like to see what I've been anticipating since becoming a Christian in 1957. I wouldn't even mind telling John Hagee, if I see him afterwards, that I'm glad he was right about the blood moon thing.

However, what if nothing in particular happens tomorrow or in the wake of this particularly notable tetrad? How many people have made fools of themselves by finding clues in the Bible and astronomy or history, then prophesying great events which didn't then occur as predicted? Many of these self-appointed prophets line their pockets with book sales while stirring up either apprehension or anticipation, while sometimes hedging their bets with a slight but deliberate vagueness about what exactly is going to happen, and then reminding people after nothing really does, "I never said it would, only that it could."

Monday morning, it will all be over but the shouting. If that's a shout of Hallelujah, fine. Great! If it's the usual yelling by all the unhappy people over the usual array of things (Hillary at the vast, right wing conspiracy, Trump at all the idiots running against him, Iranian terrorists who wish "death to America," angry African-Americans who insist that Black lives matter, etc.), well, okay. The second coming will take place eventually. Until then, we'll carry on. We don't have much choice.

Suffer the Little Ones

It was a scene right out of the New Testament. Pope Francis was in a motorcade through Washington when a little girl came through the barricade on the side of the road and ran toward him bearing a sheet of coloring paper. Security people immediately snatched the child up and carried her back towards the barricade and her waiting parents. But the Pope stopped his vehicle and reached toward the girl, telling his security detail to let her come to him.

It took me back more than forty years to when I sang in the John W. Peterson musical, "No Greater Love," about the life of Christ. In a women's chorus depicting a famous scene, they sang lyrics in which were embedded the words of Jesus:

"Every boy and girl is welcome / Every tiny tot. / Suffer the little ones to come unto me / And forbid them not." (Luke 18:16).

Actually, I wouldn't be at all surprised if the scene with the Pope and the little girl had been staged to reproduce this memorable lesson about Christ's love of children. I hope some enterprising reporter went to find the parents of this little girl and asked them, "When security people enlisted you to send your child running to the Pope, did they tell you they would first act like she couldn't come, but not to worry, because the Pope would let her come anyway, and your little one will be on TV?" No, it wouldn't surprise me at all.

If, on the other hand, the event was not at all staged, I give the Pope credit for recognizing instantly the opportunity he had to follow in the footsteps of Jesus. I don't doubt that he has the Christian character to respond that way genuinely.

That said, I'm really tired of the fawning of the US press over the Pope. I realize that of those people in the press who are Christians, a great number of them are probably Roman Catholic, especially in New York, and I understand that Catholics get excited about the Pope. I don't. I don't see them fawning over Protestant religious leaders; admittedly, there are few of them with major national notariety. I guess when Billy Graham was younger and was still a national religious force to be reckoned with, he got a good bit of press, but nothing like the Pope. Then again, Graham didn't go around with all the pomp and circumstance the Pope does, and no one was wowed by his surroundings; he didn't have robes and gold and silver ornaments and he didn't kiss chalices and crosses and make superstitious hand signals in ornate cathedrals. That sort of thing impresses some people. Not me.

Don't get me wrong: I'm not contemptuous of the Catholic Church; after all, it was the Roman Catholic Church that was largely responsible for keeping Christianity alive, if in a somewhat distorted way, during the Middle Ages. But the Protestant Reformation called Christians back to the Bible as their only authority for faith and practice (not church tradition), and back to Jesus Christ as the way, the truth, and the life without the need of a pope or a hierarchy of priests (to say nothing of "saints") to intervene on their behalf and get them to heaven.

Far from the idea that Catholics propose—that Protestants should 'come back home' to Catholicism—it is Catholics who should leave the impediments of Catholicism and join Evangelicals in following Jesus under his sole Lordship. They need no pope to tell them what the Word of God says. Every believer in Jesus Christ can know and follow Jesus for himself, through the presence and power of the Holy Spirit.

I'll let the political pundits sort out whether the Pope is a Marxist (I think he is), and whether his view of capitalism is distorted (I know it is). At least for today. Tomorrow, I may not be able to contain myself. For now, I'm relatively certain he's also a good actor, and I think the kid and the coloring book was staged.

I Was Right

Update:

Minutes after the now famous encounter of Pope Francis and a little girl in his Washington, D.C. motorcade, I wrote that I wouldn't be surprised if the event had been staged. It was too perfect as an opportunity for the Pope to reenact Jesus' instructions to his disciples to "suffer the little children to come unto me, and forbid them not."

It turns out I was right, if only in part for now. The event had been planned for a year and rehearsed to get it just right. The Pope himself may—may—not have been in on the plan, however.

The Associated Press reported that an L.A. based organization, Full Rights for Immigrants Coalition, started planning the faked reality when they learned the Pope was coming to America.[32] Juan Jose Gutierrez, of the Coalition, told AP about the stunt. (He didn't call it that; I did, because that's what it was.) In fact, this same group pulled off a similar stunt a year ago in Rome.

The Washington reprise wasn't a one-time plan, either. If the little girl, whose name is Sophie, hadn't succeeded in getting to the Pope in Washington, she would have been taken to New York and, if necessary, Philadelphia to make other attempts.

AP's report, citing the heavy security around the Pope, opined that in spite of the planning and rehearsal, it "required a lot of luck" for Sophie to get to him. Was it all luck, I wonder (and I don't believe in luck, anyway)? The "luck" Sophie had makes me continue to be skeptical about the Pope's innocence in the matter. I will not be surprised if we learn in another week or so that he knew about it and consented to it.

One has to give the Coalition credit for being enterprising in their devotion to their cause, although their cause includes amnesty for illegal immigrants, with which I disagree. But if the Pope, or even only his security detail, was complicit in this manufactured event, it would further lower my already low opinion of the papacy.

---

[32] Alicia Caldwell, "The Dance Behind Sophie's Meeting With Francis," *(http://www.usnews.com/news/politics/articles/2015/09/25/la-immigration-group-a t-center-of-girls-encounter-with-pope,* The Internet, 21 Sep 2015).

Does God Not Exist Because You Got Hurt?

Most people believe there is a god. Others reject that belief for all sorts of reasons.

Professional philosophers (I suppose you can make a profession out of that—college professors who teach philosophy might be called that) who do not believe in a god generally disbelieve for, well, philosophical reasons. At least, they would say so, I think. They would say they agree with this or that philosopher from a century or more ago and their disciples up to the present, who have reasoned that there is no god. It seems evident that some professional philosophers did and do believe there is a god—Anselm, Descartes, Liebniz and their disciples, but I suspect you wouldn't be able to coax a simple answer out of them that there either is or isn't a deity.

Most people, who aren't philosophical scholars or theologians, just regular people who reach conclusions from life and everyday thinking, have decided, both simply and profoundly, that there is a god. To put that conclusion into the more typical Christian idiom, most people believe in God. In America, despite the mix of other, minority religions, the Jewish or Christian belief in the God of one or both Testaments is the prevailing conviction.

That said, sometimes people who once accepted the general notion of a god or the God of the Bible at some point in their lives may suddenly reject that belief. Unfortunately, they do so for less than valid reasons, but understandable ones nonetheless.

Take Julianne Moore, the actress, who suffered the loss of her mother, Anne Smith, in 2009, to septic shock. Smith was only 68 at the time. Moore was extremely distraught. She allowed her pain to bring her to a conclusion that there is no God. She said, "I learned that there is no 'there' there." The reason for this conclusion and rejection of belief in God, which Moore had maintained in a cursory way previous to her mother's death, was that Moore reasoned that because God allowed her mother to die, he must not exist.

Some of you who are paying close attention have noted the contradiction in logic in that statement. If God doesn't exist, then he didn't exist to allow someone to die, or to enable them to live, either. The argument is often poorly stated, but in its more consistent expression it's the old "how can an all loving God allow suffering in the world" argument. Scads of people have used it, but it has never become a substantial argument against God's existence in spite of its frequently being employed. At the very least, it's a logically flawed argument, since it generalizes from a restrictive set of specifics. (Otherwise, we could equally state that God must exist because we feel blessed.)

The argument is based on the assumption that if God exists, he must be all good and loving, and if he is all good and loving, he would not allow evil in the world. That assumption is deeply flawed, making leaps in logic that are not justified by the premises, and not resting on premises that are logically derived themselves.

That said, I sympathize with Moore and with everyone who thinks of that argument when grief, tragedy or violence mars his or her life. I realize that people who resort to that argument are simply trying to deal with their disillusionment, disappointment, shock, anger, sorrow, and contradiction to their previous assumptions.

Moore was trying to do that. In addition to her blunt assertion that there is no "there" there, Moore said, "We impose order and narrative on everything in order to understand it. Otherwise, there's nothing but chaos."

However, although I am deeply sympathetic with people who lose loved ones and have a tough time dealing with their loss mentally and emotionally, another side of me wants to respond to Moore and others with a bit of sarcasm: "Well, I'm glad we got that settled. People have been debating and thinking and writing and studying about the question of God's existence for millennia. Thank you, Julianne Moore, for figuring it all out for us. Why didn't we think of just going to someone who just lost her mother and ask her if there's a god or not. How stupid of us: of course there's no God. Julianne Moore's tragic loss proved it. Let's all scrap all our other reasoning, tear down all our churches and synagogues, and do something more profitable with our time and energy—there is no God!"

Really, how arrogant it is to presume to tell the American public that your private experience of grief has settled the divide at the heart of humanity for all history!

That said, Julianne, we are all sorry for your loss (if a bit belatedly said).

Classic and Easily Answered Questions

Short answers to two questions, quite unrelated, that people often ask by way of expressing their doubt about the teachings of the Bible:

Hell

One question by non-Christians, usually in defense of their non-belief, is Why would a loving God send anyone to hell? They think they've stumped all of Christianity by posing this thorny problem, but it's thorny only for those who haven't done much study of the Bible and haven't really availed themselves of sources for good answers—like the Bible and church.

People often think the question is rhetorical, that the answer is obvious and that it's something like, 'He wouldn't, and that proves there's no hell.' Unfortunately, the question presupposes some ideas that misrepresent the Bible's teachings about several things.

A better question than how a loving God could send anyone to hell is: how could a just God let anyone into heaven. The same Bible from which we get our typical doctrine of hell teaches us that God is holy and just, and it also tells us in no uncertain terms that every one of us has sinned and deserves to be separated from God forever. So how can God be just and still let us into heaven? The real mystery is not how any human being winds up separated from God forever and misses out on the joy and perfection of heavenly life; instead, the mystery is how any sinful human being is allowed to join the eternal citizens of heaven as if he had never rebelled against the holy God and earned his wrath instead of his reward.

The answer is that entry into heaven—which the Bible calls "salvation," is allowed only through the provision of someone to absorb the punishment of sin for us. That someone was Jesus Christ. No one deserves heaven, but through repentance and faith in Christ, we can go there by God's grace.

Bearing Arms

Another question that some non-Christian critics and even some misled Christian ones ask has to do with guns and such. Many if not most conservative American Christians are supporters of the Constitution's Second Amendment right to keep and bear arms. Some people ask how bearing arms and being ready to use them fits with what Jesus said about turning the other cheek. Didn't Jesus preach non-violence?

Indeed Jesus did teach that in interpersonal relationships we should turn the other cheek. Most people ignore the context and the limits that are implied. First, Jesus' teaching had to do with circumstances in which it's just you and your adversary. Second, the circumstances did not involve serious injury or threat to life, merely an insult or irksome challenge. Third, Jesus never suggested that if anyone threatened someone else with physical harm, you should not protect that person.

Paul surely understood Jesus' teachings, and when he generalized on the Christian's obligation to make and keep peace, he said, "Insofar as is *possible*, live at peace with all men." Further, we are confronted with a startling piece of advice from Jesus himself just before he was crucified: "he that hath a purse, let him take it, and likewise his scrip: and he that hath no sword, let him sell his garment, and buy one" (Luke 22:36). While earlier in his ministry he told his disciples to go on a missionary trip with no wallet, money [or weapon], to demonstrate the ideal, Jesus later advised his followers to live realistically, paying reasonable attention to financial security, as well as physical security. He was giving them permission to defend themselves if it became necessary.

A classic hypothetical illustration imagines a man and his family accosted by a would-be rapist and murderer. Should the father do nothing to prevent his wife's or daughter's rape? Should he acquiesce to their murder? Should he welcome his own murder, on the principle of turning the other cheek?

I have never met anyone who dared to answer Yes to any of these questions. I've met many people who try to avoid saying Yes by posing argumentative questions themselves, such as 'People who carry guns are often shot with their own weapons,' but these people know they're not thinking right if they try to carry pacifistic ideas, purporting to be based on the Bible, to such an extreme.

The larger point of Jesus' teaching about turning the other cheek is that his followers—Christians—should love when hated, and that when they are persecuted *for their faith and witness,* they should place their priority on exhibiting the love of God to their persecutors. The bottom line is that if what is at stake is the witness's message of the love of God, then the Christian is obligated to respond in a way that will preserve that message.

What then is that obligation? To oversimplify, we might say that if an persecutor comes up to a Christian preaching on the street and socks him in the face, the preacher might well determine that the most

Christlike response would be to turn the other cheek, whatever that involves; it would be the only response that shows his love for the persecutor. On the other hand, if a husband is accosted by a man who threatens to kill him or his wife, the question of whom the husband should love—his wife or the attacker—presents itself. I know that I, myself, would choose to kill the attacker if necessary, to demonstrate love for my wife, or love for my own life.

We simply cannot force the Bible to support the idea generally that Christians should allow criminals to harm or kill them. Particularly is this true when it comes to threats of violence that have nothing to do with a Christian's witness. There is no Bible text that implies in any way that if I am mugged I must spread my arms and invite my own demise, or that if my wife is attacked, I should stand by and not interfere, or that I should decline to keep myself armed in my home against the threat of invasion. Anyone who suggests that the Christian must be this kind of pacifist is being intellectually dishonest about the balance of the Bible's teaching about self defense.

Science Cannot Know God

An article on *salon.com* by John Messerly recently went on and on about the problem that religion has with smart people: really intelligent people, says Messerly, don't believe in God. The more education one has, the less likely he is to believe in God. That's the theme the writer pounds away at, again and again.

There's some truth to the proposition, of course. It's no secret that Christian faith, for instance, has more adherents, proportionately, among the poorly educated of this country than among the erudite. It's also true that among the rich there are few Christians, compared to those among the poor. Jesus himself observed that not many rich people will be in the kingdom of heaven, and he was glad to say that the good news came to the poor and oppressed.

To make the leap to a conclusion, however, that the rich or educated, because of their riches or education, are right in drawing the conclusion that there is no God, is unwarranted and illogical. Yet Messerly goes on, paragraph after paragraph, pronouncing the foolishness of religious people to continue believing in God.

In a moment of unintentional disclosure of Messerly's defective reasoning, however, he castigates religious people for critiquing scientists who attempt to debunk religion. Messerly is aghast that religious people would dare to question the conclusions of experts in science. He states: "How else to explain the hubris of the philosopher or theologian who knows little of biology or physics yet denies the findings of those sciences? It is arrogant of those with no scientific credentials and no experience in the field or laboratory, to reject the hard-earned knowledge of the science. Still they do it."[33]

It struck me *instantly* upon reading that statement that in the rest of his article Messerly ironically demonstrates that he would not question for a moment the right of educated elitists to critique religion. I might adapt his own statement: "How else to explain the hubris of the scientist who has little experience with religion yet denies the experience and faith of that religion? It is arrogant of those with no religious qualifications and no experience in faith to reject the propositions of divine revelation. Still, they do it."

---

[33]John G. Messerly, "Religion's Smart-People Problem," *(http:// www.salon.com/ 2014/ 12/ 21/ religions_smart_people_problem_the_shaky_intellectual _foundations_of_absolute_faith/,* Dec 21, 2014, The Internet).

Messerly, along with many others like him, has accepted uncritically the idea that science is not to be questioned by anyone and that education is self-evidently supreme in the human experience. The problem is when science does not stick to what it can know and instead starts pontificating about what it can't. The problem is also when education becomes indoctrination in the *religion of science*.

In other words, the problem is when science becomes the religion of the educated masses. When science is religion, the deity is man himself. Man worships himself through his exaltation of science—his ability to understand this world in quantifiable ways.

The prophets of this religion of science have told the world with brash confidence that nothing cannot be explained by one realm of science or another. The folly of that kind of assertion is that we cannot know that we cannot know what we don't know. To deny there is something beyond what we know empirically, on the assumption that we know all we need to know about knowing by way of empirical knowledge, is supreme folly.

I'll let you sort through that last statement on your own. You have the rest of the class period.

Flash!
Parts of the Bible Could Be True!

An article written by Sasha Bogursky and published on FoxNews.com this week announces to the world that there is just possibly, just maybe, a slim, slight possibility that some of the stories in the Bible may actually be true![34]

Imagine that!

The exciting news, hotly debated by more reasonable, rational, scientifically minded, sane archeologists, is that a cracked jug probably used for wine has an inscription that refers to "inferior wine" and they date the pot during the thirtieth year of Solomon's reign. Called the Ophel inscription, it is believed by Haifa University professor Gershon Galil to prove that Solomon was a real king of Israel, that Hebrews at the time of Solomon knew how to write, and that Solomon built the temple—just like the Bible says!

Imagine that!

I'm constantly amazed at how amazed some people are that accounts in the Bible might actually be true. Of course, I grew up in a home where the Bible was loved and taught, and in churches where the Bible was believed and studied. Eventually I discovered that many people have absolutely no belief in the factual nature of biblical histories, much less in the truth of its spiritual message. I suppose it has taken me most of my life since this discovery to believe that people can be so skeptical and close minded.

One of the reasons people disbelieve the Bible is that they accept a principle of critical analysis that essentially says to doubt everything, especially if religious people said it. It's good to demand that accounts purporting to be historical measure up to some standards of authenticity. Bible scholars for centuries have studied the texts in comparison with other ancient writings, and biblical archeologists have amassed a great deal of corroboration for the texts of the scriptures.

As if no one had ever provided any documentation at all of the Bible's historicity (where it presents itself as history, anyway), determined skeptics deny that it can be trusted to tell us anything factual

---

[34]Sasha Bogursky, ""Message decoded: 3,000-year-old text sheds light on biblical history," *(http://www.foxnews.com/science/2013/07/31/3000-year-old-inscription-translated-biblical-history.html,* The Internet, 31 Jul 2013).

at all. The watchword of these deniers of the Bible is that it is a collection of myths that have no reliability at whatsoever.

One wonders what it takes to prove to such skeptics that the Bible can be trusted. One wonders if these people ever trust what someone else tells them. If your father told you what his father told him, and you tell it to me, am I justified then in telling you what you believe is a lie simply because someone else didn't hear it, didn't write it down, and the story you were told cannot therefore be corroborated? Well, Hebrew history was for many centuries handed down by oral tradition, by people who reduced that tradition to accounts that could be memorized verbatim and then passed on to successive generations. When writers got around to including some of these stories in their accounts, and those accounts turned into parts of the Old Testament, the resulting books should have been considered highly reliable.

The problem, of course, is not intellectual or rational. It is spiritual. People don't disbelieve the Bible because they have done solid study and found overwhelming evidence to discredit it. They disbelieve the Bible because they have an internal disincentive to believe anything that purports to tell them what God says to man. If they can convince themselves the Bible has no shred of reliability to tell us truth, they will feel more comfortable ignoring what it says.

The fact that the fundamental reason for determined disbelief in the Bible on any level is spiritual and not intellectual does not mean that biblical archeologists shouldn't continue to try to discover and interpret more evidence of the Bible's accuracy. It does mean, however, that if Christians hope to overcome denial, they will have to confront it with spiritual means and not simply more scholarship.

Terrorism and Islam

Criminals Become Terrorists

A recent news story about a beheading in India illustrated a fundamental truth about what is simplistically called terrorism: most terrorists are morally bankrupt criminals first and foremost, and religious fanatics second, if much at all.

The news reports that two brothers in Lucknow, India, beheaded their sister (who didn't have much luck, now, did she?), because she had an affair with a cousin. After they killed her, they carried her head through their village. The news story called the atrocity "an honor killing," which, if you keep up with your religious extremists, is a term describing a family execution of someone who, as far as they are concerned, has brought dishonor to the rest of the clan. Honor killings are reportedly common in India, and they're particularly common among Muslims.

These brothers apparently are not terrorists, but they are extremists: they hold extreme views and do extreme things in the name of their religious beliefs. As extremists, they aptly illustrate terrorism, which is a specific kind of extremism. *Islam breeds extremists.*

I'm going to say that again slowly, because I know you think you didn't hear me right, or you're aghast that I would say something like that. Islam - breeds - extremists.

It's not alone in breeding extremism, of course. Any religion or sect thereof, or value system that is:

1. Rooted in a narrow cultural setting, idealizes that setting, and attempts to project it upon the world, or
2. Rejects the equal contribution of all the sciences to the facts that shape a world view, or
3. Originates in the visions and writings of a single person whose nature is self-evidently no more than fallibly human,

will breed extremism. Islam falls under all three categories:

1. It arose in Mecca, in what we know today as Saudi Arabia. Of course, every religion starts somewhere on the globe, but Islam made a core tenet of the expectation that every one of its followers would make a pilgrimage to Mecca in his lifetime if possible, and in the meantime, every Muslim is supposed to bow down toward Mecca five times every day.

2. The orthodox core of Muslims hold that the Quran describes a cultural setting that should be reproduced throughout the world. Among the last people on the globe to admit that the world was, in fact, a globe were Muslims (read the history of Abdul Aziz, 1875-1953). Some of them won't admit it in 2015, but they still believe the world is flat.
3. And Islam was begun by Muhammad, revered by Muslims as "the Prophet" but not thought to be other than a fallible human being.

It should be no mystery that the cultural-religious settings that produce the most terrorists in the world today are Islamic countries. But how come vast numbers of Muslims, in those countries and around the world, are not *all* terrorists? Manifestly, they aren't.

This doesn't mean that Muslims in general disavow the purportedly religious aspirations and goals of terrorists; they don't in fact. But those same passive Muslims are not themselves terrorists and aren't about to be. It's the criminal element among them, the young men, mostly, who have developed a deep-seated anger about the world, who imagine that they have been downtrodden and cheated, and who have come to want to kill someone as the ultimate demonstration of that anger—it's they who become terrorists. They have been fooled into thinking they want to kill for Allah; in reality, they just want to kill.

The fact is, terrorists are largely a criminal element first; the religious angle of terrorism comes later. They may be enlisted as youths, but so are gang members. Actually, if you compare the way kids in the hood get sucked into gangs to the way disaffected and alienated young people get recruited into radical Islam, you find troubling similarities.

The 9/11 terrorists were people with criminal character and intent, indoctrinated in a dogmatic Islamic setting to bring out their fundamentally immoral core. That may not be what their indoctrinators purport to be doing, but that's the bottom line. Islam's myopic morality ironically failed to include the principle that outlaws murder. Rather, radical Islam deceitfully attempts to *justify* cold blooded murder by the concept of jihad, the struggle of Muslims to prevail eventually throughout the world, resulting in unexceptional acceptance of Islam. And radical Islam then attempts to motivate prospective bombers and shooters with a Quranic promise of paradise, but the criminal intent is frightfully transparent. So is the fact that the organizers and preachers of the blessedness of murder-suicide keep a comfortable distance from their mischief.

The religious angle of terrorism, of course, may suggest a far more sinister element, an element that is in fact other-worldly: it is demonic. The essence of demon activity is the focused and concentrated effort to bring chaos and death to followers of the Son of God, Jesus Christ. Nothing in history has ever qualified as demonic as much as radical Islamism. I suspect nothing ever will. I anticipate, in fact, that this particular incarnation of demonic activity will usher us into the end times.

It may already have.

Strains of Revelation

Any Christian, not just a conservative one, but any Christian who has any familiarity with the last book of the Bible, Revelation, would have to be a dullard not to hear its strains reverberating in current events.

Rev 6:9-10: I saw under the altar the souls of those who had been slain for the word of God and for the witness they had borne. They cried out with a loud voice, "O Sovereign Lord, holy and true, how long before you will judge and avenge our blood on those who dwell on the earth?

The attacks of 9/11 were devised by Al Qaeda as an assault on what militant Islam regards as the Great Satan, otherwise known as the United States. To be clear, Al Qaeda is certainly an avowed enemy of Christianity, but the attack in 2001 was not on Christians only, but on the West in general, based as its culture is on Judeo Christian heritage and a form of governance derived from Christian principles.

Since 9/11, however, we have seen the steady rise of even more militant, even more hateful, even more repressive, even more violent, even more jihadist terrorist groups, based on the theology of Islam and committed to wiping out Christians and persons of any other religion, so as to create an immense Caliphate. Their goal is to force the world to accept Islam, or else to kill all those who refuse to submit to Allah.

For several years, the main competition to Al Qaeda has been The Islamic State, also known by its acronym(s) ISIS or ISIL. In recent years, several horrific events have been splashed across the media as people around the world have been confronted with the beheadings of numerous persons, some of them Middle Eastern, some of them American, French, and Japanese. Increasingly, ISIS is making a point of stating clearly before the video executions that the persons being killed are Christians.

Of course, some terrorist attacks recently have been directed at Jews. ISIS and Al Qaeda hate anyone not Muslim, and Jews and Christians are the primary targets.

In one attack, twenty-one men from Egypt were beheaded in Libya on a beach, after the demonic terrorists who carried out the gruesome event made it very clear to their video cameras that the victims were Christians and were being executed because they were Christians.

Again, any Christian—dare I say anyone—who watches these events and has even a scant knowledge of Revelation, cannot help but think its prophecies are coming true in our times:

> Rev 20:4: I saw the souls of those who had been beheaded for the testimony of Jesus and for the word of God.

Amazingly, our Denier-in-Chief still refuses to acknowledge that this brand of terrorism is solidly based on Islam, consists of Muslims, is being carried out for the purpose of Islamic Jihad, and is intent on wiping out all other religions, principally Christianity and Judaism. What more evidence does Obama need?

On the other hand, it should be clear to all by now, and certainly is clear to me, that the President is sympathetic toward Islam. Those who have maintained for years that Obama is a closet Muslim have a strong argument in the way he has treated terrorism in its connection to Islam. Whether or not this is true, his sympathy toward Islam is wholly evident, and he reveals his fundamental stupidity in not realizing that there will be no conciliation with jihadists. They do not want jobs or a better economy or capitalism or anything else they associate with the West. They want submission to Allah—"Islam" means "submission." Islamic terrorists are evil and they must be wiped out. Nothing more fully fits the definition of either a just war or simply self preservation than a war on terrorists fought in self defense.

I really don't care much if Muslims think that a war on Islamic terrorism is too close to being a war on Islam itself. In fact, I want a Muslim who is not presently a terrorist to think twice and three times before he even remotely considers becoming one. I want the United States, and the Western world in general, to declare war on Islamic terrorism and to pour resources into covert and overt military operations to kill these Muslim extremists before they force upon this world of ours the fulfillment of biblical prophecy from Revelation, Islamic-style.

Atheist Terrorism

Right off the bat I want to make sure that nobody thinks I really believe that atheists are terrorists. At the same time, I wish to make it clear that I believe that today's radical atheists are similar to terrorists in their fundamental philosophy. Let me explain.

It used to be that atheists as a whole were pretty much satisfied to tolerate the majority's belief in God. Finding themselves in a conversation about the subject, atheists could be expected to be vigorous advocates for their denial of the existence of any god, but otherwise they understood that they were swimming upstream. They had their organizations, but public atheist figures making an issue of their beliefs such as Madelyn Murray O'Hair, or more recently Richard Dawkins, have been the exception rather than the rule.

What was happening during the 20th century up until the 60s or 70s, however, was the laying of a foundation for the widespread uprising of atheists we are seeing today. The outspoken radicals such as Madelyn O'Hair managed to carry out successful assaults on critical targets, and atheists are now taking advantage of those early victories to make inroads for their anti-God religion in the general public; and make no mistake, atheism is a religion.

For instance, in 1963, in response to a lawsuit filed by O'Hair, the Supreme Court reached a decision in the matter of teacher-led prayer or Bible reading in public schools that has been troublesome for Christians. The decision prohibited public school employees from requiring students to read the Bible or to pray, but the greatest impact on Christians has not come from the decision itself. School teachers and administrators tend to go beyond mere compliance with the law; instead, either fearful of being sued or dismissed, some teachers exaggerate the requirements of the Supreme Court's decision by disallowing student initiated religious activities, or by purging school holiday decorations of any religious symbolism. Worse, dedicated atheist school teachers berate and persecute students who choose to write on religious themes or who wear religious jewelry or who bring Bibles with them to school for use on personal time.

In the news in mid 2016 was the story of an elementary school principal who confiscated a student's slips of paper with Bible verses on them, which the boy had given to a few fellow students who were interested in them. The principal defended the action as complying with "the separation of church and state." The particulars of this story suggested that the people who clamped down on a little Christian boy were taking advantage of a misreading of law to carry out their own private war against Christianity. In many circumstances, however, those who exaggerate the constraints of the First Amendment's prohibition of establishment of religion do so because they're afraid of getting in trouble for allowing religion where it might not belong.

The fear struck in the hearts of teachers and principals who otherwise might not go overboard comes from the rising tide of atheistic warfare on Christianity, in particular. Thousands of incidents all over the country have convinced Christians that any attempt to speak of their faith or merely to represent themselves as Christians in a public setting will be met with personal assault against them and possibly lawsuits threatening their very livelihood and future. Frequently when one of these incidents makes the newspaper, the account will say that a single letter from an atheist complaining about a religious symbol or speech will prompt the people in charge of an activity to ban any Christian expression, even what is specifically protected by the First Amendment.

Atheists have come into their own. The war on God in America is no longer a phenomenon made up of sporadic ambushes by the exceptional fanatics. It is now a wave of anti-theistic attacks, coordinated by an unseen demonic source. Like terrorists, atheists strike fear in the hearts of many timid Christians, whose main hope in life is simply to get through it and go to heaven without suffering for their faith. Unfortunately, that hope is getting dimmer for this country.

Unlike suicide bombers among actual terrorists, however, the atheist terrorist is more like the militant who devises and plants IEDs. When they go off, the terrorist is not usually hurt. He lives and becomes a minor hero to his fellows, striking again when the opportunity arises.

Atheists are like today's Islamic terrorists in one essential way. They are not satisfied to believe what they believe and to attempt to *convince* other people they are right—that's a basic American freedom. No, they are committed to *forcing* you become atheists. If they cannot actually change your mind and heart by their intimidating public condemnation and tactical bullying, they will be satisfied if they can at least scare you into submission such that you don't reveal by your behavior what you secretly believe.

The tactic of atheists today is to attempt to use the Constitution against Christians by intimidating a generation of schoolteachers, lawmakers and jurists into censoring textbooks and public practices of all kinds, removing anything having the remotest of religious significance. If they can convince a generation, perhaps two, that if they take their religious beliefs outside their homes they risk intimidation, lawsuit, or even criminal charges, then atheists will be able to see the end of Christianity on the horizon in the U.S.

I realize my reader may suggest that I'm overestimating the power of the atheist lobby or the atheist component of the public. However, if, in the year 1800 or even 1900, you had prophesied to a Christian the state of the atheist-Christian struggle today, he would have thought you mad.

Truth is Truth

As if we needed another reason to declare the utter folly of the Western world's tolerating the idea of Islamic government, or Islamic education, or just about anything else Islamic, witness the declaration of the Islamic, Saudi Arabian Sheik Bandar al-Khaibari that Earth does not rotate. SABAK (don't ask me to keep typing that name out in full) thinks Earth is stationary and non-rotating in space. (My source didn't say if he thinks it's flat, as well, but he may.)

His argument is simplistic: if the earth rotated, planes wouldn't be able to travel any distance at all in the direction of rotation because the earth would always be traveling away from them, as fast or faster than the plane could fly. If you tried to fly the other direction, against the rotation, you wouldn't have to fly far at all to go a long distance, since the earth would be coming toward you as fast or faster than you were flying. In other words, if you took off from Saudi Arabia towards China, your destination would rush towards you.

I don't need to point out the silliness of this argument to my readers, unless you are students of SABAK, but it should go without saying that the "reasoning" of the Sheik is senseless on several levels. First of all, he has his rotational notion all wrong. If he took off from Saudi Arabia and headed towards China, the earth would be rotating away from him, not towards him.

Second, of course, the good Sheik apparently has no understanding at all of physics or astrophysics. Without going into these sciences to explain, I offer simply that airplanes can fly any direction they want without being helped or hindered by the earth's rotation for the same general reason that you can ride in a bus going 75 m.p.h. and walk to the front or back of the bus without being pushed or shoved.

Third, the Sheik is attempting to disprove proven fact by citing a phenomenon that he simply doesn't understand. It reminds me of a scene from Mark Twain's *Huckleberry Finn,* where Jim argued to Huck that the stars didn't just happen, but that "the moon laid 'em." Huck thought that sounded reasonable because he had seen a frog lay "most as many." Neither one of them had a clue.

Neither does the good Sheik, for his basic argument is that of the cognoscenti of the world in Galileo's time, that the Earth is stationary in space and that the Sun and stars revolve around it.

Granted, there are probably a good many Muslims who don't hold to the Sheik's view, but I would love to see a poll. How many Islamic clerics, to say nothing of Muslims on the street, have this antiquated cosmology? I wouldn't be surprised to find that a significant number of them do, especially since it would pair well with their Dark-Ages view of jurisprudence, morality, ethics, gender station, and governance.

Islamists want to take us back to those bad ole days of yore when there was no basic human freedom, when governments lopped off body parts for crimes of all sorts, when women were chattel, when no one could worship as he pleased, and when the earth, as it was supposed, was the center of the universe. As to that last one, the jury was in, a long time ago. Any person, Sheik or otherwise, who attempts to disprove the rotation of the earth, its position in the solar system, and the solar system's place in one of millions or billions of galaxies, is almost hopelessly ignorant. I say "almost" only because I don't know everything, and there may actually be a way to educate such a deeply rooted fool.

In a way, of course, I should cut the Sheik some slack, because he's just reflecting what his religion has persisted in teaching its adherents. Most of us hold on to some foolish ideas that have long been disproven by solid science but that we learned from our culture.

It's not that we who don't doubt that the earth rotates, or that the universe is unfathomably immense, or that germs cause sickness, cannot ourselves be stumped by some confrontation with scientific discovery. Clearly we can. Until a hundred years ago, our best minds did not know that there was more than one galaxy in the universe. Until less than a hundred years ago, we didn't know that we could split the "fundamental" particle, the atom. Until even less time than that ago, we didn't realize that matter could be eaten up by black holes and spit out into other universes we can't even detect. That last one may or may not be true, but the data are adding up to that conclusion.

The point is, we must all be ready, all the time, to be confronted with facts that may disturb previous notions, and then with proven truths that may upend previous beliefs. We have to demand that the proof of such truths be incontrovertible before we revise our world views, or even our religious ideas. However, once the proof cannot be contradicted from reason, we have to be willing to base our lives on what actually *is,* not on what we've always heard, even if we heard it from our Imams, preachers, priests, parents, grandparents, or other venerable sources.

Truth, if it really is truth, is truth, no matter the source, and folly is always folly, no matter how venerable.

As Seen on TV!

Drugs in the Morning

The collective view of pharmaceutical companies that advertise between six and eight o'clock in the morning is apparently that TV viewers at that hour are: asthmatic, type II diabetics with rheumatoid arthritis; who've had chemotherapy and suffer from COPD and blood clotting; who had trouble going to sleep, what with alternating constipation and diarrhea; are up early because they have chronic migraine and can't sleep; and they might as well be up because between ED for one spouse and post menopausal vaginal discomfort for the other, no one would get lucky in bed anyway.

There used to be some things the FCC czars would not allow to be advertised on TV or radio. Those things included prescription drugs. Now, it's commonplace for men to hear, "Guys, you can get and keep an erection with Viagra," and "Gals, it doesn't have to hurt for you to have sexual intercourse." So pharmaceutical companies are going full steam telling us all about their phenomenally expensive drugs, for what are apparently frighteningly widespread diseases.

Companies advertise all times of day and night, of course, but I have noticed a glut of drug ads between the time I get up and sit down with a cup of coffee to watch the news, and the time I walk out the door to go make a dime. I got out of bed because I had just slept eight hours and it was time to begin a new day—nothing more than that; but apparently a good portion of the rest of the viewing public is seriously sick. I'm sorry for them, all joking aside, but I wish there were a Pharmaceutical Channel where they could tune to get help, leaving the rest of us to be bored by the usual mix of routine commercials.

My generic name for these prescriptions is Wonderol. It would be a blessing to hear about Wonderol, of course, if we could be reasonably certain that taking it would almost certainly help us if not heal us, with little to no down side. Unfortunately that's not the case. For the privilege of advertising Wonderol, the drug companies have to warn us why we shouldn't take it. We're warned not to take these miracle drugs if we're allergic to them or any of their ingredients—well duh! We're warned not to take one of them if we have an infection or another of them if we have a history of medullary thyroid disease, and to be certain we tell our doctors if we've been to a region where "certain" fungal diseases are common. Which ones, I wonder? Further, we are warned that the drug they urge us to take might actually make our conditions worse.

What's really alarming, however, is how likely it is that taking Wonderol may in fact kill you. In the case of all these ads I've seen, compared with the seconds spent in positive promotion, more time is spent giving you a run down of the side effects of taking the cure, which are enough to send a rational person running in the opposite direction. The spokesperson will tell you, in a level, unexcited voice, that taking Wonderol may have serious negative consequences. He or she tells you this while the images on the TV screen show overly-smiling people enjoying life, while happy music distracts you from the terrifying message being quickly and softly recited.

My laptop lives beside my corner of the sofa, and over a period of weeks while watching TV I was able to log fifty prescription drug ads almost all during my breakfast and waking-up hour. I found it both fascinating and horrifying to listen carefully to all the warnings about side effects. A sampling across the board includes: sudden or severe pain in your left upper stomach spreading up to your shoulder, rapid breathing or feeling short of breath, weakness, confusion, memory problems, fever, swelling, weight gain, urinating less than usual or not at all, vomiting, diarrhea, nosebleed, insomnia, unusual dreams, thoughts of suicide, unusual bleeding, bleeding that will not stop, dehydration, low blood sugar, upper respiratory tract infection, high cholesterol, kidney disease, sinus infections, severe cellulitis, Lupus-like syndrome, severe rash, and sepsis. This list includes examples from a dozen or so of the ads I've logged, and the list of almost every drug's side effects is longer than this one. Some of the side effects in the above list can lead to death, and a couple of these drugs' makers admit (again, in dulcet tones) that you may develop pancreatitis and die from taking their concoctions.

Nearly every time I endure one of these ads, I say to myself, why would I risk killing myself by taking one of these things? The ads all say, "Ask your doctor if Wonderol is right for you!" Why would I do that either? Doesn't he know already? And if he doesn't know and hasn't already prescribed something for me, should I confront him with the amazing claims of Wonderol and put him in the difficult position of writing a scrip if he hasn't reviewed all the literature?

In all probability, of course, he has been thoroughly introduced to Wonderol, because all the drug reps who've visited him have given him the spiel and a boat load of samples. Since I don't go to doctors who I think have any remote chance of being quacks, if one of my MDs were to think my chances were much, much better of showing significant improvement on Wonderol than of experiencing anything more than a pesky but minor side effect, I might—might, mind you—fill the scrip and take the stuff. On the other hand, I might risk the disease.

I'm aware that you might infer from my rant that I lack sympathy with those folks who suffer from the diseases these drug companies are trying to treat. However, I don't. I know that people who have come down with chronic, life altering, sometimes life threatening diseases are often desperate to find any relief, any mitigation, any successful management of their symptoms they can. Who knows but that tomorrow I may be in the same boat. All I want is for the TV to stop serving up a constant string of advertisements implicitly warning me that I'm about to be old, ill, and falling apart. I don't need that when I'm eating my granola.

I Don't Watch Football

Christian news viewers are sometimes outraged by stories about high schools where referees penalize a team because some player celebrated a touchdown or other great play by pointing heavenward or kneeling to pray. On one level, Christians have a right to be outraged, especially if the penalty is intended specifically to squelch religious expression and no penalty is called against other displays of celebration.

That's not the situation, however, at least as far as I have observed. Celebratory displays of all kinds are being discouraged or outlawed in high schools, and for all I know, lower schools. It's a good thing, because what those little wide receivers do in the end zone of their middle schools and what those quarterbacks do in the end zones under their Friday Night Lights they will do on Saturday afternoons at college and later in the NFL. They already are. People who bunch around their big screen TVs on Monday nights watch players prancing into the end zone and going into pre-planned, well rehearsed, carefully choreographed performances celebrating themselves. It is conceit on parade.

The variety of these self-aggrandizing performances is endless. In fact, that's part of the plan of the performers. They try to be unique in how they call attention to themselves. Some players motion for pre-selected partners to come to them, and then the two or three of them launch into their routine. Others have solo acts consisting of quasi dance steps and probably lyrics. The most common display is mostly just hopping, arms tightly at the sides, head bobbing, hooting about one's prowess.

This is one of the reasons I don't and won't watch football on television. I've watched the occasional pairing of teams connected to members of my family by college loyalties, and the rare Superbowl because someone in the family or at church wanted to. Otherwise, I just don't stay in the room if football is on. The reason is no more complicated than this, that players who are full of themselves subject the viewer to arrogant displays of me-ism, little dances designed not only to praise themselves but also to flaunt their victories in the faces of their opponents. Such celebrations are the essence of poor sportsmanship, as well as being stark evidence of the poor character of the players involved.

This kind of self-centered exhibitionism turns my stomach. It has no place in sports, except that apparently it does. Many high schools have tried to discourage the activity with penalties that some people have found a little silly, or a little offensive. But if they could just teach youthful players that dancing in the end zone, or after a great tackle, or when you intercept a pass, or when you recover a fumble, is not appropriate, then maybe it wouldn't be a problem in college. And if colleges would keep up the pressure as well, maybe players who make it to the NFL won't automatically go into narcissistic gyrations when they make a good play.

I should say that I haven't watched football for many years; in fact, I haven't ever been a football fan. In high school, I went to football games, but mostly for other reasons. I was in the marching band my freshman year in high school, so there was that. The other three years of high school I often dated to football games—it was something to do and since it was usually cold it provided an excuse to put my arms around my date. In college, however, I went to only two football games, and one of them I went to only because it was homecoming and, on one of the few occasions she did so, my hometown sweetheart visited me at my campus.

In some part, my lack of interest in football traced to the behavior of football players. Arrogant dances were not a feature of football when I was young, but arrogant football players were. Many of them were bullies, and I had a continuing problem with bullies when I was young. Then in college, I quickly became aware that football players were given a leg up on their studies, given special food and other special treatment, and that the athletic program was favored above all others. For instance, I was a theater major, and I spent my college years rehearsing and performing in a modified level of the library, while athletes got new stadiums, new facilities, new everything, and breaks on grades. It made me a little bitter. So if they didn't come see my plays (and they didn't), I wouldn't go see theirs. And I didn't.

And I don't. And I won't, as long as proud, preening, prancing players dance around on the field inviting everyone to worship them for a few seconds. It's nauseating. And if penalizing high school players for even the most inoffensive displays can discourage the most offensive performances later, I'm all for it.

Kick Soccer Back to the World

I have no interest in soccer. None. I never have, and I'm confident in saying I never will.

Even so, because my wife thought it would be interesting to turn on the TV and watch the women's world championship game with Japan in 2015, we watched the last thirty minutes or so of it, and of course, we saw the U.S. win. Woo hoo. I'm still unimpressed.

If I have it right, the original word in Spanish for the sport of soccer was balompié. The Dictionary of the Royal Spanish Academy confirms my conclusion, reached independently, that the American word "football" was "adapted to Spanish"—"futbol." Their older word is not used commonly anymore among them. They adapted our word for one reason, in my opinion: to try to popularize their sport in the United States, where we play a far more interesting game by that name. While I find our version largely uninteresting, too, it's soccer that leaves me thoroughly unmoved.

I didn't grow up with soccer. Virtually no one in my generation did. We were proud to play, watch, and root for a thoroughly American sport. Think of it as part of American exceptionalism: we are a country that has a unique political system in the world, and its own culture to go along with it. Our three major sports were made in America: baseball, football and basketball. In my opinion, we don't need to accrete the pastimes of other countries. The Canadians long ago infiltrated the northern border states with hockey, but it's been slow to catch on in the south, and I wish it were even slower. Some of the ivy league schools think they're being delightfully English and Oxford-ian to play rugby, but we'd be just fine without it. Same with soccer, or futbol. Let the Japanese, the Brazilians, the Mexicans, and whoever else in the world that goes gaga about soccer keep it.

Soccer is sort of like basketball, only played with the feet. As I watched the world championship (was it a cup?), I was struck by the resemblance to basketball teams moving back and forth on the court. A soccer field is roughly three times as long and wide as a basketball court, but that accords with the idea of kicking a ball with the feet rather than moving it in a smaller range with the precision of the hand. The field is marked similarly, and there's a net as a goal in both, but rather larger for soccer. The players move constantly, as in basketball, and there's a similar lack of identifiable "plays" in both sports, more a general "theory" that seems to shift constantly. Because of the size of the field and the inherent loss of ball control between players, there are more "turnovers," if you can call them that, in soccer, resulting in a sense that no one really gets to do anything much in the way of a strategy for very long before being interrupted.

The greatest difference in soccer and basketball, it seems to me, is that basketball scores can be wildly high, while in soccer it isn't unusual for a game to end in a 1-0 score. I suppose that explains why soccer commentators are so elated when one team finally gets the ball into the goal that they yell "Go-o-o-o-o-o-o-o-o-o-o-o-o-o-o-o-o-o-l" (goal, in English). The absence of "plays," greater distances, frequent turnovers, and the imprecision of kicking, as opposed to hand throwing, all explain the lower scoring, I suppose.

Don't get me wrong: I'm not overly enthusiastic about American sports, either.

—I like baseball, but I don't live for it. I played little league as a boy, lost interest in my teens through thirties, then re-acquired it when the Braves went from worst to first.

—Football (the one played under Friday Night Lights) doesn't really interest me. (See the previous article.)

—As for basketball, I find it uninteresting. So, it shouldn't come as surprise that I don't find soccer interesting. Like basketball, it features sheer frenzy as one of its main components, and that's tiring. I'm more interested in thoughtful activities. I played golf for many years (and yes, I do realize that golf came from Scotland: we brought it with us in the days when we still thought of ourselves as belonging to the British Isles). You have to do some thinking while you play golf, not just frenzied reacting. My interest in baseball is mostly because it's a brain game. Yes, it requires some physical strength, agility, and talent, but without a significant brain element, baseball would not exist.

Soccer doesn't seem to have much of the brain element. It's just a lot of running and reacting, furious movement with very little to show for it.

As much as anything, soccer reminds me of seeing little children turned out on their school playground to run off some energy. Often they spread out to the limits of their fenced-in areas, giddily racing around with little apparent plan, burning off the calories of their government-dictated lunches, insuring their tired teachers that when they return, they will happily get out their mats and take naps.

Lastly, I dislike soccer for what it does to the level of service in some Mexican restaurants. I was in a restaurant not long ago trying to get a waiter to notice me. All the wait staff were gathered around a 60" flat screen TV mounted near the front door, watching a soccer match. In most Mexican restaurants, the music is half for the clientele, to give them the impression they're in a Hispanic setting, and half for the staff, because they really don't like American music. But the TV is totally for the staff, because it's always tuned to soccer. They make no apology about it. If you don't like it, eat another jalapeno.

I have no illusions about soccer's diminishing in popularity in America: clearly things are going the other way. I'm not yet in the minority in my lack of interest in it. A majority still think it's a foreign sport. However, America's liberal leaders are obviously interested in making the United States like the rest of the world instead of exporting our culture to them. What a shame. There's a reason we came over here four hundred years ago. It was to do our own thing. Let's get back to it.

Not False, but Misleading

The advertising world has never been known as a bastion of high morals and ethics. Some completely honest people do get into advertising, but many slick salesmen in every arena of commerce have made a dirty name for themselves, misrepresenting their products, lying about their guarantees, and promising prospective buyers all sorts of things they never deliver.

The situation is certainly no different and in fact is markedly worse now that the Internet is here. On the Internet fly-by-night merchants can promise the moon, sell it for $39.95, never ship it out, and close down their sites before the sun comes up on their fraud.

Television, however, is still one of the most likely places to find crafty and deceptive marketing. Often it comes down to the wording of advertisements. False advertising is legally actionable, but with the right wordsmith behind the ad copy a company can appear to be making false claims without really doing so. Examples are easy to find within an hour of turning on the TV, any time of day.

A company says, "Can a protein originally found in a jellyfish actually improve your memory? Our scientists say Yes!" The product is Prevagen, and the ad goes on to claim that the product "supports healthy brain function, sharper mind [and] clearer thinking."

The key to the makers of Prevagen's being able to avoid being taken to the wood shed by litigators is found in the wording: "Our scientists" is one of the phrases that help insulate Prevagen from false claims. A company can hire you, call you a scientist, and you can say "Yes!" to whatever claims they make. For that matter, you can have only a high school education but call yourself a scientist and there's no law that says you can't, because there's no official or legal definition of "scientist." Unless you falsify having a degree in one of the sciences, just saying you're a scientist, even if you don't have any training in a particular science by an accredited school, isn't illegal.

Of course, you have to be careful about what you say, and Prevagen's makers are. They say it "supports brain health." That's a very interesting phrase, and it's employed by a number of advertisers I've taken note of. What does it mean to say something "supports" your health in one way or another? Actually, it means very little. At base, all it may mean is that the product has some caloric content and therefore food value, and it can be said to support your health in all areas. A cracker supports your health. A vitamin certainly does. A glass of sweet tea supports it very nicely, thank you (and with that, I rise from my computer to go get one). In fact, bottled water has no calories but it, too, supports your health, in the most basic way. It prevents dehydration.[35] The phrase "supports your health" is so vague that it can hardly be attacked as misleading.

This is not to say that makers of snake oil are immune from suit. In fact, Prevagen's makers have been sued for false advertising. A suit was filed in a U.S. District Court in California back in January of 2015 against Quincy Bioscience, LLC, over their claims about Prevagen, most notably that it has been "clinically tested." The suit challenges that assertion and the claims about Prevagen that are said to have come from those tests. The matter has not gone to jury trial yet, but when it does, I suspect the jury, properly charged with the law, will have no choice but to find that because the ads didn't claim that Prevagen actually produces better brain health but only supports it, Quincy Bioscience successfully walked the tightrope and didn't fall off into the gulf of false advertising.

Or take the Willow Curve. Handsome Chuck Woolery, the original host of the Wheel of Fortune and also the Love Connection, made himself a familiar and harmless face by hosting other game shows and acting occasionally. Now he's advertising the Willow Curve, an electronic gadget with flashing lights that you put on your knee or shoulder, etc, and it's supposed to reduce pain. The advertising makes claims too numerous to list, and they are all vague, invented by the makers of the Curve, and supported only by studies done by people who work for the company. Most notable is a doctor who is nearing a hundred years of age whose chief claim to fame seems to be that he wrote a book about how to be an expert witness.

What I want to focus on, however, is one of Woolery's remarks in assuring the potential buying public of their satisfaction. He says the Willow Curve has a 90-day money-back guarantee; you can get a refund if it doesn't work for you. "But," he adds, "you probably won't need it [the guarantee] because I promise, the Curve could change your life." An earlier version of the ad had Woolery saying, "I promise the Curve *will* change your life." Later versions, including the one that runs on radio, have him saying only that it "could." By the way, the early

---

[35]However, for ludicrous statements to the contrary see such articles as *http://www.telegraph.co.uk/news/worldnews/europe/eu/8897662/EU-bans-claim-th at-water-can-prevent-dehydration.html.*

versions of the ad referred to Charlie Sanders, football legend, who cancelled knee surgery after using the Curve. In fact, Sanders subsequently died because his knee pain turned out to be from a cancerous tumor, which killed him.

Anyway, back to Woolery's promise. "The Curve could change your life." What does that mean? Essentially, nothing. I promise you that tomorrow it could rain. The forecast is for 0% chance, but you never know. Strange things can happen.

I remember sometime in the early 60s I found out that the Farmer's Almanac had predicted snow for one early day in June. I told everyone to expect it. In a weird turn of events, it actually did hail—I know, different thing, but the point is, near certainties sometimes are defied by flukes. So the Curve really *could* change your life, and I can *promise* you that. As long as there is the remotest of possibilities for an event to take place, a promise that it *could* is not a lie. Ergo, saying it in an ad is not a lie. Misleading, yes, but only if you infer that the ad is promising that it will happen. Since the words are what will be picked apart if someone sues over claims, the words, if carefully chosen, are the marketer's salvation.

I watch television and see this kind of ad and I think, it's so obvious how they're almost lying but not quite, which is not telling the whole truth. It reminds me of an apt definition I learned about fifty years ago: An excuse is the skin of a reason stuffed with a lie. That rings true, doesn't it! Well, these tricky ads are somewhat similar: the skin of a fact stuffed with a lie. In court with a slick lawyer they might get away with it, but in our minds they should never succeed. We should be smarter than that. Problem is, a lot of people just aren't, and the makers of snake oil walk to the bank with smiles.

Curious Observations about TV

On a somewhat different note from my usual subjects, I have in mind today a number of curious characteristics of TV programs. I enumerate some of my observations.

1. There are many more homosexuals on TV programs than in real life. Overgeneralizing, every TV show either seems to have to have a regular character who is homosexual, or the writers inject a homosexual into the story of the week on a regular basis.

Case in point, "NCIS," one of my favorite programs, recently killed off its only regular homosexual character, Ned Dorneget. Ned appeared a few seasons ago as something of a dweeb, easily fooled by Gibbs's team members eager to have a new probie to pester. Ned "came out" on the program when he and McGee were assigned to escort an exotic beauty, and Ned told McGee she wasn't his type. To McGee's, "She's every man's type, Dornie," Dorneget said, "Not mine. I'm gay."

So what, I said out loud. Who cares. His homosexuality didn't fit into the show in any significant way. It was just the producers' way of nodding their approval to the homosexual community. Now that Ned is dead, I suspect he will be replaced with a lesbian. Wanna bet a few bucks?

Of course, there's "Modern Family," a show I don't and won't watch, which features a homosexual couple, prancing and sashaying across the set. Why is it, I wonder, that we have heard the homosexual community tell the rest of the world that (male) homosexuals *aren't* necessarily effeminate, but when the pro-homosexual entertainment world puts homosexuals into television programs, they usually *are* effeminate? Curious.

When the homosexual male (rarely a lesbian—I wonder why?) is a character in a single episode, nearly always he's opposed by some religious person, whom the writers present as not merely having a moral opposition to homosexuality (which we do, on Biblical grounds), but also as being a self-righteous ass (which most of us religious types aren't). By contrast, the homosexual is presented as exemplary in every way, and certainly not promiscuous (when the truth, unfortunately for wishful thinking liberals, is that most male homosexuals are quite promiscuous). Inevitably, the point of the episode is to persuade the morally flexible public to sympathize with poor, persecuted homosexuals.

I could give several of examples of programs where in a main cast of five or so characters one of them is homosexual. Even if the producers are trying to represent the population, their casting would suggest that 20% of the population is homosexual, which they aren't. The actual incidence of homosexuality in the population is something like 3%, including both men and women. Ask yourself if TV producers are promoting homosexuality. Answer honestly.

2. No main character can become attached romantically. If they aren't already attached to a girlfriend or boyfriend, no main character will be able to sustain a romantic relationship. It may take one episode or five, but eventually the romantic prospect will move, become uninterested, turn out to be a crook, or get killed—or a combination of several of the above.

There are exceptions, especially if main characters hook up with each other, as in "Bones." But then, "Bones" has lost viewers since that turn of events. The recent series "The Closer" had the main character marrying a supporting character, and the series ended a season later. A connection? I think so. "Castle" featured Richard Castle and Detective Kate Beckett flirting and sparring with each other for a number of seasons until they finally decided that, like cats, mating was more interesting than fighting, and they got married. Stana Katic (Beckett) is leaving (—and by date of this publication, has left) the show, and CBS subsequently—and no doubt consequently—cancelled the show for the following season.

Good stories are even better when characters are complex, and some of the most interesting main characters are those with notable flaws. We're all flawed, of course, but TV characters are frequently flawed to the point of being dysfunctional, particularly in this matter of being able to initiate and sustain a romance.

Compare this theme of systematically dysfunctional characters with what used to be typical TV fare. In the 50s and 60s the popular shows featured families, such as "Father Knows Best," "The Donna Reed Show," and "Bewitched." Even "The Munsters" and the "Addams Family" were just that—families. Some of those families were missing a father or mother, like "Bonanza," "My Three Sons," and "The Andy Griffith Show" (which had Aunt Bea as a substitute), but as late as "Happy Days" we were seeing comedy and drama come out of a solid, happy, family setting. Then producers began introducing us to the idea that nobody's family was really happy and most people preferred to be miserably single. Welcome to modern TV. (But, see #6, below.)

3. Ninety percent of main characters are single, and those who aren't are in rocky marriages. This is a troubling thing in my view. It appears to me that TV producers and writers want us to believe that most of the interesting and useful people of the world are not married. Take "Law and Order" as an example. If you can keep track of the characters who have come and gone, most of them are single, and writers occasionally get mileage out of a shambles of a marriage in one of the characters' lives. Or consider "House." It featured a cast of nine doctors, only one of whom was married, and he occasionally seemed determined to cheat and mess it all up. House tried constantly to get Cuddy into bed, Cuddy insisted on adopting a daughter to raise alone, "13" was a promiscuous bisexual, Chase was a womanizer, and on and on you go.

Some shows, of course, are intentionally about singles because they clearly aim at singles in the viewing audience. "Friends," for instance, was a cast of singles, two of whom finally got married, and in three more seasons, the show ended. "Seinfeld" was a cast of zany singles, none of whom could maintain a romance for more than a few shows without screwing it up, because each of them was hilariously screwed up himself. The more recent "Big Bang Theory" consists of a cast of singles, none of whom seems anywhere near being adult enough to make a marriage work.

4. Entertainers often tell us they're against guns, but there is more gunfire on TV than anywhere in real life. Now, remember, I'm a Second Amendment supporter and I own and use guns. I'm just noting that it's common to hear Hollywood types tell us how bad guns are, and then they go to work every day and make shows about people using guns. Then again, that's just one example of Hollywood hypocrisy. The typical Hollywood liberal tells the rest of the world that we're bad people hurting the environment. They say this as they board their private jets and burn petrochemicals across the skies. Note again, I don't have anything against planes, trains and automobiles, but the two-faced entertainers' rant about the rest of us is irritating.

5. Religion is spurned by most TV characters, except the occasional villain, who is typically a priest. Most regular characters on today's TV series are agnostics or just nothings when it comes to religion. You can't say the producers are attempting to represent the population in this matter: seventy percent of Americans identify themselves as Christians. So TV producers inject regular Christians into their programs—as priests who are discovered to be diddling little boys, or Protestant

preachers who turn out to be having affairs or are racists or are bilking their congregations, etc, etc. With the exception of the occasional, milk-toast cleric who makes a walk-on appearance and is of no significance at all to the plot or the program as a whole, as an overwhelming rule religious characters are there to be ridiculed or condemned.

6. Possibly the best example of an exception to the foregoing critiques is the wildly popular "Blue Bloods." It's built around a family. The family is Catholic; I could have asked for a nice Protestant family, but the Reagans are good Catholics. (I'm not suggesting that some Catholics aren't good: Catholics themselves call themselves good or not good, in reference to their relative faithfulness to attending Mass, going to confession, etc.) The Reagan family exhibits generally exemplary moral characteristics, even though they have various crises arising out of dramatic situations. They eat a meal together in every episode and they talk and interact, as families should. They love each other. They support each other. They believe in honor and tradition. They believe in America. And among the Reagan sons and daughters there is a brother with a full fledged family, a brother looking hard for love, a sister who has had one divorce but is looking for a successful successor, and two grandkids who learn something in every episode about life, truth, and goodness.

So far, none of them is gay. There's always next season. Then I'll stop watching it. But herewith I ask the show's producers to keep reminding themselves, We're wildly popular *because* of our moral, religious, loving-family theme, not in spite of it.

Flawed Attraction

Over the years I've wondered why television tends to attract people with odd looks. I'm talking about on-air personalities. More than you might have noticed, television personalities have facial and other features that make you wonder why they wanted their images splashed across thousands of TV screens every day.

Take one of the local newscasters near me, one of four major stations in my immediate area. The anchor for many years is a fellow with a strangely triangular face, not helped by his hairstyle, and a large, dark mole near his lips. I don't mean the sort of mole that accents Cindy Crawford's face that you can quickly ignore while you admire her ageless beauty. I'm talking about the kind of growth that makes you think to yourself, "Why don't you go have that thing taken off?!"

Take the anchor of another newscast, who talks out of one side of her mouth; she has a sneer that would exceed Elvis's at the height of his curled-lip expression. She is otherwise radiant in her smile, but that contorted mouth is a constant distraction, to me anyway. I know that she never had Bell's Palsy or a stroke. She just has a defective grin.

Take the anchor of the third station in this same group. He's the prettiest boy I've seen on TV in years, except for his mouth, which is a tiny little thing that he doesn't open much when he speaks, giving the viewer the impression that he is hiding bad teeth, which he isn't.

I've also often wondered why radio seems to attract people with speech impediments. Go figure. Take Tom Brokaw, who had trouble with the R in his own name as well as anywhere else it was in a consonant blend. A local talk show host can't say his l's. He also has a problem with r's in the middle of a word, which come out sounding like w's. Jim Leher couldn't pronounce his own name properly, though I suppose however you pronounce your own name could be considered correct. Another local guy who does live reports and news on the half hour during the afternoons does absolutely the most ludicrous and stupid sounding impression of a bad broadcaster that I've ever heard, except for the fact that he's not doing an impression. I can't even type out what he sounds like. Clearly he has a bad ear, having listened to the exaggerated, sing-songy delivery of other broadcasters over the years and having then tried to copy them, but failing miserably. What surprises me about this man is that the station has kept him on for a decade or more and hasn't sent him to remedial speech classes somewhere. I turn down the volume whenever he comes on if I can reach the radio.

After I had made a lengthening list of these odd mismatches between people and their career choices, I began looking for more examples in the broader spectrum of careers, wondering if not just some but most jobs have more than an average sampling of people who really shouldn't be doing what they're doing. Some of the obvious jobs came to mind. There's a joke that a list of oxymorons should include "political ethics." These days, I think there would be no debate that politics attracts quite a few unethical, to say nothing of immoral, individuals. Rightfully, politics should be inhabited by morally superior persons. Unfortunately, I think it never has been.

Embarrassingly, religious ministry comes under the same sort of accusation. Catholic priests and pedophilia come to mind, as do high profile evangelists and prostitutes or graft. The numbers might not support a generalization that there are more sexual sinners in the ministry than in the general population, but by all rights the number should be much, much lower, given the nature of the job.

For my own part I would never presume to become a hair model, since I have very little, or aspire to do fitness commercials, which I also don't qualify for. Apparently, however, one's own disqualifying characteristics may not be something of which he is aware, which may explain why some misfits for a profession get into it anyway. I heard in a roundabout way of one of my nemeses from an earlier life who remarked, when he found out what I was doing for a living now, "What the (bleep) does he know about that?!"

If there is any explanation of this phenomenon of attraction to jobs where your flaws will be painfully obvious, it may be found in the idea that in aiming toward a career, people may unconsciously be trying to compensate for their weaknesses. People have the best chance of success if they major on their strengths, but if their weaknesses do not outweigh their strengths, perhaps the magnification of their strengths through their work can minimize at least their self consciousness of their weak points. Their strong performance in news delivery may not keep the rest of us from seeing their prominent moles and misshapen mouths, but maybe by going on camera or behind the microphone they learn to get over their shortcomings in their own minds. I suppose that's worth something.

Meanwhile, I'm considering sending an anonymous letter with a twenty-dollar bill in it to a radio station, to start a fund to send their very bad reporter to speech therapy.

Smart Woman, Dumb Man

Nationally known pundits are slow to notice it, I think, but I've noticed for a long time the prevailing theme of commercials: Woman smart, man dumb. Women in commercials are predominantly depicted as intelligent, understanding, wise, and practical, while men are depicted as bumbling idiots lacking common sense.

Many of these commercials are cast in an atmosphere of humor, but there's nothing funny about the overall lesson being taught young skulls full of mush[36] who learn about their entire world these days from what they hear on TV and see on the Internet, which is also full of commercials.

Sometimes the theme is subtle. Other times it is over the top. It's surprising how often this theme appears, but it's even more shocking that men in media tolerate it.

A sampling:

Allstate:

A woman and man are at table in restaurant. She asks him to confirm he believes men are better drivers. He says yes. She asks then why she has a check from Allstate for good driving (and he doesn't). He opens his mouth to speak and she says, "Silence!" Man wrong, woman right. He's a chauvinist and she overwhelms him factually.

AT&T - iPhone

A man at work on the phone with wife finds he has forgotten his anniversary, but he lies to his wife that he didn't, and uses his iPhone to make dinner reservations while still talking on the phone. He is a liar and a forgetful boob, while she is the opposite.

In a similar commercial, a husband and wife lie on lounge chairs at a resort. She asks if he remembered to arm the security system. He assures he he did, and then he surreptitiously activates the system from his phone. The she asks if he remembered to close the windows, and he assures her he did this, too. Cut to a scene inside the home, where pigeons are making use of an open window to roost in the couple's kitchen. Woman smart, man forgetful and deceitful.

---

[36]I was using this phrase before Rush Limbaugh took it up. I got it from John Houseman, Professor Kingsfield on "The Paper Chase" (1973).

Charter DVR

A man helps his sick wife. He recorded TV for her, but the programs he recorded are all fishing shows and other "man" programs. He is oblivious to her tastes. The woman, irritated by her husband, pushes him away and tunes to "Lola's Life." A man is portrayed as a dense buffoon.

Cheerios

A man and woman are having breakfast. The man is eating Cheerios while reading the box. "Says here Cheerios can be a part of a heart healthy diet," he says.

His wife answers, "Yes but you still have to go to the gym." She's in charge of him, in other words. She makes him go to the gym. He's under her thumb.

Clorox Disinfectant Wipes

A woman arrives home to find her absolutely doofus husband is playing with the baby on the kitchen counter. There are various foods open and spread around on the counter, and the father has the baby under its arms, helping it to dance around on the counter, quite nude. The suggestion is that the baby either has or will urinate or do something else on the counter, where food is prepared. The wife/mother puts on a look that says her childish husband has no sense at all. Dumb man, sensible woman.

Excedrin

A woman comes out to find husband on the deck with a deck washer. "Oh, you're going to wash the deck!" she says.

"Not just wash," he says, "power wash." She looks dubious. He turns on the unit and the wand goes out of control in his hands, knocking over table settings, plants, etc. She looks disapproving. Stupid man, normal woman.

FiberOne

A wife is looking at a FiberOne package: "I think you need more fiber in your diet," she says to her husband.

The husband says, "Ohhhh, fiber makes me sad." Clearly he doesn't know what fiber is. He continues, "And why are you talking about fiber when you're eating a candy bar?" He grabs half her "candy bar," which is actually a FiberOne bar, and he begins eating it.

She says, "You enjoy that," and he makes some sort of sound

indicating he loves it. Of course, it's full of fiber. She smiles knowingly and he is blithely ignorant of what he is doing. Smart woman, dumb man.

GEICO
"Can switching to GEICO really save you fifteen percent or more on car insurance?" says an ad. "Do people use smart phones to do dumb things?" Three guys in an office celebrate the end of a day or a deal by pulling out their phones and using them to party. One plays a horn, another pours bubbly, and a third makes noises with yet another app. A woman at the copier turns and sees them, and she looks completely dumbfounded, which figures, since she found them being really dumb. Dumb men, smart—or at least not dumb—woman.

Honda HRX
A man shows off his new mower. Describing its features, he doesn't know their names, and he makes up things: "It's made of...kryptonite!" Even where a man might be generally assumed to know the subject, which is hardware, the man is presented as a lightweight, a buffoon.

Hotels.com
A cartoon dad makes reservations for a family vacation in a woodsy cabin and is chased and injured by a bear while the smart mom uses her smart phone to make reservations someplace safe. Dad walks in relieved, bandaged from a bear attack.

Life Insurance
A man plans to do chores on day off, reading his list, ending with "Buy life insurance." His wife is surprised. The man at first seems smart as he explains how easy it is to call for life insurance on the phone.

Then his wife says, "Good: you'll have enough time to fix that—[some project]." She can't let the matter go without having the last word. The guy fell into her trap. He comes off finally as bested by her.

Lowes
A couple has a better yard than last year. The husband says the difference is that he put a lot of love into it. His wife says it's really because they went to Lowes.

After the ad info, the husband says, "So it wasn't me?"

She responds, "Well, you provided the love." The woman comes off as rational, sensible, and honest. The man comes off as a deceptive braggart.

Lowes

A man and woman come in for light bulbs. An associate asks if he can help them with things for the patio. The man says, No. The woman says, Yes. The man then "corrects" himself and says, Yes. The man is led by wife, who knows better, of course. Smart woman, dumb man.

McDonalds

A young man and young woman, probably dating, are sitting at a McDonald's table. She says some boy acquaintance of hers says Sundays are just for watching football—"Can you believe that?!"

The camera shows the young man frozen in fear, wondering what to say. You know he's thinking, "Well, I agree." But he knows if he says that, his girlfriend will dump him. So he thinks quickly and says, "He's a jerk."

She smiles and nods, affirming his "girl sensitive" behavior. Aside from the question of whether guys watching football on Sunday is a perfectly reasonable way to spend the afternoon, the boy has played the wimp to his girl. Perhaps this is not a dumb man, but he is a wimpy man, and his girlfriend is a controlling woman, if only unconsciously.

Another commercial in this same series has a similar situation where the boy adapts to the "sensitive" position in order to keep from sounding too masculine.

Off Clip-on

A woman advises her husband to wear insect repellant. He thinks she's going to spray him in the face with bug spray and he winces and screws up his face in fear. She just clips on a plastic unit and he is relieved. Dumb man, smart woman.

PCMatic.com

A man and wife are in the kitchen where the man is laboring over a laptop computer. The man jumps up saying he has to go to the store to get something to fix a computer virus he fears he has acquired. The wife calmly tells him he can fix it online. She demonstrates. He acts ignorant of it all. When she finishes fixing his computer, he thanks her and she takes his keys and takes the car to girls' night out. He stares dumbfounded into the camera. Dumb man, very smart woman.

Progressive

Popular spokeswoman Flo urges a male customer of Progressive to do a "model" routine for her snapshot camera. He makes a fool of himself and has to be stopped by Flo when his wife comes up behind him and sees him looking stupid.

Sears

A man uses a GPS in a store to locate another store where he can buy another brand. A woman tosses his GPS in the dryer while the man looks foolish.

SPDR Investment

A father is trying to build a wooden play structure from a large kit. He does a ridiculously terrible job that no man would ever believe was even close to right, even resorting to putting pieces together with duct tape. It looks more like a house destroyed by a hurricane than a merely defective structure. The voice-over announcer says, "Dad's aren't always worried about accuracy. Fortunately their investment company can—etc." The generalization is not even representative. Stupid man.

T-Mobile

In a series of commercials in which a slender girl asks one or more men why they are without shirts, or why they are being mugged, etc., it is revealed that they have their wireless accounts with someone else. In other words, some other company stole their shirts and is robbing them blind, etc. The fact that none of the foolish customers is a women establishes the "dumb man, smart woman" theme.

Taco Bell

A man picks up a taco and yells, "I've got a winner!" He goes wild over the taco. Two rational, calm women are standing by. One says, "What is he doing?" and the other explains, making him sound like a nut case.

Walgreens

In an ad for a pre-paid card, a man says, "I pre-load it myself, so I can't get in trouble spending."

A woman says, "I pay bills online; when I need more money, I just load more on it."

The woman is smart and admits to no shortcomings. The man is smart only because he admits he can't manage his money.

Yogurt

A wife is on the phone talking about all the dessert flavors available to her (she's thinking of her yogurt), while her husband nearby is searching the fridge to find these desserts as he listens to her. Finally, she turns and sees him: "Uh, babe, what are you doing?" He looks guilty. The man comes off a lame brain, easily fooled, while the woman is in the know.

Yogurt

The roles are reversed from the other ad. The man is on the phone talking about desserts, not as if they were yogurt flavors, but instead trying to fool the person on the phone into believing he really is eating the actual desserts. His wife comes in, opens the fridge and says, "Uh, babe?—" and the husband is 'caught' lying.

He says, "I gotta go," to the person on the phone. The man comes off as deceitful and a braggart. The woman appears as honest, keeping him in line.

Do I need to continue this list?

Why would the men in the ad agencies producing these spots tolerate this overwhelming theme ridiculing, lampooning and insulting men while making out women to be superior in every way?

And would women tolerate being typecast, stereotyped and ridiculed in the same way, if the shoe were on the other foot?

If you think they would, I have some mountains in central Kansas I'll make you a good price on.

Just How Cold Is It?

Paul Siple, an Antarctic explorer who was part of the famed Byrd expeditions in the late 1920s, along with Charles Passel, a polar scientist, developed the now familiar wind chill factor. Temperatures at the pole, of course, are dangerously frigid. However, what made the subfreezing temperatures at the pole even more dangerous to human beings was wind. Simply put, the faster the wind blew, the quicker human skin would freeze when subjected to temperatures below 32 degrees F. Coffee cools faster when you blow on it, too, even though your breath isn't particularly cool.

The explorers' idea was to invent a simple system to factor in wind speeds and tell them how cold it really felt like at any given temperature. Even with temperatures over freezing, the wind would chill the skin, and thus the whole body, more rapidly. Hypothermia, a deadly condition in which the body core is cooler than 95 degrees, sets in faster when it's not only cold, but windy. Siple and Passel's system was developed using a plastic bottle filled with water. They developed a chart based on the times it took for the bottle to freeze when subjected to various wind speeds in differing temperatures.

Eventually the idea took on a life of its own and government types fiddled with the concept and developed a complicated formula for calculating the wind chill index. For any given temperature below 50° F. (the highest temperature for which the index is calculated), you subtract the WCI (wind chill index) to get the WCET (wind chill equivalent temperature), which tells you that things will chill down at a rate commensurate with the adjusted temperature instead of the actual temperature with no wind. In its simplest application, it still amounts to saying that at any given temperature, it feels colder and colder, the stronger the wind blows.

I don't remember when TV and radio weather people first began reporting the wind chill factor, but I began noticing around twenty years ago that meteorologists, whether certified or not, were bending the theory to mean different things, or were expressing the wind chill in terms that were misleading. The simplest way for a weather person to express it was, "It's 32 degrees right now in the city, but with the wind, it feels like it's 20." That, in itself, is a subjective generalization, but it's the practical way to state the effect of the wind chill factor.

About fifteen years ago, however, I began to hear people—not weather people, just people—say things such as, "We'd better get the plants inside tonight. It's gonna be 40, but with the wind it's gonna be freezing."

Wrong.

The actual air temperature doesn't change at all just because a wind whips up. You know that. But apparently some people are easily misled into believing that wind actually lowers the temperature. Since they didn't figure out the wind chill factor for themselves, they obviously got their notions from their local TV and radio stations.

I began to listen more closely to weather forecasts to see what they were saying. Sure enough, some of the supposedly trained meteorologists were getting sloppy with their reporting. They were coming close to saying that the wind chill factor actually lowered the temperature.

One weatherman would say, "It's 25 in Smallville. Well, it's 32, but it might as well be 25."

Another weather woman would say, "It's 32 out there, but really, it's colder with the wind chill. And that's what it's all about, isn't it?—the way you feel."

I began to rant. (I do that when I get irritated with irresponsible communication.) Weather people, whose science has always been inexact, were now intentionally misleading the public. I heard people actually say the roads would be iced over, when the temperature wasn't going to be lower than 36, because the wind chill, they believed, made it 30.

It wasn't just people I don't know, who live on the other side of the intellectual tracks, who mistook the wind chill factor for actual reduction in degrees. Even a close friend of mine, hearing me point out this incorrect idea, which was being promulgated by inaccurate weather-person verbiage, said to me, "What makes you think you know more than the official meteorologist?" On many things, my dear friend, I don't. On this one, apparently I do. I study a lot.

Someone obviously has been getting on the case of many meteorologists, however, because I've heard them recently beginning to explain the WCF and being more precise and factual in telling us what it means on frigid mornings in winter. Frankly, however, I'd like for talk of the wind chill factor to just go away. It is minimally useful information anyway. Unfortunately, however, the wind chill segment of the weather forecast seems to be well ensconced.

The next, up and coming trend in erroneous weather forecasting may be dew points. I heard a weatherman tell us last night that the dew point tells us how dry it feels in your house. No, that's the humidity. When was the last time you had dew in your house? Oh, well. I think I can guess that it won't matter what I, or anyone else who thinks rationally, says about it; the weather people are going to go from one trend to another, fluffing up their basic facts with popular myths trying to make themselves indispensable to us. Just show me the radar, and I'll make my own guesses. So far, on basic stuff like whether it's going to rain on me on my 200 mile motorcycle trip, my track record is as good as any local weatherman.

Ban from TV and Everywhere Else

While people are making New Year's resolutions, linguists often propose that in a new year everyone should eliminate various words or phrases from their writing and conversation. I've never waited for the turn of a calendar page to rail on the seeming addiction some people have to colloquialisms, idioms and other phrases that either have become, or always were, pretentious, highly unnecessary, or tiresome. Many of my most hated phrases are ubiquitous on television and radio. If I were the Language Czar for a Day, these are the ones at the top of my list for eradication just now.

The reality is...

Not only is it entirely unnecessary to begin a statement with "The reality is," but doing so can actually operate to prejudice your listener or reader against the truth of the rest of your sentence. Like "To tell you the truth," when someone tells you that "the reality is," you may immediately, even unconsciously, doubt the reality of what follows.

The problem with the phrase is that most people who use it do so continually. It becomes tiresome and well worn in a short time.

The fact of the matter is...

Like "the reality is," this phrase is an entirely unnecessary preface to a statement of fact, weakening the impact of the statement rather than intensifying it.

Take it to the next level...

I suggest that we bury this phrase and never resurrect it, for any purpose whatsoever. It's used in business contexts, sports, education—practically everywhere. Reporters often stick the phrase into their stories about entrepreneurs or up and coming sports figures. I will freely acknowledge that it serves a purpose other than just to fluff up one's speech, but it suffers from two problems. The first is overuse: advertisers seem to be the chief users of this semi-idiomatic construction, and they use it often, so often that it loses impact. The second problem is that the phrase is a cheap substitution for finding words that specifically describe the contextual idea. Instead of "taking your career to the next level," why not decide what that next level actually is, and describe that specific accomplishment instead?

Give back...

I will live happily the rest of my days if I never hear anyone saying that he is giving back. Admittedly, sometimes he is, but most of the time, he isn't. He's donating. He's giving. He's sharing with people in need. He's contributing time and effort for a cause he believes in.

Often, it's someone who has been very successful and is now donating time at a soup kitchen or some such thing, who is said to be giving back. The argument would be that he didn't become successful without the help of many other people, and now that he's helping those people who helped him, he's giving back. The problem with that explanation is that most of the time these successful people didn't get where they are by anyone's giving them anything. People bought a product or paid for a service that the successful or famous person invented or devised.

What's wrong with saying someone is giving to his community—not giving *back,* just *giving?* In this case, simpler is better.

Reach out...

If a TV news person tried to reach someone for a comment, why doesn't he say only that—"WXYZ tried to reach (or called, or tried to contact) Mr. Jones for a comment, but so far there has been no response"? I suspect the current phrase, "reach out," came from the now fairly old advertising slogan of Bell Telephone (and AT&T), "Reach out and touch someone." Wherever it came from, it should go back.

Viable... Impact... Awesome... Amazing...

I have been campaigning for years to have "viable" removed from the English language except in its medical usage, with the possible exception of a political sense. Viable means "capable of surviving," and its most specific application is to fetuses (or foetae). By extension, you can probably justify its usage in describing anything that can survive past the point of its genesis and fundamental development. A political candidacy may or may not be viable after the early stages of a campaign.

There is no other word in our language, however, that has been as abused as much as this one. In a separate article I wrote several years ago, I identified at least two dozen meanings attached to "viable," none of which is even close to the idea of survivability. Anyone who pays the slightest attention to how "viable" is used will become aware in very short order that people employ it out of laziness and lack of vocabulary. It has become a generic adjective for "good."

And while you're at it:

Eliminate the adjective "awesome" from your vocabulary unless you are describing the universe or God, and drop "amazing" while you're at it, unless you are watching a magician or a nearly incredible feat of athletic ability. If everything is amazing or awesome, nothing is.

I always remember the story of the newspaper editor who came to look over the shoulder of a rookie typesetter who had just placed the headline, "JONES WINS COUNCIL ELECTION" in 200-point type at the top of page one.

Calmly he advised, "Save something for the Second Coming."

I could go on, but I would lose control of myself and not get to the rest of my list. That wouldn't be a viable option for this awesome rant.

Back in the day...

Exactly what day is it we're speaking of? I remember fathers and grandfathers prefacing mild rebukes of their complaining kids by saying, "Back in my day, we didn't have cell phones." But what day is *the* day?" The phrase isn't *terribly* irritating, but as long as I'm suggesting we dump the others on my list, take "back in the day" along with them.

The thing of it is...

Back in the day, I liked to watch Richie Brockelman, Private Eye, a very short-lived TV series in 1978, a spin off from The Rockford Files. Richie used this phrase, "The thing of it is," every few minutes on the show, and he always followed it by another "is." "The thing of it is, is" etc. It's a joke between my wife and me (not, as many would say, 'between my wife and I') to repeat the whole phrase now and then.

The phrase should probably go the way of the TV show, which ran for about a month and was never renewed. The thing of it is, is, it's entirely unnecessary, and people aren't always certain how to make a complete and proper sentence after saying it. It's fluff.

Oh, and while I'm on it, I described Richie Brockelman as a short-lived series. Keep the description of short-lived, but learn how to pronounce it. The "lived" part is not properly pronounced as in, "Where do you live?" but as in, "Was it a live performance?" "Short-lived" comes from the two words "short" and "life." A thing that has a short life is short lived–long "i". Think of a cat, which according to myth has nine lives. The cat is therefore "nine lived," as in "dived."

Actually…

Newscasters, particularly on-scene reporters, are famous for beginning every third sentence with this word. "Actually, we're on the scene right now, and you can actually see the police department behind me where the suspect was actually brought in. Actually he's probably in the jail right now. We're actually going to be here until a spokesman comes out to give us a statement."

Sometimes, I actually mute the TV until the offender is removed. Don't throw the word away, but think before you just toss it in as a connector.

One of the… is

The window of opportunity to correct this misusage in English may have shut. It is so fixed that I suspect it may never be fixed. How many people think there's anything wrong with my saying, "One of the politicians who is honest most of the time is Senator Jones"? Possibly 95% of people would see nothing wrong with that statement except the idea that any politician is honest. In fact, however, the grammar is wrong as well. It should be, "One of the politicians who are honest." The opening phrase, "One of the," creates a class of people to follow, a class described by the adjectival phrase, "who are honest." The sentence, as composed, describes politicians who are honest.

The problem most people have with such constructions is that they know the subject of their sentence is "One," so they use a singular verb in the next phrase—"who is honest." However, the verb that goes with "one" is not the verb before "honest," but the verb just before "Senator Jones." Now, you could say, "One politician who is honest is Senator Jones," but if you insist on using "one of," you're heading into that class construction zone where a plural verb is probably going to be required.

The way to avoid this problem is to think before you speak and to ask yourself quickly, 'What kind of politicians am I describing?' Answer: 'politicians who are honest.' Then, after you think twice before making such a claim about politicians in the first place, insert the proper grammatical construction into your sentence.

Massive…

A dozen times a day, on slow days, I hear someone say something is "massive." Most of the time, it isn't.

"Massive" means having great mass. In the world of science, the term "mass" has the specific and technical meaning; it's a measurement of the resistance of matter to acceleration. But the practical meaning of the adjectival form "massive" in the world of people, sofas, cars and buildings is that something has both great size and weight.

The word is relative, of course, in a universe where the objects with the smallest mass cannot be seen even with microscopes and the objects with the greatest mass are thousands of times as large as our Earth. But if we consider the relativeness of the word first with respect to the human body, which is probably the most useful marker for human beings, and then with respect to other objects in a class of things, then something of great size compared to other things may be justifiably called massive. Among all boulders a particular boulder may be massive; a seven tiered wedding cake is massive where most are between one and three; an earth moving machine is massive, dwarfing the dump trucks you see at most construction sites.

However, the word "massive" is used loosely and inaccurately most of the time these days. It's employed to describe things that have no mass at all.

An inferno cannot be massive (as I just heard on TV), since an inferno isn't an object: it's a chemical reaction, an event, but it has no mass.

Nor is the fireworks show massive (as I also heard on TV on New Years Day), because it also has no mass: it's an event.

A troop movement is not massive. It, too, is a process, or an activity. It cannot be massive.

A heart attack is not massive. It may be extensive, sudden, or something else, but not massive. In this case, the term is so firmly fixed in the common description of a medical event that I don't hold out any hope that the culture can be persuaded to stop saying it. (I'll even admit to having said it myself. Of course, it was a long time ago.)

A problem cannot be massive. It may be pervasive, considerable or comprehensive, but not massive.

Government cannot be massive. Well, ours is, but not technically. It may be enormous, vast or far-reaching (and it is), but save massive for when it really fits.

A storm isn't massive, despite its being a weather system hundreds of miles across consisting of whirling air molecules—they each have mass, but the storm doesn't. A storm may be widespread, huge or immense, but not massive.

Can "massive" be used correctly, you're thinking? Of course! I'm glad you asked.

One of the pyramids at Giza has great mass. Relative to other things in your house, that old upright piano has mass. So, a pyramid may be described as massive, as may a piano, if it's bigger or heavier than most others. In short, "massive" properly describes things that have "mass"—a lot of it.

Before you say something is massive, ask yourself if (1) it has mass at all, and (2) if it has relatively more mass than other things in its class or other things around it. If it doesn't, just say "large."

That's as many words and phrases as I will lead to the chopping block today. I simply had to execute them now and express my indignation at their having lived so long in this world, condemned but still on death row. If only it were that easy to get rid of them.

Language Czar—hmm. That prompts my next subject division.

The English Language

What Difference Does It Make?

What difference is there between these sentences?

The candidate visited three different states in one day.

The candidate visited three states in one day.

There is no difference, of course; they mean the same thing. The word different makes no difference. It's superfluous. It should be left out. You don't need it. Get rid of it. Get the idea?

Yet "different" is one of the most commonly misused words by English speakers. Placing different before a noun in a situation such as the one above is not only a superfluous use but a misuse, because the word as used doesn't mean what it means. In the typical use of "different" the speaker or writer means only to emphasize enumeration, not to say the things described actually differ from each other.

For instance, in the sentence above, the speaker didn't mean to suggest that the states the candidate visited were not the same kind of states at all; he only meant to emphasize that the candidate traveled and made campaign stops in a wide area in a very short period of time. Yet the word "different" doesn't contribute to the meaning of the sentence, and it doesn't mean what it means.

1. I had to go to seven different stores to find the right size pants.

2. I visited that house three different times before I found anyone at home.

3. The boss interviewed eighteen different people when he was looking for an assistant.

While it's possible to imagine that the stores were really different in sentence 1, that's not what the writer meant. He was looking for pants; he went to clothing stores; the stores weren't really different other than the fact that they were in their own locations and had different names. "Different" is in the sentence unnecessarily.

In sentence 2, different is entirely superfluous. The speaker didn't mean he made an effort to visit the house at markedly different times of day; he simply meant he went three times.

Sentence 3 employs "different" when anything else would be impossible. Of course they were different people—they certainly weren't the same people!

Different strokes for different folks.

Now there's a proper use of the word!

Speaking of things that don't make much difference, what about that nauseatingly ubiquitous term, "in terms of?" If you kept a pad and pen with you all day, you'd hear it more times than you could write down without getting another pad. A sampling from TV and online:

"Study says lettuce is 'three times worse than bacon' in terms of environmental impact." What difference does "terms of" make? Why not just "worse than bacon in environmental impact?"

"What will 2016 bring in terms of Government policies?" Again, "terms of" is superfluous as well as being verbal garbage in the sentence. The same is true of: "In Terms of One Outing, at Least, Max Scherzer Has Few Peers." Take out the "terms of" and you'll have the same thing, minus the worthless verbiage.

"Connecticut split in terms of holiday budgets." The article that followed this title changed the lingo when in the first sentence it led off with, "It appears Connecticut is split when it comes to holiday budgets." But then the writer couldn't help himself and reverted to the excess phrase: "Three Connecticut cities ranked in the top 100 in terms of having higher end budgets." What would have been wrong with "top 100 in higher-end budgets?" Nothing.

"…Characterizing large cardinals in terms of layered posets." This is correct. The sentence is about mathematics and the phrase is appropriate.

"The deceleration of population ageing in terms of cognition…" The British spelling distracts us American readers, but the bad usage bothers me more.

"In terms of Chelsea club politics, Roman Abramovich has a conciliatory Jose Mourinho exactly where he wants him." What's the difference in simply saying, "In Chelsea club politics…"? None at all, except, of course, that you would be more correct.

"Website Calculates Costs In Terms Of Stealth Fighters." Don't wonder what's wrong here, because nothing is. Calculating costs in money is one thing, but calculating costs by counting stealth fighters in its place is another, and it's precisely where "in terms of" is called for.

"Adele's '25' Arrives: What to Expect in Terms of Sales" No, just say, "what to expect in sales."

"In Terms of Diversity Initiatives, Tolerance is Not Enough." The addition of "In terms of" actually weakens the statement here. If I were writing it (and thankfully, because of the subject matter, I'm not), I would say, "In diversity initiatives, tolerance is not enough." Succinct.

"Athens and Piraeus control world's biggest fleet in terms of value" (title of an article). Here's a usage that's technically correct but "gooey" —the statement would be more forceful this way: "Athens and Piraeus control the world's most valuable fleet."

"We're really family oriented in terms of a restaurant." Huh? What possible contribution does "in terms of" make? None at all. "We're really a family oriented restaurant." Leave it at that.

Then there are all the news stations:

"Jack, what are we expecting in terms of rain today?"

"Jill, how are things looking in terms of traffic out there this morning?"

Don't get me started.

Wordily Redundant

I admit that occasionally I use a redundant phrase. Considering the hundreds of commonly used redundancies, it is nearly impossible not to employ one now and then, if not more than occasionally.

Sometimes we say something redundant to be emphatic. I think with affection of dear old church members called on to lead prayer in a service, waxing eloquent, at least in their own ears, in their supplication to the Almighty to "lead, guide and direct." Aside from the possibility that each of those three words may give a different shading to the basic prayer request, clearly the praying person is trying to emphasize the concept that he or she wants God to be in charge. Well, amen to that!

While we're at it, there's a fellow I know who isn't content to say "amen" only once, but must conclude all his public prayers (—I wonder if it applies to his private ones, too?) with, "Amen, and amen." The two verbal periods to his prayers are intoned in the same sing-songy manner every time, all for emphasis.

More emphatic redundancies: "polar opposites," "filled to capacity," "completely annihilate," sudden impulse," and "few in number." One could list probably several hundred more. I will resist.

Lest you be too quick to defend your own redundancies as justified by the need for emphasis, however, you should take note of a few redundant pairings that, when you think about it rationally, are sort of stupid.

Do you ever hear someone say, "The general consensus is that…"? A consensus is a *general* opinion. The same goes for "the general public." Or consider, "the final outcome." I'm sure I've said that, but it's sort of silly to double up words that mean the same thing, or to use two words where one includes the meaning of the other. How about, "foreign imports," or "new invention," or "past history"? That last one always makes me shiver. I always think, "As opposed to present or future history?" Of course, that's just my personal opinion—oh, yeah, personal opinion is redundant, too.

Some more dumb ones are: "7:00 a.m. in the morning," "as an added bonus," "the reason why," "possibly could," "could potentially," and "an armed gunman."

Sometimes, we resort to redundancies because the lone word we need isn't enough for most people to understand. If I were to say, "The joist caught him on the nape," would you need a few seconds to realize I was talking about the lower back of the neck? Most of us say, "nape of the neck," which is redundant, but generally helpful. Likely most of us have also said, "close proximity," thinking that "proximity" means only the position of one thing in relation to another." In fact, "proximity" means "nearness in space or time," or in other words, *close*.

Probably we would also include in the "helpful" category such combinations as "pre-recorded," and "circle around," although the single words we could use instead of the two would not be confusing without their redundant buddies.

A few phrases have the benefit of history, sometimes sacred history.

- "Free gift" is used in the King James Bible, translating the Greek, which itself was redundant. Then again, it was perfectly acceptable in Greek to use double negatives as a means of emphasizing something really was a "no no."
- "Some men's sins are open beforehand, going before to judgment; and some men they follow after," says the Bible. What other way is there to follow than after?
- "We gather together to ask the Lord's blessing," some of us sing at Thanksgiving, though gathering would have been enough.
- "Join together in the singing of a hymn," say ministers of music from time immemorial, as if joining were not sufficient. So it is with, "join together this man and this woman." Let's make sure the couple is joined really well.

One particularly thorny patch of English is where we tread into the usage of acronymns. Many of us have become so used to using acronyms that we forget what they mean, and then we combine them with words already incorporated in them: "HIV (**h**uman **i**mmuno-deficiency **v**irus) virus," "GRE (**G**raduate **R**ecord **E**xamination) exam," ISBN (**I**nternational **S**tandard **B**ook **N**umber) number," "UPC (**U**niversal **P**roduct **C**ode) code," "LCD (**L**iquid **C**rystal **D**isplay) display," "VIN (**V**ehicle **I**dentification **N**umber) number," "PIN (**P**ersonal **I**dentification **N**umber) number," "ATM (**A**utomated **T**eller **M**achine) machine," and "please RSVP." "Please" is "s'il vous plait" in French, which is where we get the SVP.

Finally, please don't "return back" or "remember back" or do anything else "back" that begins with "re-" since "re-" means back or again. Think about what you're saying and you'll probably avoid most redundancies. Plan ahead! (Oh, and if you want to get picky about it, that's redundant, too.)

Somewhat Grammatical

I often hear people say, "somewhat of a problem" or some other word after "somewhat of a". This doesn't sound right to my ear, and it should grate on yours, too.

I'm not just being picky. Or maybe I am, but I don't care. It is possible, of course, to be obnoxious about such things, and I would have to plead guilty to occasionally crossing that line, myself.[37]

"Somewhat of a problem" is somewhat wrong. "Somewhat" is defined in some web dictionaries as an adjective, an adverb or a noun, depending on how it's used. I think you'll find that "somewhat" is not a noun, unless used incorrectly. A good example is the phrase cited. What the speaker should have said is, "some*thing* of a problem." "Thing" is a noun, and "something" is, too.

The speaker could have said, "somewhat problematic," and that would have been correct because both words are adjectives; "of a" ties them together into a sort of compound adjective. In other words, the parts of speech should match.

As of yet...

Idioms sometimes make idiots of us, and like "somewhat of" and "something of," we're sometimes confused by "as of." There's "as of now," or "as of last week," or "as of this moment," which are correct. But then you hear—or I do, anyway—"as of yet."

"Whether he is going to run again for mayor he hasn't said as of yet."

"As of" should be followed with a noun or noun phrase. Drop the "as of" in the sentence above. "Yet" means "as of now." So, you could say that "as of yet" is both incorrect syntax and also a redundancy.

Try and...?

Which is proper: "try and hit the target;" or, "try to hit the target?" Can you imagine saying, "I'm going to attempt and hit the target?" Of course not. It's very common colloquially to say, "try *and* do something," but it's wrong all day long. Try to remember this one.

---

[37] Reader's Digest, Feb 9 (I think): "I used to love correcting people's grammar until I realized what I loved more was having friends."

I done it...

I am amazed at the number of people with not only high school but also college degrees who say, "I done it," or "I seen it." I'm not sure whether to blame them for not soaking in what was taught in English classes or to hold the English teachers and the schools responsible for not having taught English in the first place.

I'm also surprised that most of the time people who graduated from high school or went to college, while they may *say* "I done it," would *write,* "I did it." A modicum of congratulation is in order, but when one still goes around talking as if he were from Barefoot Backwoods he leaves the impression that he is ignorant.

I would like never again to hear anyone say, "I seen it," or "I done it." Unfortunately, this will never happen. Speakers guilty of these deliberate regressions into bad grammar are usually proud of their avoidance of correct speech, and almost certainly they are not teachable. In the vernacular, they're too far gone.

Paring Down the Language

1,025,109.8—that's how many words the Global Language Monitor estimates are in the English language (as of this writing). The estimate is something like the National Debt Clock, which projects the debt based on several factors and may or may not be right. Still, more than a million is a lot of words. It's probably too many, in fact. So let me propose eliminating some of them, or at least cutting back on their usage.

Insensitive

—A news article reported that a top official at the IRS admitted that the agency's targeting of conservative groups for denial of 501(C)(4) status, "was wrong, that was absolutely incorrect, insensitive and inappropriate." Insensitive does not belong in this list (and the responsible persons at the IRS do not belong in their jobs anymore). It should have been replaced by outrageous or reprehensible. Insensitive is a weenie word to describe what the IRS did.

—Sony Pictures Entertainment chairman Amy Paschal admitted she made racially prejudicial remarks about President Obama in email. She said, "The content of my emails …were [sic] insensitive and inappropriate but are not an accurate reflection of who I am." Aside from the fact that she's trying to convince us that what she says and does when she thinks no one is looking is not who she is—when it manifestly is—"insensitive" as a descriptor of racism is awkward at best. At worst, it sorely downplays the nature of her remarks.

Very unique

I'd like to eliminate the often heard "very unique," or any combination of "unique" with a modifier. I'm convinced that "unique" cannot be sensibly modified, because it means something that is one of a kind—unlike anything else.

For a while I considered the possibility that I might sometimes want to say that the uniqueness of one thing within its own sphere might be far more significant and extensive than the uniqueness of something else in another sphere. For instance, suppose you were making up a travel game where everyone had to name something that was unique. One person says, "The seashell picture I bought at the beach." It was in a store with lots of other seashell pictures, but there wasn't another one like it—or another one like any of the others, for that matter.

Another person in the car says, "I can top that. On 'American Pickers' the other night they had a Harley bicycle frame made into a bench with a grindstone powered by the pedals and chain." The bench was unlike anything else because it was truly one of a kind. It wasn't just a one-off art work in the style of others. The seashell picture would deserve the adjective "unique" in the sense that there wasn't any other picture *exactly* or even almost exactly like it; but the bench was unique in the sense that there wasn't anything *at all* like it (as far as we know).

Couldn't we then say that the bench was "more unique" or even "very unique," considering the comparison we've hypothesized? It's arguable.

On the other hand, people almost never have such circumstances in mind. Mostly they are using "unique" as a synonym for "different" or even "interesting." For all practical purposes "unique" is not properly modified. A thing is unique, or it isn't, period.

Homophobic

I gag at this non-word which, sadly, our dictionaries will probably add if they haven't already. There are many phobias, and their names include the appropriate Latin or Greek roots. "Phobia" is Greek for "fear." "Homo" means "same" in Greek, leading to the word "homosexual" in English, meaning "same sex," or being attracted to the same sex as oneself. "Homophobic" would mean "fear of the same." To leave out "sexual" or some root word for it makes "homophobic" virtually meaningless. We must remember, however, that this non-word comes from the same folks who stole "gay" from the English language and made it mean something oddly contradictory.

Interestingly, since homosexuals gave us this non-word "homophobic," one wonders why they chose to shorten the word "homosexual" to "homo" for purposes of the contrivance. "Homo" is considered by homosexuals to be a slur against them. Why would they lop off "-sexual" to make a word they expect to be taken as a serious term? Curious.

Make a difference

If, in our quest to reduce the size of the language, we single out silly words and useless phrases so as to really make a difference, we should also ban "make a difference." Hitler made a difference. The Boston Strangler made a difference. We should really be more specific about what kind of difference we want to make. Better still, we should avoid the phrase altogether, with or without specifics. Just tell us what you want to do that's supposed to make things different for the rest of us.

Proactive

Finally, we should ban "proactive." If any dictionaries have started including "proactive" in their printed volumes, they should be ashamed. It isn't a proper word. Be active; that's enough. If you need "proactive" then you probably need to coin "antiactive" at the same time. The world of biology already uses anti-active in its subject-restrictive jargon. On the street, however, there's no use for "proactive." You don't even need it as the opposite of reactive. Active is enough.

With these proactive suggestions, I'm just trying to be sensitive by reaching out to you in a very unique way, hoping to make a difference by giving back to you who have faithfully read my musings. Now quit it!

This and That

Drug Deaths

Every time another entertainer dies in a drug or alcohol related incident, I think of the long line of actors, musicians and other famous people who have exited this life by their own hands, one way or another. In a very few cases I think briefly about how I might miss seeing someone on the silver screen whose talents I appreciated, or how I might miss hearing a voice or an instrument that stood out from the crowd. With these deaths I experience a mixture of regret and contempt: regret for the talent suddenly gone and contempt for the cause of it.

Dying of a drug overdose, whether "accidental" or intentional, seems to me to be like dying from a game of Russian Roulette: if you keep playing the game, it will have fatal results. In a way I hate to say it but I will, because I'm feeling blunt just now: Most of the time I don't really feel sorry for people who kill themselves with drugs. Usually they don't mean to kill themselves—hence, the term "accidental overdose." Most often they just mean to get high, and sometimes they're addicted to getting high. That's the part that takes away most of my compassion.

Again, I hate to say it, because by some standards I'm supposed to feel compassion, but most of the compassion is erased by the impression I get that these people aren't victims of anything: they're deliberate actors. Nobody shot them up with heroin against their will or forced them to snort cocaine. They did it because they wanted to, because they had a lot of money lying around from their success in selling us records and movie tickets, and they chose to run with a crowd that got its kicks from drugs. Then they pushed the envelope and left this world in a buzz that turned the lights out. On the other side, surprise, life in this world is over.

There is, of course, some compassion left in me. I'm sad that some entertainers are so screwed up or so spiritually empty that they feel they have to go looking for something to give them a falsely transcendent feeling. I wish more people in the entertainment world had a purpose for life that came from God rather than merely from their craft. If they did, fewer of them would be looking desperately for drug highs because they would have spiritual peace.

Unfortunately, the entertainment world is known for its excesses, and its spiritual character is very irreligious. Despite the few fine Christians or Jews who are actors, singers and such, the culture typified by the Hollywood, Nashville, New York axis seems unaffected by the atypical good examples living among the crowd. Like Lot, a righteous man in Sodom, the rare Christian actor or musician does not seem to make much of an impact on the larger culture.

In the past ten years, we have learned of the drug or alcohol deaths of some very well known performers: Philip Seymour Hoffman, Lisa Robin Kelly, Heath Ledger, Cory Monteith, Ike Turner, Amy Winehouse, and Prince, to name a few. Someone you may not have known died of an alcohol-drug combination was Thomas Kinkade, the "painter of light." I was sorry to see him go. The others leave me with mixed reactions.

Of course, over the course of my lifetime a lot more very famous people, mostly entertainers, killed themselves, whether they meant to or not: Marilyn Monroe, Judy Garland, Jim Morrison, Corey Haim, Jimi Hendrix, Chris Farley, John Belushi, Lenny Bruce, Hank Williams, Alan Wilson, Brian Cole, Elvis Presley, Gram Parsons, Janis Joplin, Sid Vicious, and on and on. In fact, there are people who keep lists of just such things, and those lists are much, much longer than this one.

I browsed some of them and picked out about one in twenty-five names with which I was familiar. The rest are unknown to me, though I'm sure that people who know rock music well would know all the beloved drummers, guitarists, bassists and singers who got high just one too many times. In some cases, when they were absolutely sure they wanted to leave this world, they took the old fashioned route of shooting themselves—no question about the results that way. If you broaden the list to include entertainers who killed themselves some way other than by drugs or alcohol or both, you would be talking about thousands of people.

Just now, however, I'm thinking about this demon of drug use that keeps rearing its ugly head, and I'm struggling to feel something more than simply disgust. What started me thinking about it today just after New Years in 2016 was the news of Natalie Cole's death. Complications from congestive heart failure, said the first report. Immediately I figured it had to be more than that, and it was. It's well known, of course, that Natalie, the daughter of Nat King Cole, became a heroin addict in the 70s and then a cocaine addict in the 80s. She contracted Hepatitis-C from being an IV drug user; the chemotherapy she took to save her from the Hep-C killed her kidneys, and her death resulted from a combination of things connected to all of it. Maybe she isn't quite on the list of entertainers who died of drug overdoses, but drugs certainly put her on the downhill slope towards her death.

The whole matter reminds me in a grim way of the the Darwin

Awards, a tongue-in-cheek honor concocted by Usenet discussions in the mid 80s. Awards are announced annually for people who, as Wikipedia puts it, "contributed to human evolution by selecting themselves out of the gene pool via death or sterilization by their own actions." For instance, in the year 2000 a 19-year-old Texas man died attempting to play Russian Roulette with a semi-automatic pistol instead of a revolver. Drug use is similar, and it tends to say similar things about its subjects: they are both victimizers and victims. They have no one to blame but themselves.

Sometimes I see the word "tragic" in the report of yet another entertainer's having died from taking drugs, legal or illegal, or from alcohol abuse. When I think of some punk rocker or foul-mouthed rapper killing himself with a needle, I don't usually think of the word "tragic."

In other cases, however, perhaps the word "tragic" is justified in the classic sense, where tragedy describes a reversal of fortunes caused by a person's hubris. To arrogantly assume one can dance with the devil and not be damned is hubris. Drugs are the devil of the entertainment world. When drugs ruin or end a career, they do one of two things: either they rob the rest of the world of the enjoyment it might have had from the entertainer's gift; or they just invoke the Darwinian principle by taking their misguided users out of the gene pool.

Really Handicapped

Recently in the land down under, after she returned to the parking lot following her shopping, Justine Van Den Borne found a snarky note on her car. Someone thought she should not have parked in a handicapped space.

Van Den Borne's car bore a legitimate handicapped permit. Apparently the issue for the note writer was not that he/she could not see the permit, but that he *could* see Van Den Borne as she exited her car and went into the shopping center. What the note writer saw left the impression on him or her that the handicapped woman was not sufficiently handicapped to need the sticker or to use it.

The note simply asked if she had forgotten her wheelchair. Van Den Borne took to Facebook to respond, and the response "went viral." Predictably, her note defended her legitimate use of her permit due to her having Multiple Sclerosis. She was having a good day that particular day, but some days she couldn't walk without help. Her rebuke of the note writer's "abusing me on my good days for using a facility I am entitled to" evoked sympathy broadly. "Just because you can't see it doesn't mean a person isn't struggling to put one foot in front of the other," she said.

Some time back, I had a severe injury to my right knee that required surgery to repair. When I was finally able to drive again, I carried a cane and walked with substantial pain. While still on crutches, I had acquired a prescription for a handicapped permit, which my wife used when ferrying me around. When I ditched the crutches and got back to driving, I went to using a cane, and I displayed the handicapped permit when I went on little errands to the grocery store, the pharmacy, and other places. At work I already had my own space close to my building. My goal, however, was to lose the cane and to recover normal walking strength and stamina.

Eventually I found that while the cane was no longer necessary, at least for a while I was not going to have the strength or stamina I had before my accident. I had good days and bad days, but no days described in ServPro fashion—"like it never even happened." I was glad to have the handicapped permit, which I hung from my rear view mirror when I parked.

I hadn't been off the cane more than a few days, however, before I began thinking that while I could justify using the handicapped permit to park close to the store, I didn't really need to. It was uncomfortable to walk, but it wasn't going to injure me to walk five or ten parking spaces farther. And there were people whose injuries, illnesses, or sheer age made them twice as much in need of close-in spaces as I was.

Consequently, I decided to let my permit expire and not renew it. Even on my bad days I could still walk. It hurt; some days it made me moan with every step, and some days it still does. But I could walk. I determined I would forego my legal privilege because compared to others I was not handicapped. Not that most people could see. Not yet.

Now, I'm going to risk an *ad hominem* attack. My situation isn't completely analogous to Ms. Van Der Borne; however, she admitted to her anonymous note writer that she was having a good day and could walk unassisted. Everything she said in her Facebook reply suggested that she wasn't in any danger of suddenly collapsing. I just wonder if it crossed her mind that on that good day, when she could walk on her own, perhaps she should park in a regular space, if only to celebrate the fact that on that day she felt better. An unseen struggle to put one foot in front of another does not by itself make using a handicapped privilege imperative.

All that aside, for every Justine Van Den Borne who legitimately has a handicapped permit and whose use of it is legally justified all the time, there are a dozen people who have handicapped tags who don't really need them when compared to those who are seriously incapacitated. As well, there are probably fifty others who misuse a relative's tag by driving without the permitted person in the car, or by parking in a handicapped space and going into the store while the actual handicapped person stays in the vehicle.

Bottom line, those who have legitimate permits should use them without guilt as long as they really need to, but never use them unethically.

Another day, I'll rail on all those self-centered drivers who park in handicapped spaces illegally because, after all, they're only going to be inside the store a minute.

They Can't Help Themselves

Here we go again. Archaeologists, doing what archaeologists do, have gone and dug up another skeleton in Africa—actually, they sort of found it in a cave, a cave so hard to get to and get into that one wonders why they were there in the first place. The find was actually made about two years ago, near Magaliesburg, South Africa; it was a collection of bones representing possibly fifteen individual primates. Major announcements of this sort of thing usually await some sort of reconstruction of the bones and, in this day and time, a piece of computer assisted art depicting what scientists say the "individual" (not to say "person") may have looked like.

The artwork from the Magaliesburg finding looks rather startlingly like some present day Africans, except for the mostly missing external nasal structure. Some subjective decisions go into these re-creations, and I've often felt that the resemblance of the artist's rendition of most of these alleged ancestors of *homo sapiens* to modern man was tweaked to convince the dubious.

The researchers, who made their announcement in September 2015, were quick to say that *homo naledi,* which is what they're naming the creatures the bones came from, were probably not direct ancestors of modern human beings. Other experts who had gotten a look at the bones concurred in even more certain terms. I often chronicle the back-and-forth claims of archaeologists about where man came from and how early, and I've noted how humorous it is that the tree of man's supposed evolution gets redrawn every few years, but how they're always certain that *this* time they've got it right. This particular discovery is a tangent, because the finders are not claiming that ultra-great-grandma and grandpa were *homo naledi.*

What was interesting to me, however, was how Rick Potts, director of the human origins program at the Smithsonian Institution's Natural History Museum, just couldn't help himself when he described *homo naledi* as "the evolutionary experimentation that was going on."[38] Experimentation is something people do. This sort of language is strikingly common in articles on evolution. Evolutionary scientists regularly personify the process of evolution, or they speak more generally of "nature" as if it were an intelligent being. On the one hand,

---

[38]Rick Potts, quoted in "Scientists discover new human species relative: Homo naledi," Associated Press, 10 Sept 2015, The Internet.

they describe evolution itself as a process of random mutations over millions of years, filtered through natural selection, by which the most successful procreators survive and dominate. But then they give nature or evolution a personality and credit her (nature is a mother, you know) with trying this and experimenting with that, with providing this and giving that.

In other words, in spite of the fact that most evolutionary scientists are adamantly against the concept of a creator God, they can't help themselves: they just have to vest inanimate and non-material processes with a personality and conceive of them as godlike forces.

I think it's telling that people who will snicker at backwoods Christians for believing in a Creator can't eliminate from their speech the telltale signs that somewhere in their hard hearts they know there is a God.

Disqualified by Failure

Larry King, 8; Zsa Zsa Gabor, 9; Richard Pryor, 7; Billy Bob Thornton, 5; Elizabeth Taylor, 8; Geraldo Rivera, 5; Lana Turner, 8; Heddy Lamar, 6; Danielle Steel, 5; Barbara Walters, 4; Martin Scorsese, 5; Frank Sinatra, 4; Jennifer O'Neill, 9; Mickey Rooney, 8.

By the time this list reached Elizabeth Taylor, you probably guessed what the numbers following the names are: the number of marriages these people have had. Gleeful critics of Rush Limbaugh add his name to the list of famous people who have failed in marriage again and again. Rush is on his fourth marriage. For a few critics of his recently, Rush's failed marriages disqualify him as a proponent of the sanctity of marriage or as an opponent of homosexual "marriage" on the basis of its endangering heterosexual marriage.

Really?

To examine the validity of that sort of criticism, let's look first at the situation of Rush's marriages. As a young man, when he was working radio jobs near his hometown, Rush married for the first time. Her name was Roxy. She divorced him three years later for incompatibility.

Three years later he married again while he was working for the KC Royals. Wife number two divorced him seven years later, to marry someone else within the year. Hmm.

Rush waited four years and married Marta Fitzgerald, after he had come to national fame on the radio. Marta had been married thrice herself. Apparently she didn't take well to the public exposure their private lives got, and she moved out within the year. When she did, Rush asked her for a divorce.

Rush married his current wife only after dating for three years, having met her at a celebrity golf tournament in which he played. They married in 2010. While it's never wise to bet on the future of fallible human beings, this marriage may last: (1) it was preceded by sufficient time to get to know each other well; (2) it was and continues to be less in the limelight than Rush's marriage to Marta; (3) Rush, and wife Kathryn, are much more mature than Rush and any of his previous exes were; and (4) Rush and Kathryn have a business venture together and seem to be partners in a more significant way than he and any previous wife were.

One of Rush's critics lambasts him in the loudest of tones and declares that no one who has "killed four marriages himself" has any right to preach that gay marriage will destroy the institution of heterosexual marriage in the U.S. or the world.

Analyze that for a moment. First, the writer apparently doesn't know Rush's personal history. Rush's three first wives ended their marriages with him, the third by abandoning him leaving him little alternative but to file for divorce. The other two apparently could not cope with the vagaries and publicity of the life of someone in the public eye. This same dynamic goes a long way to explaining the high divorce rate of entertainers, news people, sports stars, or anyone who goes to work to the notice or adulation of millions and comes home to someone who lives in the shadows. That's why it's rare and newsworthy to learn of Hollywood couples who've been married for forty or fifty years with no sign of calling it quits.

Second, the critic accepts, apparently without question, the casual but deeply flawed idea that in order to proclaim the wisdom of something, one must never have failed in that very thing.

What a blind and foolish notion that is! Sometimes the most effective and convincing proponents of a moral, social, cultural, medical, or legal piece of wisdom is someone who has failed miserably and learned the hard way. Then he hopes, and tries with all his might, to convince everyone else not to make the same mistake.

Some wits and wise men insist, in fact, that there is no other way to learn but the hard way. Kenny Rogers sang of it: "Promise me, son, not to do the things I've done; walk away from trouble if you can: you don't have to fight to be a man."

When I was in high school, during the last century, we had to watch a film about drunk driving, which included a scene where a driver was pulled out from under a wrecked car, dead of course, folded over like a book, limp like a bloody lasagna noodle. It made some kids wretch. It was supposed to. It was advice from a dead guy not to do what he had done.

What do you think makes "Scared Straight" so effective? It's that the message of warning to young hoodlums comes from men and women who followed that path themselves and wound up in prison for life.

Who knows better that it's not wise to marry when you've known someone only a month: someone who never made that mistake or someone who did?

Who knows better that sleeping around creates an inordinate thirst for variety that likely dooms any future marriage: someone who never slept around, or someone who did, and who then couldn't make marriage to one and only one person succeed?

I heard a little story years ago about three ministers out for a day of fishing, when one of them boasted he could walk on water. He stepped over the side of the boat and walked around, then returned. The second one did the same thing, to the third one's amazement. The third minister then said, "If you can, I can," and he stepped over the side, only to sink over his head. When the others dragged him into the boat, he blubbered, "How come I couldn't do it?" The first minister said to the second, "You think we should tell him where the stumps are?"

It works the other way around in real life. Some years ago my brother and I were fishing in a lake where a friend of mine and I had previously fished. My brother was driving the boat and I suddenly told him to go slowly and avoid the path he was on. I remembered vividly having run over a barely submerged stump when with my friend a few years before, and it resulted in the loss of the motor's lower unit. My experience was painful, but rather than make me shy and zip-lipped, it compelled me to speak. I had to warn my brother where the stumps were.

Those who have no experience with a thing may have conviction, and there's no reason they shouldn't preach from that conviction. Those who have failed in something, whether previously they preached against it or not, have not only conviction but also experience. Experience is a powerful persuader. Most people who fall can tell you what put them off balance, what tripped them up, what others should watch out for, what pitfalls loom.

The Apostle Paul is a good example. He killed Christians; then he became one. Better than most people he knew how to reach stubborn hearts with the gospel.

Recently I heard a presentation by a lawyer who gave some statistics from his own profession. He said that lawyers admitted that when their kids told them they wanted to be lawyers, too, 80% of lawyers advised their children to be anything else but lawyers. They didn't want their kids to know the heartaches and headaches of their profession.

Wisdom is a wonderful thing: it flows in its fullest and unexceptional glory from the one who authored it, who personifies it, and who cannot breach it—God; it richly rewards the lives of people who have followed it rather than violating it; it redeems the lives of people who have spurned it and then discovered it. While it is hypocrisy to *pretend* never to have done what you criticize in others, often the most effective critique is to warn others, if you know from experience, where the stumps are.

Pondering My Own Antiquity

Recently I've regrettably caught myself thinking about the impending diminution of physique and mentality associated with aging, trying to be honest enough with myself to admit that it's no longer pending, but happening. I fight it, of course, heeding the urging of Dylan Thomas, "Do not go gentle into that good night, / Old age should burn and rave at close of day; / Rage, rage against the dying of the light." I suspect if I hope to stave off or just slow the natural processes, my rage will have to intensify every year, every month, even every day as the years continue to come on. At some point, however, I will have to admit that I have been overcome.

The doctor who repaired my badly broken leg in 2014 advised me soberly that I am no longer forty-two. He picked that number out of the air, I think, because six months later he had revised it to nineteen. Apparently he observed that I am actively engaged in mimicking someone a great deal younger than I. While I assured him I knew I was considerably older than nineteen or even forty-two, I also assured him that I wasn't going to go gentle into that good night.

A recent news story out of the UK startled me with its illustration of a very opposite view of life. A British woman who worked in a nursing home became convinced that she wanted no part of advanced aging, and she went to a suicide clinic in Basel, Switzerland, to end her life while she still had no "serious health issues." The woman, whose name was Gill Pharoah, was seventy-five.[39]

There's no doubt that getting old usually brings multiple health problems. A few people are hale and hearty up until a sudden end that comes mercifully through a heart attack or stroke in their sleep. Most people, however, develop one disease or another and also experience diminished visual, auditory and other capacities, and take more and more expensive medicines to alleviate this and that, until they finally succumb to one or the other of what they've been fighting for years. A growing number of people lose their presence of mind before meeting the infinite mind in death.

While I contemplate this reality, still I have to say I think there's something defeatist and spiritually alarming about Gill Pharoah's decision to commit suicide. People commit suicide every day, of course,

---

[39]Ollie Gillman, "Healthy ex-nurse, 75, kills herself…" (*DailyMail.com,* 2 Aug 2015, The Internet).

but almost always because of some terrible event going on at present in their lives: they lose a fortune in the stock market (witness the crash of 1929); they commit a terrible crime and don't want to be captured and tried for it (Bryce Williams in the recent Virginia, on-air shooting, e.g.); they realize they're hopeless failures in life and they don't see any light at the end of the tunnel. Some people have even committed suicide after finding out they have a terrible disease that will end their lives within a year, after it also robs them of every normal human ability. Rarely if ever, however, have I heard of someone committing suicide as a preventative measure. It's disturbing, and if it became a trend, it would be alarming.

It may already have become a trend. The article reporting Pharaoh's suicide said that 611 Britons did the same thing during the two year period of 2011-2012. I'm officially alarmed.

Why? Because it illustrates powerfully the spiritual vacuum of any modern culture in which such a practice could arise. Where people can determine that the mere anticipation of the possibility of physical and mental incapacity is all they really need to know to end their lives on earth is fairly powerful proof that they have no realization that they have lives beyond this earth. Even if they had a rudimentary belief in life beyond the grave, the decision to end their lives prematurely on the speculation that it would get more difficult proves that they're not thinking of the more likely possibility that their lives would have value to the people around them if they stayed—even if they stayed in terrible health—which isn't anywhere near certain in the first place.

Gill Pharaoh, for instance, said that her decision was occasioned in part by her concern for her children, that they shouldn't have to take care of her in her old age. I'm certain that most of us can see her point and can sympathize with it to the extent that we all hope we will not have to be taken care of. Are we not more wisely counseled, however, to weigh our worth as human beings, the value of our thoughts, words and activities, the worth of our wisdom and experience, and the value of our day-to-day relationships with the people we love, against our mostly selfish desire to be spared declining health? I think, in fact, that the idea that killing oneself would be a favor to his or her children is mostly self deception.

Yes, grown children often will say of a parent who dies after a protracted illness in which they, the children, were constant caregivers, "It was a mercy." They will also feel relieved and freed themselves. That doesn't mean they wish their parent had keeled over a long time ago. If they do, they tell us a lot about themselves, don't they?

My father died after a protracted illness, himself. He didn't linger years, only about six months after his illness became serious. Several things about his experience, and ours with him, demonstrated the value of those months.

He echoed the sentiment of others that "growing old isn't for sissies." His courage in facing those increasingly awful days proved his mettle and challenged the rest of us to braver living.

He found a renewed purpose in testifying to his caregivers about spiritual truths. Some people who visited him to minister to him found themselves going away feeling more that he had ministered to them.

He fulfilled the ancient parental role of blessing his children before he went to be with the Lord. Each of us who sat with him and talked with him in those last days had some heart-to-heart conversations that left us with enriching or challenging thoughts and truths.

Finally, when he went, he didn't leave us with any reason later to feel that he had cheated us of any portion of his life that might be valuable. We couldn't say to ourselves, ten years down the road, that Daddy had denied us the privilege of his taking part in our son's wedding, or seeing his grandchildren in our line, or helping us understand something about our own approach to aging. Daddy went when there was nothing he could to to prevent his going, not when he decided to take a short cut out of fear, selfishness or defeat.

So I'm sitting here thinking about my age and the probability that things will get worse progressively, and I recall a time some thirty or forty years ago when I was engaged in portraying an old man theatrically. I developed what I thought was a fairly good characterization of a seventy-year old, and in pondering the matter philosophically I thought to myself, I think I'll make a pretty good old man. I am now about four years away from the age of the man I once portrayed from a distance. Pondering my own antiquity is no longer theoretical; it's quite realistic, and I'm trying to ask myself if I still think I'll make a pretty good old man.

Having pondered what I think is a wrong-headed, wrong-hearted act on the part of some woman I didn't know an ocean away, I'm thinking now that I will be even more committed to making sure that I'm the old man my children need me to be, no matter how my health may turn out. I'm thinking that I need to be the old man my wife wants me to be, discounting the complications that I can't do anything about. I'm thinking I want to be the kind of old man I myself want to be, raging against the dying of the light, not acquiescing to the inevitable but struggling against it—not bitterly, but with great, joyous energy, being young at heart to the last, insistent on squeezing every last drop of life out of life, until I am taken home where all of life returns to me, and more.

Why a Flag Should Fly, or Not

The nation, via its presses of varying degrees of responsibility, has been focused on events in South Carolina recently, since the racially motivated murder of nine persons attending a church in Charleston. The shooter was a young White man, barely more than a boy, later discovered to have been radicalized in cult-like, racist doctrines and sporting a Confederate Flag as one of his symbols. The church was historically Black.

The governor of South Carolina, Nikki Haley, announced quickly that it was time for the Confederate Flag to come down from the statehouse grounds, where it was moved a few years ago to a memorial rather than the statehouse dome. The General Assembly of South Carolina agreed to take up a bill to remove the flag, the state was set afire emotionally about the issue, both pro and con, and in a rapidity of legislative fury that must rival any measure ever undertaken by South Carolina's or any other state's assembly, the bill was passed, Haley signed it the same day, and the flag came down within hours.

A day after the descent of the Confederate Flag from the statehouse grounds and its placement in a museum of the Confederacy, the chatter on talk stations and television, and in gatherings of all kinds, was hot with debate about the removal and what prompted it. I weighed in as well.

Lewis Grizzard—God rest his soul—of *Atlanta Journal & Constitution* fame, and more nationally of stand up humorist fame, would be introduced for his comedy show by someone saying he was "an American by birth and a Southerner by the grace of God." I feel a similar sense of affection for my heritage as a Southerner. I was born in Martin County, North Carolina, "down east," as they say in the State. I was reared in Richmond, Virgina, the capital of the Confederacy. My teen years were spent in the Upstate of South Carolina, the first state to secede from the Union. I attended and graduated from a North Carolina university. I went to grad school in Texas. I've lived in the two Carolinas since. I am a Southerner, through and through. No one has any grounds for doubting my affections for the Southern way of life.

That said, I have never been a fan of the modern incarnation of the Confederacy, populated as it is with wannabe rebels. I have never owned a Confederate Flag, never had a Confederate Flag sticker or decal, and never wanted to. It's not from lack of familiarity with my culture. I studied the Civil War in school. In the 7th grade I wrote a mini-book on it. I painted army men blue and gray and played Civil War with friends when I was still doing that sort of thing. But none of this made me like the guy who lived across the hall from me in college whose room was a shrine to the Confederacy and who loved most of all his figurine of "The Little Rebel," who was captioned as saying angrily, "Hell, no, we won't fergit!" This guy also chewed tobacco, brewed his own beer, partied hearty, and flunked out of school because he was such a hell raiser.

Nor am I like a cousin of mine by marriage who is a Civil War re-enactor, spending who knows how much every year on his moth-eaten hobby, that probably is a lot of fun, but that simply doesn't inspire me. I'm an American. I'm not a Confederate-American, just an American.

And since I'm a Caucasian, it almost goes without saying that I don't have the anti-Confederate sentiments that most Blacks do (not all, you should understand, but clearly most).

So I haven't debated anyone about whether or not the Confederate Flag should—or now, should have—come down from South Carolina's statehouse grounds, on the basis of my love of the South or my appreciation of my heritage. I have, however, briefly debated the issue, just on other grounds.

To me, you see, the issue is not how you feel about the South, or how you feel about the Confederacy, or how you feel about the Constitution or feel about the encroaching hand of the federal government or feel about racism or feel about bigots or feel about segregation or inequality or anything else. All arguments for or against taking down a Confederate Flag from statehouse or state grounds in S.C. or anywhere else that rely on *feelings* about this or that issue are quite beside the point, in my opinion.

One thing and one thing alone should determine the issue. It is a principle, time honored and followed by nations throughout history:

It is singularly inappropriate for the flag of a defeated cause to fly over government buildings or grounds where the victor's flag flies.

The Confederacy was defeated. The Confederate Flag should never be flown over any state's grounds where the state now belongs to the United States of America, no longer to the Confederacy, which no longer exists.

Would it be appropriate for the Union Jack to fly over the U.S. Capitol? No.

Would it be tolerable for the Nazi flag to fly over government buildings in Berlin? No.

Case closed.

Except, of course, that it isn't, because people imagine that taking down the Confederate Flag means disrespecting the history and heritage of the South. It doesn't. And if an enthusiast of the cause mounts a Confederate Flag in the back of his pickup truck and drives it in the wind all around town (as some people did in my area shortly after the flag went down at the Statehouse), it doesn't necessarily mean that the driver is a hating, racist bigot—though it may.

The point is that anyone in this great country can fly a flag of his choice from his truck, in his yard, or anywhere else where he has the freedom of speech and expression. He's telling you how he feels.

If anyone gets angry and agitated and cries and bellows about taking a flag down, she's telling you how she feels, as one South Carolina Representative did on the floor of the Assembly, leading to that body's approval of the measure to bring down the battle flag of Northern Virginia (which is what the most commonly displayed Confederate Flag is). But all that debate is over feelings, and feelings are not what should determine whether or not a state flies a certain flag. A state should fly only the flags that are valid representations of governmental entities that have authority in them. The Confederacy does not qualify.

What people do with the Stars and Bars on their own property is up to them. May the South and its way of life be preserved. May those who fought for a cause they believed was the true spirit of America be honored in their place. May those who honorably surrendered to the victor continue to be revered. May history not be sanitized and thus fictionalized. May we also not long for days we did not experience, for a life that was fundamentally inequitable to great numbers of Americans, or for a past that might not have led to the utopia some believe it would have.

May we instead celebrate the United States of America, for all its weaknesses and sins still the best the world has to offer. "America, America, God mend thine every flaw; Confirm thy soul in self control, Thy liberty in law."

What Marriage is Like

I don't subscribe to the Huffington Post, and I never visit its website, but I see an article from it now and then via another news site I frequent. A recent one on the subject of marriage caught my attention. It contained the highlights of a rather superficial survey via Twitter of people's opinions of marriage. It seems Huff Post asked people to summarize marriage in 140 characters or less by way of a Tweet, and then Huff Post reported out the answers they say "perfectly capture what married life is really like."

What disturbed me about the article was first that so many people think of marriage in negative terms. That's sad; it shouldn't be that way. I was also disturbed by what I think is obvious, that Huffington Post appeared to be cheering the critics of marriage. In part I infer this purpose of theirs by the fact that not a single Tweet they selected affirmed the goodness and value of marriage, and by the fact that they think overwhelmingly negative views of marriage are entirely on target. Apparently nobody involved with the article at Huffington Post has a decent marriage.

But we readers have no way of knowing if the Tweets the Huffington Post thought were the best were really representative of all the submissions. Further, no doubt the process of soliciting the Tweets was in no way scientific, and thus the Tweets cannot represent the general population. They would come closer to representing the Huffington Posts' readership, and that would be liberal left in politics and social issues. The makeup of its readership probably accounts for the skew of these opinions of marriage.

With that disclaimer on their behalf, I'd like to weigh in on the top Tweets. In all cases I'm convinced that it's not marriage that failed the Tweeters, but they who failed it. In many cases, they came to the altar expecting the wrong things, having counterproductive moral inadequacies, or looking at the opposite sex in a superficial or even perverted way.

1. *"Marriage is mostly just walking behind your wife carrying heavy things,"* said one Tweeter. This is funny, in a way, because it is based on a rather common sight. Men on average are stronger than women, and they may also act like gentlemen and do the heavy lifting when the couple are together. I give the Tweet a passing grade because it's meant in a lighthearted way—I think. Still, it's in the negative range of opinions.

2. *"Marriage is the IKEA of relationships. Easy to walk into, confusing to piece together, and difficult to exit."* This makes me sad. The Tweeter apparently was casual about her marriage, probably casual about the relationship, and suffered the consequences, finding divorce the bitter result. That the writer of the Tweet chose this subject to typify marriage suggests that it was the most significant thing about marriage that he or she had on his or her mind. That would be the case in all of the following Tweets as well.

3. *"Marriage is like a public toilet. Those waiting outside are desperate to get in. Those inside are desperate to get out."* Like the first Tweeter, marriage to this one is mostly about his failure in it. And it can't be good that his marriage reminded him of a Porta-potty.

4. *"Marriage:is like going to a restaurant: you order what you want, then when you see what the other person has, you wish you had ordered that."* Here's a fellow (I'm making an assumption, of course; it could be a woman) who went into marriage not really ready to commit himself to one woman for life. In all likelihood, he had multiple sex partners before deciding to marry, and having gotten a taste for promiscuity, he found it hard to be monogamous. Sad.

5. *"Marriage is like waiting in line for a ride at an amusement park. You spend 99% of the time pissed off for 1% of intense pleasure."* Here's a guy whose idea of a relationship with the opposite sex is far more focused on sex than is healthy or mature for a marriage. Men in particular have a weakness to this attitude, simply by nature. But men who don't learn that marriage is much more than sex, and who fail to develop the ability to build broadly based relationships, are doomed to marital failure.

6. *"Marriage is like deleting all the apps on your phone except one."* Interesting. The tone, however, suggests a negative opinion. Deleting all your phone apps is not something you would do for any positive reason. You would do it only if dared or forced. The Tweeter felt trapped into getting married, and instantly resented and regretted giving way. Imagine living every day wishing you had someone else for a spouse. Sad.

7. *"Marriage is like playing bridge. If you don't have a good partner, you'd better have a good hand."* I will be reserved in my comment. I assume his or her opinion is the result of having come to the marriage with an unfounded

idea about sexual compatibility. That concept is mostly bunk, made up to excuse sleeping around before marriage, like shopping.

8. *"Marriage is like a constant struggle to solve a jigsaw puzzle whose pieces keep on changing shapes every minute."* Of all the Tweets, this one was probably the most positive, in that it was the least negative. Most marriages do experience changing struggles and challenges. But if the Tweeter was talking about the partners themselves changing, that suggests that he or she has spent less time on getting to know the other than he should have.

9. *"Starts off easy, then gets harder, and eventually you go online and find a way to cheat."* One of the saddest of all the Tweets, here's a wife or husband who in all probability has never been committed to her spouse. Cheating was inevitable only because faithfulness was never really vowed.

10. *"Marriage is like playing Monopoly. It starts out as fun, gets a little boring, then someone steals money from the bank and no one ever wins."* I confess I'm not entirely sure what this Tweet is about. It's sort of like the comment of a young woman on a radio commercial by the Catholic Church, where an interviewer asked people on the street to compare marriage to a sport. The woman said with a little laugh, "Baseball. It lasts a long time and not a lot happens!" The bank heist in this Tweeter's comment suggests he's thinking of some event in his or her own marriage that further soured an already unsatisfactory relationship. Counseling could have helped. So could some simple, human maturity.

11. *"Put your GPS on full volume for your daily commute if you want to know what marriage is like."* A common complaint, particularly of men, is that women (the voice on the GPS is almost always female) are always telling them what to do. What's sad about this complaint is that many men get off to a bad start *allowing* women to tell them what to do, instead of having a conversation in which both persons get to contribute, and no one lords it over the other. I have been saddened for years seeing men who allow themselves to be henpecked. These are the guys who, if they don't end the marriage early, turn into doormats. Sad.

12. *"Marriage is like a sweet romance story till you get to the lame M. Night Shyamalan twist where you realize you've been dead for years."* Again, here's a tragic consequence of not keeping marriage alive with affection,

conversation, mutual activity, sharing, and work.

13. *"A bad marriage is like a horrible job. You are happy to have one but always [on the] lookout for other options."* The Tweeter married for the wrong reasons, I'm confident to say. Desperation? Bad reason to get married. I understand it, but you can't blame marriage itself, as an institution, for your failure to come to the altar with a heartfelt and well considered commitment to one person for the rest of your life. And the tag line about looking for options illustrates my urgent criticism of the modern approach of people to marriage. They tend to believe that it isn't important to go into marriage intending never to leave it; instead, they anticipate, even sometimes plan on, a second marriage. What a terrible attitude!

14. *"Marriage is like a phone call in the night: first the ring, and then you wake up."* With a play on "ring," the Tweeter is trying to say that getting married often takes place in an atmosphere of unreality, asleep in fantasy. That may be true for some, like the Tweeter, but it need not be true of all, and it isn't true of quite a few people I know.

15. *"Marriage is like a beanbag; comfortable for a while then bloody difficult to get out of."* This final word returns to the familiar idea of divorce. Again, very sad.

My views of marriage are reflections not only of my own marriage but of the unions of most of the people I know. Yes, I know some people who failed at marriage and are trying it again. Yes, I know a few people who stayed single for fear of marriage, and some who just preferred single living. But I know countless married people, and most of those have been married happily for a long time.

I wouldn't know how to Tweet what marriage, my marriage, is like in 140 characters (I don't have a Twitter account and have never sent a Tweet), but here are a few more characters than that:

After forty plus years of marriage, I find my wife to be my best friend. Actually, I'm not sure I expected that at first, because friendship seemed like something more easily achieved with fellows of the same gender. I expected something more exalted, somehow. I expected my wife to be my romantic partner, and I think I thought everything we did would be charged with the romantic angle. Turns out my concept was limited. As I grew, we grew, and we grew to be good friends.

Revisiting that wag's opinion of marriage like a sport, I tend to agree, it's like a baseball game: it lasts a good long time, if you're blessed and if you work at it and are committed to it. It has rhythm and structure, but it has moments of breathless excitement and restful interludes. It builds teamwork and profits from it. It makes use of the talents of each partner and the strength of cooperation. In the course of play you develop memories. It's a day in your lives lived in the sunshine of a divine-human opportunity on a field of dreams. You win some and you lose some in the complete season, but it's always worth playing, because there's nothing like it anywhere else in the world.

Another New Age of Man

I've written previously about the ongoing stabs experts take at when and whence man began to evolve. I've noted that archeologists and biologists will from time to time tell us excitedly about some new discovery and announce to us that the relative certainty with which some of their fellow scientists have told us that man is X number of years old, was misplaced, and that modern man is X-Y or X+Y years older than that. Man's place of origins has also shifted from eastern Africa to southern Africa to the Middle East and other places, depending on what new studies have been done. It's hard to keep up with where we came from and when, if you even agree with the general proposition being offered.

A new study just released, done on 2,636 people from Iceland, claims to give us yet another adjustment to man's origins. The study, actually four of them, were published in *Nature Genetics,* put out by the Nature Publishing Group. According to Kari Stefansson, co-author of the studies, one conclusion that can be drawn from them is that the most recent, common male ancestor of the human species lived about 239,000 years ago.

That figure significantly differs from the recent University of Arizona study that declared our oldest common "father" lived about 340,000 years ago. The new study's number is closer to, but not really close to, the age of our oldest, common female ancestor, also known as the Mitochondrial Eve, revealed to us in a 1987 study. According to Cann, Stoneking and Wilson, who conducted that study, Eve lived about 200,000 years ago. (It makes for some interesting speculation as to how Mitochondrial Eve and this new, genetic father got together.)

So the see-saw teeters back toward the other side—again, if you are counting on the veracity of all these studies for your view of humanity. The problem, however, is not only the implications of the inaccuracy of these studies based on their repeated contradiction of one another, but also the manner in which the studies are conducted, as you learn when you dig into them further.

In this case, one of the contributing studies was based on previous ones done on persons with a disease. The fact that the people sampled were sick means the study contains an inherent bias (not a personal bias, but a shift in the sample itself making it unrepresentative). As a result, the sample cannot be taken as representative of the actual population of Iceland.

Not only so, but Iceland is unusually isolated as a populace, compared to other parts of the world, as, for instance, the mainland of Europe. Again as a result, even if the sample fairly represented Iceland, which it doesn't, it wouldn't come close to representing the human population in general, in any statistically meaningful fashion.

Even faced with these weaknesses of the fundamental concept of the study, Stefansson said that the results were likely to apply to other populations outside Iceland.

Not likely, in my view. The flawed bases of the studies suggest almost overwhelmingly that they cannot be extrapolated to apply to the general human population. Consequently, they shouldn't be heralded as a new discovery about the age of man.

My readers probably have gathered by now that I'm not of the opinion that man is only 6,000 to 10,000 years old, but I'm not in the Leakey camp either.[40] I'm being entertained watching the competing researchers revise each other's scientific pronouncements every few years. It's like being at a tennis match, though I have a sneaky suspicion that in this case, nobody on the court is going to win.

---

[40]Louis and other Leakeys estimate the age of legitimate *homo* species in upwards of two million years.

Whole Lot of Killing Going On

Lately in life I have been reading a lot of English history. I've read numerous books about the early Britons, back into Roman times, and the progress of society, culture and government through the medieval period and up through the time of the war ro reclaim the American colonies. Of all the interesting things I have learned, the one fact that strikes me beyond all others is how many people were executed. I knew this, of course, but having saturated myself with stories of English kings and queens for a number of months, I have been confronted every other day or so with another tale of someone who looked cross-eyed at a monarch or noble and had his head chopped off for it. England could be a terribly violent place.

Every school child in my generation learned the names of significant persons in English and American history. Among them was Sir Walter Raleigh, who famously and gallantly laid down his cloak for Queen Elizabeth to walk over rather than get her feet muddy.[41] Most of us never learned, however, that Raleigh was ultimately beheaded for displeasing the head of state—not Elizabeth, but King James who succeeded her. Nor was the offense all that serious. But it seems that when a monarch wanted to dispose of someone, he figured out a way to call that someone's offense treasonous, and then, "Off with his head!" People were also imprisoned routinely for things that we in America, or in modern England for that matter, wouldn't dream of considering even jail-able offenses.

Running a close second to executions were assassinations, which are almost uncountable. Kings and queens were particularly vulnerable, of course, but their children as well, and other nobles and court personalities. The deadly game played from generation to generation by British royalty, dukes and earls, and other people concerned first in life about being in power in their little worlds, so colored the history of England that in my mind it is difficult to see how the country ever survived to the present day. Obviously, at some point the idea of succession by assassination waned and disappeared (in England, anyway, but clearly not in some countries in other parts of the world). Just as obviously, the rule of law—law that is far more civilized—eliminated execution for all but the most serious crimes, until the UK abolished the death penalty for murder in 1965, retaining it for

---

[41]The historicity of this tale is broadly disputed.

treason, but abolishing even that in 1998.

Reading the accounts of kings murdered and displaced by rival kings, disputed claimants to the throne, or even sons who were a bit eager to succeed their fathers, I find it difficult to see how a just system of laws emerged from the English culture, and yet it did. The credit goes in some part to key monarchs along the way who were unusually just, and in some part to the system of popular governance which spread power more thinly and thus made being the monarch less worth dying, or killing, for. More than these things, however, it seems to me that the influence of Christian teaching, particularly in the setting of Protestantism, finally brought greater justice into government.

Yes, it's true that the state-church was involved with violent solutions to less than earth-shaking problems. Opponents of Christianity love to point out the church's involvement with wars. It is worth noting, however, that whenever "the church" was involved with violence, it is almost exclusively the state-church being talked about. When the Roman Emperor Constantine became a Christian (on the books, anyway) in A.D. 325 and married his Empire to the Church (Roman Catholic), he started something that was to pervert and plague Christianity for a solid 1,200 years. The state-church, first the church of the Holy Roman Empire and then even the Church of England (after Henry VIII), was an unholy marriage of institutions that invited superficial claims to piety on the state side, and prompted perverted interpretations of the Bible on the church side. The result was a great many actions by the church that were in no way representative of true Christianity.

So when the Church of England, itself a body separated from Roman Catholicism, suppressed the emergence of still other groups that protested the control of the state church, and when the state church executed Christians who dissented, it was almost the last throes of resistance to the transformation that Christianity itself marches toward.

The colonization and then emergence of the United States of America marked a major shift in society's abandonment of violence as a means of governing. While some crimes remain punishable by death, the intense debate over this fact is evidence that the citizenry would not tolerate the culture's moving back toward executions to control any lesser offenses—such as Muslim law includes, for instance. And though assassinations still occur now and then, they are universally condemned.

I don't know if the trend, if it continues, would ever result in the complete elimination of capital punishment in the United States. I don't think we're ready to do away with a remedy that seems entirely appropriate as punishment for first degree murder. On the other hand, very few murderers are executed these days, considering how many of them are spending life behind bars at our expense. I'm not sure that the threat of the death penalty is much of a deterrent where it isn't enforced.

There's a Bible verse that speaks to that matter: " Because sentence against an evil work is not executed speedily, therefore the heart of the sons of men is fully set in them to do evil" (Ecclesiastes 8:11).

Is All Money the Government's?

A bill before Congress would eliminate the inheritance tax.[42] Taken by itself, who could object to this? Notice that I said, taken by itself. If you happen to be a political party or a recipient of government largesse that profits off the tax levied on people's inheritances, you're likely to object to the tax's elimination, so your opinion is biased. Take the issue in its principle only.

A person works 45 years and pays tax every year on his income. In fact, he pays a *confiscatory* tax on his income, but that's a subject for another article. He pays federal tax, a lot of it, and then what he has left is his. He invests some of it. He pays tax on the profits from his investments. Every year, after April 15 or whenever he files his tax return, his balance with the government is $0.00. He's very careful to make sure of that.

Then he dies. And the IRS says, "Hmmm. You're rich. You made too much money. We're going to take half of it."

It's a death tax. Those who named it that named it well. Furthermore, it's double taxation, which in anyone's mind should be automatically labeled as unjust.

Still further, we can't leave the matter without asking what's so important up in Washington that they have to steal a person's estate when he dies? That opens the door to a lot of analysis of how much of the federal budget is really necessary or even constitutional. I can't get into that subject right now either, except to say that my own estimate would be that more than half the federal budget should be eliminated. There are too many giveaways, too much welfare, too many wasteful purchases, too many grants for things the federal government shouldn't be doing, etc., etc.

The point is that the government wants the tax on inheritances simply to be able to fund everything it does in its bloated way.

What I find remarkable about the objections being voiced to the move to eliminate the death tax is how they reveal the perverted thinking of largely Democrats as to the ownership of the nation's collective wealth. Democrats call the possible repeal of the tax "a giveaway to the rich." Think about that for a minute.

To give something away, you must have it and it must be yours to

---

[42]Passed by the House on 16 April 2015. The Obama Administration said a veto was likely.

give away; am I correct so far? Yes, I am. So according to Democrats, the tax now being levied on inheritances belongs to the government, yes? In their opinion, yes. If they wanted to take twice as much, or even all of an inheritance, whatever they took would still belong to them, right? That's what they think. In other words, your inheritance from your parents or your estate to pass on to your children doesn't belong to you; it belongs to the government. If they let you have ten percent back of what you're paying now, they're being generous with what really belongs to them—in their opinion. If they give it all back to you, that's a giveaway, because it's not really yours.

That's the perverted opinion of the Democrat Party.[43] All the wealth of the nation belongs to the government. "If you have a business, you didn't build that," according to El Presidente Obama.

This perverted view of America's wealth is stated in another way by the White House, which is threatening to veto the repeal, if it passes. The White House says a repeal would add $269 billion to the budget deficit over the next ten years.

Wait a minute: why? There's only one reason: the government doesn't intend to spend less. *Ever.* The government is a massive beast, a Godzilla that never reaches maximum size. It consumes ever more and grows ever larger. If somehow a grass roots movement results in a small strike at the federal diet by correcting a fundamental inequity like the inheritance tax, the head of Godzilla whips around and roars menacingly and screams that it will never, *ever* stop growing, it will never spend less, so that if it doesn't get fed one way, it will steal from the people another way. Spending is deficit spending only if the government says, "Well, we don't have the money, but we aren't going to control our spending, so we're going to borrow from China or from thin air if we have to, and the debt will be paid by the taxpayers today, tomorrow, and throughout your children's and grandchildren's lives.

Finally, objections to the bill to repeal the tax are based on a resentment or hatred of people who have more money than the objectors (presumably). Rep. Jim McDermott, D-Wash. says, "What are they doing? Shoveling a quarter of a trillion dollars out the door to the richest." Do you hear the vitriol in that? The envy?

I'm not rich. Never have been. Never will be. But I don't have

---

[43] You may have noticed that I refer to the Democrat Party rather than the Democratic Party, because I don't want you to be confused. There's less and less *democratic* about the Democratic Party these days.

anything against people simply because they have a lot more money than I do. I've worked for some of them. I'm related to some of them. And you know what? I hope that people who have half or even less of what I have to live on aren't envious of me, or angry at me, just because I have had a little more success than they have. I would hope I'm not called ugly names by someone just because he doesn't have as much.

I suspect that the objection voiced by Democrats to rich people's being able to keep their estates and inheritances is disingenuous. Probably it's calculated merely to play off the envy of lower middle class and lower class Democrat voters who have been trained by their party demagogues to think that there's only so much money in the country and if someone has more of it than you, it's only because he's figured out a way to get it at your expense. It's the old zero sum game.

What I can't figure out is why people go on believing this sort of nonsense in the face of so much evidence against it. In the face of so much logic against it. In the face of so much history against it. I suspect the reason comes down to the understandable ignorance of so many people of how the economy and the government really work, and the cynical and Machiavellian shrewdness of Democrats (and occasionally misled Republicans) who take advantage of this ignorance and envy for their own power and enrichment.

Whatever the explanation, it's vile and reprehensible. Income tax is vile itself, but stealing inheritances is particularly evil.

Anti-Gun Nonsense

A predictable article on the Mother Nature Network (MNN) by Laura Moss bears the title, "Guns Really Do Change the Way You Think" (29 Jan 2015). Moss opines as an opener that "owning a firearm, holding one or even simply looking at a picture of one has an effect on your brain." The title and the lead assertion, not backed up with serious data, then shift to an anti-gun rant based on the spurious notion that while most people may think guns make them safer, actually they don't.

Moss writes: "Guns might make us feel safer, but studies show they actually make us less safe. Statistically, if you own a gun, it's more likely to be used to kill you or someone you love than a stranger in self-defense."

Moss is off her rocker, and apparently she doesn't know how to read or research statistics. She should have paid attention to the venerable wisdom articulated by Mark Twain: "There are three kinds of lies: lies, damned lies, and statistics." Moss doesn't cite the statistics supposed to support her contention, largely, I suspect, because she can't. Her article is full of unsupported assertions, illogical conclusions and prejudicial innuendo.

Moss cited a reenactment of the Charlie Hebdo shooting in which a single armed civilian was inserted into the mix. The reenactors used paintball guns. The results of several scenarios in which the armed good guy tried to defend the public were the death of the good guy in every case.

The first thing you have to know about the re-enactment is that it was staged by an organization called The Truth About Guns. In other words, the fix was in. This group had no intention of staging an experiment in which they didn't know the outcome and where the outcome was not helpful to their cause. It's like the study done at Harvard a few years ago in which "scientists" concluded that homosexuality was genetically determined. The study was done by an all-gay group of students. The results were eventually dismissed as invalidated by bias and manipulation of data.

The second thing you have to realize about the re-enactment is that it was not a scientifically conducted study. It's just bunk.

Moss goes on to opine that guns are like snakes and spiders: we're genetically predisposed to fear them. Ergo, we are scared to see guns or use them, and therefore we cannot be trusted to do so without overall disastrous effects.

If that were true, the only logical conclusion would be that we must immediately disarm all the police, because they are also human beings and no good can come from their having guns.

Moss's conclusions are not true, however, because even if some people have a deep-seated, nervous fear of weapons, many others do not, and still others overcome their fear of necessity because of the kind of world we live in. We live in a world plagued by evil of all kinds, some of it focused on you, me, our children, or our neighbors. Moss thinks you shouldn't try to protecting yourself and others. It's too dangerous!

Moss is a fool.

Some of the simplest mottos of the supporters of gun rights continue to communicate unassailable logic and incontrovertible wisdom:

> If you outlaw guns, only the outlaws will have guns.

> Gun control is like trying to reduce drunk driving
> by making it tougher for sober people to own cars.

> If more sane people were armed,
> the crazy people would get off fewer shots.

And Moss's object of ridicule, but one of my favorites:

> The only thing that stops a bad guy with a gun
> is a good guy with a gun.

I defy you to make a logical, sensible, supportable argument against any of these terse slogans.

Do it without resorting to lies, damn lies, or statistics.

Cell Phone Zombies

Cell phones have changed the world. Certainly we could name many things that have changed the world, or their own part of the world, in some way, but think about the cell phone for a minute.

Twenty-five years ago if you wanted to call someone and you were in your car, you had to stop at a pay phone (unless you were really rich and had a radio car phone, and even then your range was severely limited.) Today you just reach in your pocket for your cell phone, or just touch a button on your blue tooth ear phone.

A mere quarter century ago you had to get out a map to find your way, and you had to have separate paper maps for cities. Now you just tap the map app on your phone and find your way, down to the block and building, and the app calculates your route in a fraction of a second.

A score of years ago you used to have to use the yellow pages to find restaurants, and since no one carried a yellow pages book around in his car, if you were traveling you had to stop and find that pay phone again. But no more. In fact, you can just say to your phone, "Find Mexican restaurants," and it will tell you politely there's one two blocks away.

Of course, cell phones are so much more than phones. They're cameras, connections to banks and stores, a means of finding out about weather, and a way to access the entire world of Internet commerce, education, news and entertainment. In fact, it's impossible to describe in a short space what a smart cell phone can do, and how it has changed the daily lives of people everywhere.

Many of these changes are beneficial. What I really had in mind when I started this article, however, is the terrible things cell phones have done to the world around each of us.

I sit at a stoplight on my way to work in the morning or on the way home in the afternoon and I watch people go by, an astounding number of them on their cell phones. Automobile accidents are increasing steadily across the nation and many of them involve people on their cell phones. Obviously texting is one of the worst things to do when you're driving, but there they go, down the road, their heads down while they type out texts, instead of looking at the road where they're about to ram the driver in front of them that just put on his brakes.

Another cell phone user is sitting at a light that turned green five seconds ago and he hasn't seen it yet because he's somewhere else in his mind. A woman pokes down the Interstate highway at 50 m.p.h. in a 70 m.p.h. zone because she's talking with someone and paying only about

25% of her available attention to the road. Another woman speeds past her doing 90, also on her phone, oblivious to the fact that she's putting herself and others in danger.

A woman gets in her car to go out and the first thing she does is call someone. For ten miles to her destination, she's on the phone. Who in the world can she be talking to? Some people never drive that they don't also talk on the cell phone. What? Because they can, they do?

In the restaurant, a family comes in with three kids in tow, and they're seated across from me. All five of them are using their cell phones for something. Mom looks like she's on Facebook. Dad is looking at news or sports. The three kids are either texting or playing some sort of game app. The waitress comes to take their orders. The adults manage to tear themselves away from their phones long enough to order for themselves and their kids, who have mumbled something about what they wanted. Then everyone returns to his phone, until the food comes, and even then the kids alternate bites with manipulation of their phones.

At work, a client approaches the window of my office and a clerk asks him what he needs. He doesn't respond right away. He's on his cell phone. The clerk finally walks off. When his call ends, the guy looks in the window and wonders why he has been abandoned.

Out on the street people walk by, somebody barely missing being hit by a car in a crosswalk because she's head down in her cell phone. A pedestrian walks into another pedestrian. He didn't see him. He was on his cell phone.

Any one of us could go on and on. Cell phones have created zombies out of human beings who had a chance at rational life, but who have been taken control of, by a digital force. Cell phones have seduced not just the young generation but most of us, and they have encouraged an appalling lack of courtesy, to say nothing of sensible behavior, everywhere you go.

The cost is not just to etiquette and traffic; digital providers, which include cell phone, tablet and computer access in their services, have created a need in the American public and they are filling it at an astounding cost in dollars. A family that brings in three thousand dollars a month may transfer a fourth or more of their income to digital providers for unlimited calls, Internet access and texting on their cell phones, and for high speed, unlimited Internet on their tablets, laptops and desktop computers.

Not only is such a luxury not limited to the wealthy these days, the government has started providing people living below the poverty line with cell phones and Internet access. That person in the line in front of you at the Posh People Supermarket, who is perfectly capable of working but doesn't, not only gets much of her food for free from the government, not only most of her rent paid by the government, but right now she's talking on her top-of-the-line cell phone, rudely chatting with her girlfriend while the clerk is trying to complete the sale of her cart full of prepared dinners.

Cell phones have come upon us almost too quickly. As a culture we weren't ready to be interconnected and instantly available so rapidly as we have actually become. We didn't have etiquette in place, and we've made ourselves into rude fools as we've become cell phone maniacs overnight. And none of the foregoing description even touches on the inappropriate creation of exhibitionist selfies or the use of cell phones as a means of harassment.

I appreciate the value of a cell phone, but lately I've become convinced I could do without one. I would save money, and I would be free of any hypocrisy when I yelled at that guy in front of me who isn't watching where he's going, "Get off your cell phone!"

Afraid of Marriage?

A Fox News story that came out of New Rochelle some time back told a bizarre tale: Fernando Brazier committed suicide over being pressured to marry Trudian Hay. His extreme solution to a future he chose under duress typifies the deeply troubling attitude of increasing numbers of young American men. Marriage rates have been going down since the sixties, largely because of that era's philosophy of free love. But the beatnik-then-hippie generation rebellion became a rejection of not just the concept of the sexual uniqueness of marriage but the concept of marriage altogether. Now a third generation away from the youth who made love not war, today's twenty-somethings are making war on love.

It really is love that is targeted, not marriage. Young people today who have a phobia of commitment are really afraid of true, life-engulfing love and the commitment that such love joyfully embraces. It isn't just marriage that young adults are afraid of, it's loving someone else enough to choose, without reservation, to devote one's life to that someone, "forsaking all others." Young people have become so used to the idea that casual sex is not only normal but virtually obligatory that the thought that they might be limited—oh horrors!—to one partner for the rest of their lives brings on shivers of fear.

Instead of taking the big leap into marriage, Fernando Brazier took a leap into the Harlem River. One has to think there were other factors involved in his lacking the basic human desire to live, but according to his note, left for his bride of just a few hours, it was being pressured into marriage that pushed him over the edge. And it wasn't like Fernando hadn't already gotten significantly involved with Trudian. In fact they had dated since they were teenagers, and had done a bit more than date, because they had two children together, ages five and two.

Here's part of the problem. Fernando, and Trudian too, like so many young people today, considered sex to be their human right, an activity that not only predictably but also reasonably and justifiably took place in the normal course of dating. Sex, this most intimate, soul-bonding activity of human beings that has always been considered by the mainstream of societies everywhere to be the province of marriage, and in fact to be one of the distinguishing acts and characteristics of marriage, has in just the last fifty years or so become recreation or entertainment. While the most conservative of folks still hold sex to be the exclusive right of the married, they are derided or dismissed as irrelevant by modern culture.

Sex has consequences, and one of them is that it has an inexplicable way of joining the hearts and souls of the people who engage in it. If you join your body with just one other person than the one you wind up spending your life with (if you ever do), the union you have with that one person from years ago will haunt you the rest of your life. Join your body with dozens or even more other persons in your youth, and if you ever do decide to settle down, one or two things will happen: one, you may have very little sense of the special nature of sex with your mate, because it isn't unique to the two of you; or two, you will have created such an appetite for variety in partners that you may find it virtually impossible to be faithful to your spouse.

Apparently, many young men and women simply cannot fathom the idea of never having sex with anyone else. At root, it may be because they have confused sex with love, and having spread their sexual selves around, they have diluted the act to nearly the commonplace, and with it has gone their capacity to feel that one very special person is the one. In essence, reducing sex to a routine date night activity has damaged their ability to fall in love. It is that wonderful phenomenon of falling in love that overwhelms other, less important matters of emotional indecision and convinces a person to enter into a lifetime covenant.

Mind you, I'm realistic. Even many people who believe sex should be exclusively for the married will have sex outside of marriage; because of the powerful nature of the temptation, it's a common human failing to go against your own beliefs. What has happened in our culture, however, is that the inevitable failures of some, or even of many, has now become the official philosophy of this generation. If we don't reverse it, it will become universally and permanently accepted behavior.

Moral principles are not things that everybody flawlessly lives up to; they are ideals that we should strive for and teach the next generation to live by, calling on the experience of our failures as well as our successes. If we don't have ideals, we won't strive toward anything. Dispensing with the ideal of sexual uniqueness in marriage leaves us with very little if anything to stand as the model of goodness in that whole regard. The working motto of this generation is to have sex when you feel you're ready. In practice, that question is decided by hormones. As a determinant of such important matters, that stinks.

No GW

Natalie Wolchover wrote an article describing the belief of some people that a planet like ours is in orbit around our sun past Pluto, and will someday hit the earth.[44] Calling on a well known scientist to refute what Wolchover calls lunacy, she wrote:

"Renowned astrophysicist Carl Sagan once described a "baloney detection kit" — a set of tools that skeptical thinkers use to investigate any new concept. A few of the key tools include: a healthy distrust of information that isn't independently verified; critically assessing an idea rather than becoming irrationally attached to it simply because it's intriguing; and a preference for simple explanations over wildly speculative ones."[45]

Sagan's intention, quite obviously, was to create a logical platform for debunking rather obvious nonsense. Unintentionally, however, Sagan was laying out a method for critiquing even the fallacious "science" of the left. Chief among the left's pseudo-scientific lunacy is human-caused global warming.

The global warming crowd, running from the negative associations that have now stuck to that term, have renamed it climate change. Next year it may be something else, but the facts will still be the facts: **there is no global warming**. Right now, there is none at all. For the past seventeen years, NASA confirms, there has been no change in the mean temperature of the earth's atmosphere.

This hasn't kept the global warming (let's call it "GW") crowd from preaching this nonsense, of course. Hollywood stars join scientific entertainers—those scientists whose main work seems to consist of getting themselves on TV and in print in pop-science magazines—in promoting a lie.

Even measurements of the amount of ozone in the upper atmosphere have improved over my lifetime. From the pronouncements of the left, you'd expect that every indicator of coming disaster would be going up, but they're not. CO_2 in the atmosphere is

---

[44]The planet may, in fact, exist. If it does, it's about ten times the mass of Earth and takes up to 20,000 years to orbit once around the sun. It is not likely to hit the earth however.

[45]Natalie Wolchover, *Beleivers in Mysterious Planet Nibiru Await Earth's End* (LiveScience.com, July 5, 2011).

not going up, either. Even if it did slightly, the effect would not be to heat up the earth to toasting temperature but to feed the trees and plants, all of which use CO_2 to make their food. That would help rebuild those precious rainforests (jungles to the non-politically-correct) that we're told we need to preserve.

But to the tree-hugging crowd, any development in the news at all is proof of GW. Storms? GW. Drought? GW. No snow? GW. Too much snow? GW. It's insane.

Use Sagan's method to critique the GW theory:

"Healthy distrust of information that isn't independently verified," he said. So, instead of blind acceptance of the claims of GW, stop, question, and ask for evidence. The "confirmation" of GW is coming from left leaning politico-scientists. People who think for themselves are breaking off from the left wing of the scientific community and telling us there isn't hard evidence for GW. Many studies are deeply flawed, and some data has been entirely fabricated. Just the fact that the GW theme is thoroughly political and always has been, should give us pause.

Then Sagan said, *"Critically assessing an idea rather than becoming irrationally attached to it simply because it's intriguing."* The intriguing element, in this case, is the strange lure of any prophecy of doom, a characteristic that engulfs the GW movement. Statistics appear and mount, proving that GW is a hoax, but its proponents continue to believe it irrationally.

"Preference for simple explanations over wildly speculative ones," Sagan said. The GW crowd is looking for an explanation for climatic shifts here and there—which again have not changed the global mean temperature one whit—shifts like colder winters here and warmer winters there, droughts, melting icebergs, etc. There's no debate over the fact that the earth has experienced cycles of climate change over the millennia. There have been mini-ice ages, decades of extremely cold winters, now and then in recorded history. The middle of the seventeen hundreds was one of those times. Then things warm up again. We're somewhere between those extremes now, and things are pretty stable.

But the GW followers are devising some scenario of human extinction caused by our own hands. If I remember correctly, New York was supposed to be mostly under water about now, according to prophecies made by one of our pseudo-scientist-politicians twenty years ago. Oh, I forgot: Obama was elected, and he promised that when he was, "the seas will begin receding."

The question of why anyone would want to perpetrate such a hoax is challenging. Or more accurately, your believing the answer is challenging. My belief is that most people who believe in GW are somewhat credulous people (even though they would deny it) who have a strong streak of fear in them and who have been taught to believe that modernity is implicitly evil. We'll call them GW Supporters. In addition to the Supporters there are also left leaning political figures who know there is no such thing as GW but are engaged in manipulating the fearful Supporters into pressuring government to take over more and more of the country in the name of saving the planet. These are the GW Leaders. The GW Leaders crave the power to rule the country, even all countries that glom onto the fearful bandwagon. And in their quest to keep the Supporters on the wagon, a mounting number of GW Leaders have been producing a growing number of falsified reports and statistics. I started to list a dozen or so of those incidents here and decided it was something you could do on your own. Try Google-ing "falsified global warming statistics."

Sagan wouldn't want his own method used to critique what he happens to believe in, but I think it's dog gone appropriate. **There is no global warming.** It's a hoax.

But it gives leftie scientists something to do.

Down with Demigods

I've been somewhere between annoyed and alarmed for years about the culture's growing adoration of anyone and everyone in the entertainment industry. It seems to me that people's fascination with, and obsession over, actors and entertainers has grown steadily during the age of television and the Internet. What concerns me is not that people find the lifestyles of the rich and famous interesting, but that in their quest to follow every detail of these public figures' lives they displace more important subjects to know and care about. Those things include current events of real significance, politics, the forefronts of science, pressing moral and ethical issues, their own communities' goings-on, and their own families.

A news site I frequent on the Internet includes a "Features" section headlining fourteen items every day that change regularly. The balance of subjects in those articles seems to me to be about the same, day to day. Today, seven of those features—50%—were about entertainers. If the website producers know their audience, we may conclude that people actually want to know: what a dozen Hollywood beauties look like without makeup; what so-and-so actually did before becoming famous; who's marrying this star; why that star cut her hair short; who was a bad boy on the movie set; and what another entertainer said about rumors going around about him.

I say, who cares?

Obviously a lot of people do. I'm not one of them. I say, "who cares," not to suggest that no one does but to say that no one should. In my opinion, we should ignore their personal lives. They make movies, TV shows and records. Enjoy those. Let what they do in their bedrooms, backstage, and in their Bugattis remain private. In fact, make them keep it private, by refusing to buy the magazines that cater to voyeurs of Hollywoodland.

I realize, of course, that the mystique, the aura, the sense that these people are something other than human beings like the rest of us, is a longstanding part of this culture. Magazines about the stars are practically as old as the entertainment industry itself. And, it's part of the way they make their money: they make money when their art makes money and when the studios and producers make money selling them and their art to the public. So, marketing the people in the pictures sells the pictures, and makes them all money. Money that was in our pockets.

I'm willing to pay some money for good entertainment. I appreciate well told stories; movies and TV supply quite a few of them. I have some favorite actors, too. What I don't have is any interest in the personal lives of those actors. I know a man who said one time he would never go see another movie with a certain actor in it because he learned of the actor's religious intolerance. He also swore he would never listen to another song by a certain singer because of his political persuasion. If I took the same approach, I would have to stop going to movies altogether, and not turn on the TV again either.

That might be good for me anyway, but it would be unreasonable. I enjoy actors' art, and I'm not interested in anything else about them.

Several times I have seen interviews by a reporter on the street with people passing by, as he asked them about some current issue or event, or asked what they knew about, or thought about, a certain public figure who was not an entertainer. Most of the interviewees were young, under thirty. It was alarming how many people did not know who presidential candidates were, who their own mayor was, or what had happened in the last week in the news, but they knew who sang a certain pop song or starred in a particular movie. The cap the interviewer put on the segment was this: "And these people vote."

I don't know that there's a single culprit to point the finger at for the idolatry practiced by a vast segment of the American (and the Western world's) people. Certainly our public schools need to be active in keeping students' attention focused on what's going on in the world rather than on what celebrities are doing in Hollywood. More importantly, parents should raise their children to be more informed about the real world than the world of make believe.

We should all be very concerned about the civic, social, political, moral, cultural, and historical awareness of the people of this country. We should care less—much less—about who wore a low cut gown to an awards ceremony.

Our Future with Cuba

Obama's startling move in July, 2015, to normalize relations with Cuba drew ire and fire from both sides of the aisle in Congress, and it's understandable, but I'm not so certain it was a bad move to make at this juncture of history.

Self-evidently, the move is in keeping with Obama's egocentric desire to create a legacy for himself, which is basically bad only if the actions he takes are themselves bad. Obama's other major initiatives have not been good for the country, in my estimation. America did not need to be fundamentally transformed, to use Obama's words. It could be that reversing a half a century of keeping Cuba at greater than arm's length will turn out to be similarly bad for America's interests. However, the policy shift may work out to benefit the greater goals of both America and the world.

Sun Tzu, in The Art of War, (sixth century B.C.) advised a power to keep friends close and enemies closer. The principle has been proven wise consistently over the course of history, and if it's worth anything to those who believe that The Godfather is the repository of all the practical wisdom needed by man, Michael Corleone repeated the maxim to his henchmen.

It's worth considering that any deleterious effects Cuba's government might have upon the United States might be better repulsed by having diplomatic relations with it. It should be clear by now that if the U.S. were hoping to pressure Cuba into giving up its communist course by isolating it from us, it's not working. Perhaps having diplomatic relations instead will work, simply on the theory of trying something new.

It's also worth considering that Nixon decided to go to China and try to dispel tensions and pave the way for better things. China is still communist, but think of what good things have descended from Nixon's initiative.

While we're considering things, think of our relationship with the Soviet Union when it still existed. They were too big to isolate, you might argue, but the point is that they were the major communist power of the world, and we didn't try to cut *them* off. Why just Cuba?

It was simply because we could, and because they are so close. Still, the isolation hasn't done what we hoped it would.

Finally, if anything has become clear to us it should be the principle that economic exchange usually overcomes politics and transforms countries' most significant relations. Why would China, for instance, really want to destroy the U.S. when we are its best customer? Ruining us would ruin China's economy, and they know that. When people trade, they learn to get along.

We should not lay aside our concerns about the infiltration of communism, yet we should admit that isolating Cuba hasn't kept the Democrat Party from adopting socialist beliefs and practices all by itself since the 60s. Maybe we can export the philosophy of our democratic republic, such as it is, 90 miles south from our southernmost shore.

I'm willing to consider argument to the contrary.

The Bane of Facebook

I'm appalled at the extent to which people: display their activities; disclose their lives; flaunt their enmity toward one another; or engage in mutual, virtual combat on the Internet sandlot of Facebook.

Clearly, Facebook creates an artificial world in which people have come to believe that they are insulated from the regular rules of social discourse. While people may not act in anonymity on Facebook, they seem to assume that their insults, threats, counter-threats and general disagreeableness will not come back to haunt them.

Facebook invites: symbolic, indecent exposure; rampant, vicious gossip; irresponsible criticism; and unrestrained vulgarity; all with the presumption of impunity. While Facebook also may have created a pleasant virtual park where mutually courteous persons may enjoy the news of family and friends, it has also created an online battlefield where undisciplined and overtly violent people argue, intimidate and assault.

When Facebook is the field of contest for feuding parties, people who live their lives on Facebook seem unable to disconnect themselves from it when it becomes abundantly wise to do so. (It's similar to people's self-destructive addition to cell phones, which, of course, they use to access Facebook.)

People's astounding lack of self discipline on Facebook sometimes lands them in court, or in jail. Victims of harassment often file for restraining orders over complaints that feature Facebook messages and images in a major way. There are controls on Facebook that allow the account owner to prohibit certain persons from adding their comments or posting material, and some people seem unable simply to cut off other people, or, in the short term, to disregard them.

You have no more right to type an abusive message into a Facebook post than you do to approach a person in public and insult or threaten him or her. What is unacceptable in private or public is just as unacceptable online. What is illegal to say to someone at his house or in a public place is just as illegal to say electronically. If you give free reign to your dark side by vowing to harm someone, you should brought to justice for it.

An Internet message is not a "pretend" threat. It is not less real simply because it is in cyberspace, and you are not able to hide behind a mask from the law just because you represent yourself with an avatar.

People under twenty don't remember when there was no Facebook.

Media people sometimes generalize that 'everyone is on Facebook.' While people used to be able to leave feedback for a business through a simple "comments" field, now most businesses are asking customers to use Facebook to respond. Some people assume life cannot be lived without Facebook, or indeed, without the Internet.

Well, look over here: here is one person who does not "do" Facebook. I don't do Twitter, either. In fact, I don't know the first thing about sending a Tweet. I believe, with good reason, that my life is substantially better for not participating in these overly "gushy" social habits. Think of the time I save to actually do things. Plus, I don't have to worry about repercussions from excessive self disclosure.

A long time ago I made a rule for my life, a general rule that I don't break unless it manifestly does not apply or the practical benefits are overwhelmingly convincing. I don't break the rule often. The rule is simple: don't jump on bandwagons. Facebook is one of those things that virtually everyone is doing. To me, that's reason enough not to join the crowd.

Natives and Other Americans

The recent flurry of overblown indignation over the name of Washington D.C.'s football team continues and exacerbates the issue of Native Americans. A very effective "commercial" campaigning for the change of the Washington Redskins name, an ad that ran around the middle of 2014, listed half a dozen other names by which various American Indians did and still call themselves, followed by the assertion that one thing they never called themselves is—and there followed no words but only a picture of a Redskins football helmet. It's a powerful argument, but frankly I think the whole matter has been blown entirely out of proportion.[46]

As to Native Americans, however, the larger issue is the opinion of many of them, and a lot of guilt ridden White people who have been misinformed about American history, that Europeans stole the North American continent from them. If they can't have it back now (and obviously they can't), then at least they should receive perennial apologies and special dispensations from the Federal government. This is generally the position of the liberal left.

This special treatment of Native Americans is premised on the idea that the American Indian was living an idyllic existence on this continent, numerous tribes coexisting and fulfilling some ideal image of human life. Then, ruthless, disease ridden, land grabbing, violent, lying, evil Europeans swarmed over the continent stealing the Indians' land, carrying out a pogram of genocide against them, herding them into little confines and starving them, freezing them, or intentionally turning them into alcoholics, with the end game that they would all die and cease to exist as peoples, eventually being lost in the mists of history.

The problem with this story is that while it is built on observations about history that have a grain of truth to them, it connects the dots with a lot of half truths, anti-Christian prejudices, and a whole lot of revisionist foolishness, otherwise known as lies.

The truth is that the American Indians (my preferred term) consisted of many tribes all over the continent, some of them avowed enemies of each other as long as they existed. Governments among these tribes were skeletal; there were virtually no writings establishing governments, codifying laws or defining borders and other things associated with

---

[46]In mid 2016 a survey of American Indians showed that more than nine out of ten of them were not offended by the Washington team's name.

developed cultures. The first European settlers reached agreements with the Indians they encountered so as to coexist. The difficulties that developed afterward resulted from a mixture of contract disputes, mutual breaches, and Indian activities that today would be classified as gross violations of international law if not outright terrorism.

The European discovery of another continent was inevitable. The expansion of the colonies and then the United States from sea to shining sea was inevitable, and I would say destined. There was no way it wasn't going to happen, and there really wasn't any reason it shouldn't have. The argument that American Indians of one tribe or another already existed here and there in the continent is not sufficient to defeat the case for the expansion of the American experiment. After all, it brought liberty in law to a vast area and provided for a future of democratic governance within the greatest set of principles yet devised among human beings. The resulting prosperity and progress proves the rightness of exploration, immigration, colonization, expansion, and the establishment of the United States of America.

One of the contentions of the pro-Indian side of the ongoing debate is that the Indians are *the* Native Americans. The problem with this tenet is that it is true only in a limited way, and perhaps a defective way.

First of all, we don't know there weren't peoples on this continent before the tribes who would become the American Indians came across Asia into North America. Even if the Indians were the first, does that give them a perpetual claim to the continent? If that principle were applied to all continents and peoples, and some ad hoc world government were to try to put everyone back where they were the first occupying peoples, there would be hopeless confusion.

Further, there is some implicit obligation, I think, for a people to do something with the land they move into. If they don't, they may not deserve to keep on occupying it when expanding populations around them have a better plan and a greater need.

I don't intend to make a simplistic argument that would underwrite wholesale invasion by empires. I just think that when the world still contained vast areas considered undiscovered, even though some natives here and there had wandered into these remote areas over the centuries, the constructive and responsible expansion of developed cultures into the whole globe was entirely justified.

One more thing. I'm a native American. About a dozen generations of my family have been born and lived in America. I belong here, and I don't apologize to anyone for my being here. I don't apologize for the United States, its culture, its government, or its rise to greatness in the world. I wish President Obama felt the same way. I hope we replace him with someone who is proud to be an American and will say so.

Stay Out of Hospitals

I had the misfortune recently of being in an accident requiring my hospitalization for two days.[47] It was my first such experience since I was about four, when I had my tonsils out. My memories of that time are very faint, consisting mostly of recollections of being given ether before surgery and ice cream afterwards. Over the years, of course, I visited other people in hospital rooms, some family and many, many more who were not, and I gained an extensive knowledge from an objective perspective of what going to the hospital does to a person. Finally being the patient myself, however, was obviously different.

I was in the hospital because of the fact that I was hurt and needed fixing, and I will be the first to thank the doctor treating me for his expertise and perfectionism at his work. I found I had no anxiety about the surgery required, the treatment, or anything else the doctor did on my behalf. Because of my helplessness as the result of injury, I sensed powerfully that I was at one of those crisis times in which I had to surrender myself to someone else's knowledge and care. Normally independent and self-reliant, I needed help at the most basic ambulatory level, and that wasn't going to change until someone else did some medical magic on my behalf.

Something in me told me that while what lay ahead of me would not be enjoyable, it would be an adventure. It was not what I had planned for myself, but it would be interesting. It was not going to be cheap, but it was going to be valuable to me, somehow, somewhere, beyond the impact of money.

I will also acknowledge freely the warm, personal care of several of my RNs, most of whom were genuinely caring. They came and went too frequently, however, and just as I was creating rapport with one, his or her shift would end.

I can't say as much about the "patient care assistants." One spent a lot of time in my room, but mostly talked a mile a minute to my wife about miscellaneous superficialities. Another signed in, told me her name, and never returned, even just to check on me. Still another popped in cheerily, said something that sounded like a Valley Girl, promised to send a nurse for my request, and apparently never did pass along the message.

---

[47]I know, I've referred to my accident several times in this book. You learn things from accidents, you know. I try to pass along the lessons.

Other people at the hospital did just about everything they could to make me miserable. Someone came every hour and a half to take vital signs, and some of them were quick and efficient. One was even nearly invisible and succeeded in being almost finished with his work during the middle of the night before I even woke up. Others, however, announced their presence during the wee hours with hearty greetings and loud knocks, intent on making sure I was startled out of sleep just to accommodate their sphygmomanometer, thermometer and pulse oximeter. I suppose they assumed I would immediately be able to go back to sleep as if nothing happened. Unfortunately, that doesn't happen in the hospital.

The worst experience, far worse than surgery, which everyone not only let me sleep through but insisted I sleep through, was spending the rest of the day and night being unable to go to the bathroom as I usually do. I shall use my father's expression here: they would not let me "drain out" while standing up. Doctor's orders for the post-operative 24-hours were to stay in bed and under no circumstances to put weight on my hurt leg. Bottom line was that I was supposed to drain out while lying down. There was no way. I wore out my abdominal muscles trying. As I told my changing shifts of attendants, I *un*learned how to eliminate while lying down when I graduated from diapers to big boy pants. They found that moderately amusing, as they hooked up another 1000 ml bag of Ringer's Lactate to further make life difficult.

Finally during the middle of the night I convinced (with what I'm sure sounded like politely articulated threats) my nurse to get a tech and assist me in standing on my good leg to see what I could do. The following day I related my frustration to my doctor when he came in for early morning rounds. Basically when he asked how I was doing I told him there wasn't much wrong with me that standing in a bathroom wouldn't cure. He laughed and understood. To his credit, he also took note of how wonderfully I was doing, made sure that the physical therapists concurred, and released me later that day.

Leaving the hospital gave people more opportunities to drive me to desperation. It took four hours after the doctor himself said, "You can go home," until the papers were actually drawn up, my signature was applied, techs undid this and took off that, and then transport personnel actually showed up and let me get in a wheelchair to leave.

At home, life was different with suddenly much less mobility than before the whole ordeal began, but at least I could get myself into my own bathroom, as man was meant to do. It took me two days to get rid of the excess fluids they pumped into me so I would feel better.

Unfortunately, I had to go back for another procedure, which meant facing enemy lines all over again. I look back on the adventure with the eye of a raconteur, but I still have the same advice for anyone who will listen:

Try to stay out of the hospital if you can.

Hands-Off Government

Government types have been warning us in increasingly shrill tones about the wealth gap. The rich are getting richer and the poor are staying poor. There's some disagreement as to whether or not the statistics include factors that they should in order to be really accurate, but in the main, the figures don't lie.

The question is whether or not this trend is going to be destructive to the American economy. Only after answering that question can you reasonably pose a follow up question of what to do about the wealth gap.

Unfortunately, political liberals are quick to assume that the wealth gap is bad for the economy, and they constantly prescribe badly worn government fixes such as raising taxes on the rich and raising the minimum wage. Raising taxes, of course, simply rakes money into federal coffers. It doesn't really act as a disincentive to making a lot of money. In fact, it may do the opposite. But the practical effect is largely to just put more money in the federal pocket making possible government largesse to the have-nots. The short term for that is income redistribution, and the even shorter term for that is socialism.

Raising the minimum wage may artificially narrow the income gap very slightly, but it has the adverse effect of prompting businesses to eliminate minimum wage jobs. It also acts as a disincentive to the lowest earners to look for better paying jobs.

But again, the answer to the first question is not altogether clear. Is the income gap bad for the economy? Political liberals, those people who right off the bat assume that government should take from the rich to give to the poor, dismiss any thought of the possibility that increasing wealth will have a beneficial impact on the economy. There was such a pooh poohing of the term "trickle down economics" during the 80s that conservative economists, who know the principle works, struggle to convince people of that fact. Rich people don't burn their money, and they don't even mostly hoard their money. They spend it.

What happens when people spend their money? Businesses that sell what rich people buy hire people and pay people more to make more stuff to sell to the rich people. Industries expand. And when rich people's money is not spent but donated instead, non-profits and individuals are benefitted.

In essence, all prosperity is trickle-down. Money doesn't trickle up. It gets taxed up, but that doesn't prosper anyone. It merely adds cost to the money, and when money is redistributed, it is less valuable. Government does not produce wealth: it is a drag on wealth.

Granted, we need some government, and thus government's drag on wealth must be tolerated. But the United States government has gone far beyond the minimal oversight, regulation and enforcement necessary to an orderly and prosperous society. To this present situation of the wealth gap, I think it cannot be reasonably contradicted that Ronald Reagan's assessment is right on target. Government is not the solution to the problem: government *is* the problem. The more the government tries to force the economy into a preconceived mold of who makes what, the more problems the economy develops. Government should take its hands off the economy and let American people do what they've always done: prosper.